Charles Gavard

A Diplomat in London. Letters and Notes (1871-1877)

Charles Gavard

A Diplomat in London. Letters and Notes (1871-1877)

ISBN/EAN: 9783743338517

Manufactured in Europe, USA, Canada, Australia, Japa

Cover: Foto ©ninafisch / pixelio.de

Manufactured and distributed by brebook publishing software
(www.brebook.com)

Charles Gavard

A Diplomat in London. Letters and Notes (1871-1877)

A DIPLOMAT IN LONDON

𝕷etters and 𝕹otes
1871–1877

TRANSLATED FROM THE FRENCH
OF
CHARLES GAVARD

NEW YORK
HENRY HOLT AND COMPANY
1897

Copyright, 1897,
BY
HENRY HOLT & CO.

PRINTED BY ROBERT DRUMMOND, NEW YORK.

PREFACE.

THE Letters and Notes contained in this volume were not written for publication. Their author, M. Charles Gavard, who died in July, 1893, was a member from 1871 to 1877 of the French Embassy at London, first as Chief Secretary, and then as Minister Plenipotentiary acting as *Chargé d'Affaires*. Having had the art to make himself a welcome guest, not only among political circles in England, but also in society, he was in a position to see a great many things that he felt would be of interest to his family, and that he accordingly described from day to day in his letters home. Also, once relieved from active service, he jotted down certain of his recollections for his own use. It has been thought that extracts from these letters and notes might be of general interest. The public, to whom they are submitted, must be the judge.

It seems not improper to reprint here two notices of M. Gavard that were published immediately after his decease.

The first of them, written by the Duc de Broglie for the *Correspondant* of July 25th, 1893, is as follows:

" In a study that has just appeared in to-day's *Correspondant*, I was led to dwell at some length on the difficulties of the situation in which M. Thiers placed the ambassador he sent to London when he commissioned him in the name of France (then suffering under so cruel an ordeal) to take part in a European conference. By a melancholy coincidence, the *Correspondant* in the same issue announced to its readers the premature death of one of its former contributors—M. Charles Gavard. It was this M. Charles Gavard who accompanied the French Ambassador on the painful mission above referred to, and afforded him the no slight advantage of his intelligent and friendly co-operation.

"When I left Paris at M. Thiers' command, I besought M. Gavard to accompany me, mainly for the reason, that as an *attaché* of the commerce department of the Ministry of Foreign Affairs, (he had been in that Department from his youth upwards), his services had been such that he had been rapidly promoted to a high post, and because I foresaw that, to ease the difficulties growing out of our enormous war-indemnity, France would very possibly be obliged to ask the English Government to consent to certain modifications of the customs-treaty that at that time governed the relations between the two countries. More than that, the treaty of commerce, concluded in 1862 by the Empire and arranged to last for ten years, was approaching its period, and the negotiations that must attend its expiration would inevitably call for special knowledge of the sort that M. Gavard possessed. But I soon recognized also in him an intelligence of a high order in matters of politics—good judgment, delicate tact, a prompt knowledge of men—all the qualities, in a word, that go to make up a diplomatic agent to whom the care of interests of all kinds may be confided.

"We were surprised at London by the news of the momentary success of the insurrection at Paris. When I found myself obliged to hasten back to Versailles, where my duties as a member of the National Assembly called me, M. Gavard was anxious to go with me—to bear his part in the strange events, the gravity of which we felt it was impossible at a distance rightly to estimate. We passed the sea, (uncertain in what state we should find France), in the company of a traveller whose *incognito* we had promised to respect. He was *Robert le Fort*, who had donned once more the simple officer's uniform he had presented to the Prussian bullets, and was going to offer his services to aid in the preservation of society. M. Gavard felt a hereditary attachment to the princes of the ruling house in France, and the memory of this night of anxiety passed in common did not tend to diminish the confidence with which they have always honored him.

"M. Thiers conferred on M. Gavard the post of First Secretary of the Embassy at London, which (save during an interval which he passed in Paris as the chief of the minister's cabinet) he held for nearly seven years. It is very uncommon nowadays for a post of that sort to be held for so long a period. And it is but right to add that during M. Gavard's term of office the French Ambassador to London was several times changed—M. Gavard was called upon first and last to serve under a number of superiors, and to all of them he rendered services on which they justly set a high value. Whenever his chief was absent, M. Gavard was called upon to exercise the functions of Minister Plenipotentiary. In this capacity he found himself obliged a number of times to deal, on his own responsibility, with questions of great delicacy; and in the cases in which he did so he received the prompt approbation of the Duc Decazes—the accomplished minister who was then in charge of our Foreign Affairs.

"Such occasions were really for M. Gavard but so many opportunities to show a prudence, a precision of language, and a trustworthiness, that brought him in England, where such qualities are highly appreciated, a number of valuable friendships. When his turn came to bear his share in the political misfortunes of his friends and to retire to private life, these attachments subsisted in spite of absence and lapse of time, and such and such an important parliamentary personage, such and such a great lord of the upper house even, such and such a distinguished writer or representative of the press, never passed through Paris without coming to shake hands with him and pay their respects to his household, where a reception of an amiable and charming simplicity always awaited them.

"More than that, these steadfast friends of his corresponded with him, kept him informed of the little incidents that promised to prove of importance in the English political world—the world of which the French know so little. It was they who supplied him with the materials for the articles he contributed regularly to the *Français* and the *Moniteur*, and not infrequently to the *Correspondant*. In especial the reader may remember a most interesting series of studies on the electoral crisis of 1885—the one which brought Gladstone, after his sudden conversion to Home Rule, back to power. The consequences of this belated change of front on the part of the old parliamentary leader, the new classification of parties that would result from it, the new features of the coming struggle, were all described beforehand with a freshness of prevision that the events day after day confirmed. Unhappily, three years ago a cruel illness put a period to M. Gavard's writing; and those who knew him intimately saw with pain the steady progress of his malady and the suffering which he referred to so seldom and endured with such courageous and Christian resignation."

The following is from the pen of M. Paul Mureau-Dogin. It appeared in the *Moniteur* for July 12th, 1893.

" The *Moniteur* has just suffered a severe loss. Our friend and former contributor, M. Charles Gavard, succumbed last night to the malady which long since interrupted his labors. Our readers have surely not forgotten the admirable articles signed J. J. with their distinction, their clever turns, their light, sure touch. Foreign politics have seldom been discussed so competently. But M. Gavard brought to the task an acquisition that journalists by profession rarely possess—a personal experience in great diplomatic affairs.

" He entered the ministry of Foreign Affairs when

he was a young man; he won the notice of his superiors, was sent to London after the war of 1870, and filled there for many years the post of Chief Secretary, then that of Minister Plenipotentiary and *Chargé d'Affaires*. Serving as he did under a succession of Ambassadors who were one after another incessantly being recalled for reasons of party politics, M. Gavard found himself called upon to play a rôle above his title: he was more than once obliged in circumstances of great gravity to act as the sole representative of France at the court of St. James; and by his coolness, his foresight, his tact, his knowledge of men and things, his standing in English 'Society,' he proved always equal to the occasion. A diplomatist of the old school, he did not (as too many others do) call special attention to the dangers he had conjured away,—at the risk of causing them to reappear again; but some day, we hope, the services he rendered his country will be known, and how, for instance, at such and such a time, the measures he took, on his own responsibility, with one of the members of the British cabinet frustrated the evil designs of Prince Bismarck. M. Gavard's long sojourn at London was interrupted for the few months only, in 1873, during which the Duc de Broglie was Minister of Foreign Affairs: the Duc de Broglie appreciated his friend's value and appointed him chief of his cabinet.

" M. Gavard's loyalty to his own party exposed him to a hostility in certain quarters, that a man of his independent spirit naturally disdained to take precautions against, and when the Left Wing came to power, in spite of all the patriotic reasons in favor of M. Gavard's being kept at London he was one of the first victims of the change of administration. He made use of his freedom to defend his convictions in the press. First as a contributor to the *Français*, then of the *Moniteur* (after the consolidation of the two papers), he concerned himself in the main with the questions, to-day so important, of Foreign Affairs. He was not, however, indifferent to the other aspects of politics. An enlightened liberal, a monarchist by conviction, the Princes had always found in him a friend and had always placed in him especial confidence.

"Much sought after in Parisian society for the grace of his wit and the soundness of his character, seconded in his own household by the rare concurrence of an exquisite affability and a superior intelligence, his salon was one of the few in which one still found good talk. Need I speak of the man as he revealed himself to those who penetrated beyond the barrier of a somewhat proud reserve? behind which he habitually took refuge from the curiosity of the public? His uprightness, the mingled warmth and discretion of his temperament, his devoted tenderness, his disinterested fidelity were not unknown to his friends and will never by them be forgotten. Under the affliction of a long illness which undermined one after another all his powers, he was even-tempered and patient; it was to religion that he looked for his support, it is to religion that those who mourn him must look for consolation."

A DIPLOMAT IN LONDON.

THE YEAR 1871.

Extracts from the Notes of M. Gavard.

My being sent to England began with a despatch that the Duc de Broglie[1] addressed from Bordeaux to M. Jules Favre, asking for a young man, who knew English well, to go with him to London. The Duke was something surprised and much satisfied, upon his arrival in Paris, to learn that the choice of the minister had fallen on M. Gavard and that this "youthful" attaché of his staff was to be myself.[2]

I had made the acquaintance of M. Jules Favre in the cruel days of the siege. When despatches or the microscopic reductions of the "Times" were brought in by the pigeons, under their wings, I often served him as translator. The headquarters[3] of the ambulance department were near

[1] M. Thiers, immediately upon becoming head of the government, had prayed the Duc de Broglie to accept the embassy to London.
[2] M. Gavard, the sous-directeur des consulats, had been attached to the Ministry of Foreign Affairs since 1848.
[3] The direction of the ambulance was in the hands of M. Gavard during the siege of Paris.

his office—were not uncommonly *at* his office, to say the truth, for he had got into the habit of sending for me. I remember more than one night-sitting and the patriotic exclamations he let fall.

Our arrangements were soon made. An ambulance-wagon took the Duke and myself to the station the morning of February twenty-third.

By the twenty-fifth, Lord Granville paid a visit to the Duke at the Clarendon Hotel where we had put up, and pressed him to complete, by the concurrence of France, the consent of Europe to rehandling the treaty of 1856 and annulling the clause which declared the Black Sea neutral. You may readily conceive we were in no hurry to wipe out an arrangement which our soldiers in the Crimea, quite gratuitously in my judgment, had bought at the price of blood, and in especial to ratify with our signature the by-gone bargain between Germany and Russia for the spoliation of France. It is true that, after having given up our provinces to Germany, it was easy to give up the treaty on the Black Sea. The humiliation was for England, and she began to expiate it even before our signature was complete.

It is a pleasure to recall in what terms the Duc de Broglie gave in his consent to this deed of violence: "France, solely not to separate herself from the other powers, submits to facts accomplished without her participation." The sort of resignation that is becoming in the vanquished was not, in that remark, unseasoned by the reserve that it was proper to maintain in the presence of England's gratuitous capitulation. This reserve marked an irony that the German plenipotentiary felt only on the following day, and that the representatives of England did not choose to take notice of. It is true, that they had had fears of a protest of quite another sort, and if the Duc de Broglie had given heed to the instructions sent him at the last moment, he would have seized this occasion to annul by his declaration at London the capitulation of Paris. But that would have been to hand France over to the vengeance of Prince Bismarck.

Mr. Gladstone's cabinet meanwhile did itself the honor of yielding to the pressing instances of the Duc de Broglie and of getting Germany at his request to knock off a billion from the figure of our ransom. It is no more than just to state the efforts made by our ambassador at London, and by the ministers of Queen Victoria at Versailles, during the first days of March. When we recollect the mingled respect and fear with which it was then the custom to pronounce the Chancellor's name, we should be grateful for the representations that the Duc de Broglie obtained from them. Of Strasburg and Metz there was no word said; but the economist in Mr. Gladstone was touched by the notion of lessening the figure imposed on us; he sincerely believed that it was an impossibility for us to pay it, and since then he has often avowed to me that he has never been able to understand how the thing can have proved possible.

Extracts from the private Correspondence of M. Gavard.

LONDON, CLARENDON-HOTEL, February, 14, 1871.

Here we are at last in a land where there are no Prussians! . . Superb passage. . . I did not turn in once except for sleep. . . To be frank, nobody was seasick. Conversation hardly languished day or night. At our arrival at the Victoria Station I recognized in the dusk the whole staff of the Embassy. Since then we have been conferring and talking incessantly. We are all under the same roof—there's not a vacant room in London.

LONDON, February 26, 1871.

No doubt you know what will happen in France to-morrow: a frightful war or a more frightful peace: Both look to me equally impossible, and yet . . . it will be one or the other. I am here, but I am still more truly with you.

We have exerted ourselves day and night since our arrival. What have we gained? . . . Surely a personal success for the Duke. . . What will the step prove to be worth that he has induced Lord Granville to take?[1]

[1] As above said, at the instance of the Duc de Broglie, Lord Granville and then Mr. Gladstone brought a pressure to bear on Germany to obtain from her the reduction of a billion from the amount of our ransom.

Yesterday I went to Morgan House [1]—nobody at home. On the train from Richmond, as I was coming back, I found myself face to face with the Duchesse de Chartres and the young Princesse Marie.[2] They were pleased when I announced that the Duke would pay them a visit in a few days and made an appointment for a 'chance' meeting to-day.

The Duc de Broglie's impression, after a long conversation with the Comte de Paris, is capital. Here was this family at hand; every member of it, civil and military, is distinguished and patriotic beyond reproach, and we kicked them out to replace them by the craftsmen of our ruin and shame. There is a perfect understanding among all the members of the family; their only desire is to come back, they understand all the necessities of the case, but they offer no sacrifice to a meretricious popularity, there is no manœuvring, no intrigue—it is admirable.

LONDON, February 28, 1871.

To learn in the chimney-corner that one's house is menaced by the Prussians and the Bastille assassins at the same time ![3] I don't know what to think; I anticipated nothing of all this; I wouldn't have believed either in the Prussian occupation or in Vinoy's inertia in the presence of a riot semi-military. . .

We are at the Embassy. We should need some-

[1] Residence of the Duc de Chartres.
[2] S. A. R. Madame la Princesse Marie d'Orleans, now Princesse Waldemar of Denmark.
[3] Highwaymen had been chasing the police and throwing them into the canal.

thing like security and leisure to turn our stay to account. The Duc de Broglie has made his début by a diplomatic success—a success, alas ! merely personal, but which may become the beginning of a reaction.

Everybody here is stunned ; it is out of fear that nobody speaks out. Europe, the Society of Peoples, no longer exists, if force is permitted to move unchecked like that to the bitter end. It is a tributary and a vassal France that they are setting up, and we must bow the head. And at present, what's to be done ? We shall never be less in shape than we are now for the supreme effort of deliverance.

LONDON, March 1, 1871.

Five o'clock, and we know nothing of the day ;[1] the Duke thinks the rodomontades will vanish in smoke at the approach of the Prussians. I don't believe either that there will be any resistance ; but there is always the chance pistol-shot that precipitates things.

The uneasiness here is extreme. The English public understands, as we do, that it is a perpetual war that is beginning. It doesn't dare say anything, but it is discontented with the rôle its government has played.

Before going in to see Parliament, I paid a visit to Westminster. All these dead reunited in a place of worship and repose in the centre of the city give one an impression of union, of fatherland. Every time that I remark upon anything here, it is the

[1] The entry of the Prussians into the Bois de Boulogne.

occasion of a sad return upon ourselves. In the House of Commons I take my place in the gallery reserved for the diplomatic corps, but I'm no farther ahead, and can catch some bits of phrases here and there, that's all. There were some young colonels with their hair parted in the middle defending the Purchase of Commissions; so be it. There is something to be said, for and against; but what strikes me, gentlemen, is that you are doing what we did the day after Sadowa. Hurry up and try to do better.

Yesterday, made my first visit to the Kensington Museum. It is really very interesting and instructive: one might get one's whole education in this place; but there are too many English paintings. They begin with Gainsborough and Reynolds; I don't say no, I often admire them, even in spite of certain contrasts of color that remind me of toast-and-jam. As to the school of to-day, molasses candy—if that's what you like, there you have it, and there the mob stays; I was literally sick. . . To pull myself together again I fled to the hall that shelters Raphael's cartoons: there is breadth to them, they are great, puissant, profound; you are in the presence of a master, you look, you listen, you profit. Would you believe it, they have never found out that these seven cartoons fill a room? They have added antique chests, pictures, whatever they could to embarrass and distract the attention.

Before dinner, as I was walking with the Duke, I saw at a distance the Duc de Gramont.[1] Delicate

[1] Minister of Foreign Affairs under the Empire at the time of the declaration of war.

situation for me between my ambassador and my former minister. I had to wait for his bow, whatever it might cost me. It was done *in extremis*, and I saluted after my chief. Really, how can these poor devils live through it?

LONDON, March 2, 1871.

People here are evidently beginning to be disturbed: it is the English that are paying, by the sacrifice of the treaty of 1856, for the service Russia has rendered Prussia. There is no longer a 'balance of power,' there are no longer any guaranties for anybody, with a second Poland and a secret fund of five billions in the cashbox of Frederick, Bismarck & Co. This war-reserve will drain the markets of Europe. We hold a fine position here. We no longer have to weep at people's doors, to disturb them with unreasonable importunity, we have only to wait, to let things come our way. The Duke does so with a master-hand.

LONDON, March 5, 1871.

A dolorous telegram had just been bulletined in the clubs: The Prussians at Paris! The Prussians clear to the Place de la Concorde! Can it be? What? From to-morrow on you will be exposed to all the consequences of this barbarous and futile insult, and I not there! I dare not let my thoughts dwell on you.

I don't doubt the ill-omened treaty will be signed. The only thing to say is that it would be still more ill-omened if it were not signed. It isn't a treaty of peace, but a pact of perpetual war, one of the treaties of peace such as Napoleon signed after each of his victories. That sort of thing lasts as long as the victory does, and up to the present time fortune has been fickle. That's the last word of the theory of nationalities under which the wars of Italy, Denmark and France were begun! . . . To have done with it, they have torn a country from the bosom of its mother, to which it clung, like my unhappy town of Metz. The feeling of disapproval is universal here; it is waiting till the thing shall have been accomplished and till nothing can be done, to break out with violence. For four months now public opinion has been veering every day more and more to our side, by reason even of the madness of our resistance and of the terror our enemies inspire. People know now the object of the war ; it is this wholesale and retail pillage that more than any thing else moves this land of the ' home ' and the ' law.'

We started this morning after mass for Richmond and took the wrong railway. Still, we were at the table at Morgan House at the stated hour. The horses here are fast, and we had discovered our mistake before we were twenty leagues away. Our road ran through the country from Kew to Ham, an admirably tilled district, the trees a hundred years old, cottages everywhere, or brick houses cast in the same mold, in endless succession without life or picturesqueness ; not a bit of wild, nor a touch for the imagination. Morgan House is more than plain outside. The interior is very agreeable and on the side of the park looks out upon a great green with magnificent ruminants in it. The meadows and their old oaks constitute the magnificence of England. The young Duchesse de Chartres is always charming. There was a significant silence on the subject of the absent ones.[1] The Comtesse de Paris, very pretty, vivacious and agreeable, quitted us to verify the report of the committee of supplies.

Do you know that more than fourteen millions has already been got together for our wounded and other victims of the war?

Took a look, before I left, at Orleans House, and then at Bushy Park. Hard by there were oaks such as grow nowhere but in a land where the law has not been violated once in at least two hundred years.

We are going to install ourselves at the Embassy. Imagine a first-floor-up, in the middle of a great amphitheatre; amazons and gentlemen cavalcade about on every side. Be it said by the way that this daily exhibition, in the heart of the town, of timid young girls who break in horses while they show their own grace and audacity and bring out the contours of their bodies, constitutes an exercise that may whet their appetite for lunch, but would not appear to us bourgeois to prepare young people for the virtues of the fireside.

LONDON, March 6, 1871.

. . . Saturday evening, at the Foreign Office. In the wake of a long line of carriages we went down to the New Palace. Fine stairway, and nothing else; I looked in vain for the apartments; two or three

[1] The Princes were then at La Grave, at the Duc Decazes's.

adjoining chambers might serve for robing-rooms. Well, the scene took place on the double stairway, right and left; the crowd mounting the steps was like a picture by Veronese. The Prince of Wales upon a side-landing, watched the coming up, with a jocular air; the Princess was interesting, congenial, touched with the distinction that suffering lends beauty. At the bottom of the stairs, a scraping and blaring of violins and trumpets in uniform. Think of me, then, as in the midst of aristocratic English society; but where are the Holbein heads, and the noble personages that have walked out of the frames of Van Dyck? I sought them in vain. Our bourgeois society quite as justly satisfies the eye. Not one pretty woman anywhere; and yet in the streets, on foot or on horseback, there is no lack of brilliant complexions, nor of golden hair, real or false. I shook hands with Mr. Gladstone; it is what receiving the ribbon of the *Légion d'Honneur* would be at Paris. I was much struck by the somewhat rough expression of countenance of Mr. Lowe, the chancellor.[1] Guided by Franqueville,[2] we reached the Duc de Broglie, who was a centre of attention and attraction. His being there in a double capacity made a sensation. His remark upon encountering M. de Bernstorff, the Prussian Ambassador, was going the rounds: it came off at table before the reception. Lady Stanley had been the only person between the two belligerents and had shown herself

[1] Robert Lowe, Chancellor of the Exchequer, created Viscount Sherbrooke in 1880, died in 1892.
[2] Comte de Franqueville, now a member of the Institute.

much preoccupied with what would happen when the ladies withdrew, and the time should come to "pass the wine." "Don't be afraid, I'll find a way out of it," the Duke said to her; and then presently addressing the barbarian: "I have been distressed so long at seeing the Prussians established in my home without my having invited them, that it is a pleasure at the house of a friend to meet one of them that I can exchange courtesies with."

The company left at midnight. The next day, at seven, we were up and about, to go to the mass at the Jesuits', in a chapel in which everything was beautifully finished and choice. The service was nicely done, the priest knew what he was saying and what he was about, and it did not all move *presto* as in Italy. The faithful are there for a purpose; they pray, they take the sacrament, with devotion; it is serious worship.

At eleven we were due at York House;[1] it was France in the person of the Duc de Broglie that was paying the visit. I fancy that both of them were gratified and touched. The Prince is always simple, but perfectly adequate to his position, inspiring sympathy and confidence and displaying them himself; the young Princess is merry: a united and affectionate couple. The gay Princess Amelia,[2] with blond hair, the picture of her father as a child, is vivacious and amiable; the Duc d'Orléans is a stout youngster with hair more than blond, who contributes his share to the hubbub.

[1] Residence of his Lordship the Comte de Paris.
[2] Now Queen of Portugal.

From every side, when I enter any of the retreats here that our exiles have found, familiar images attract my eyes; everywhere portraits, faces I have loved, memories; the sketch of the Queen by Scheffer, a work of art appreciated everywhere; but I glanced at this so quickly that I cannot stop long to describe it.

Before lunching, we visited Orleans House.[1] Too much has not been said about how well the fortune of the Duc d'Aumale has been laid out. The *Stratonice*, the *Mort du duc de Guise*, the *Passage du gué*, and the extraordinary canvasses of Decamps, Morhilat, Fromentin, besides the *Vierge* of the Orleans family and the sword of the great Condé. It is vain even to try to examine the glass cases and the shelves in the library. It is all very noble and very beautiful, and framed in English scenery with a rustic, modest little river, the Thames, running through it, and green everywhere.

From York House we went to Bushy Park. There we found the Prince, yes, the Prince, with the best grace in the world—but the Prince!—the first gentleman of France, Henri IV. himself!—one would think he had stepped down from his bronze horse. Only, the *Béarnais* ought to speak more rapidly. The Prince expresses himself with the utmost good sense, all the words in their proper places, his remarks perfectly just and sure. "The Republic has come indeed," he said, "when you see princes begging for a seat in the Assembly." No more, no less: that speech indicates all that he is thinking of, the measure

[1] Residence of the Duc d'Aumale. The Prince was absent.

of his Legitimism, and all that he accepts. . . .
He recollected my father, and *I* recollected his. exclamations over the lithographs of Captain Gavard and how he found them " wonderfully like." How much has happened since, and where would France not be to-day, if on a day of glory and liberty she had not thrust this whole family out of doors, and with it the only rational system of administration. That is the Duc de Broglie's perpetual refrain.

LONDON, March 10, 1871.

Finished the day, yesterday, at Lady Burdett-Coutts's.[1] Handsome house no doubt, but not especially so for the richest woman in a private station in the world. She is a large Englishwoman, not very young, with a cordial manner. In the apartments, a pell-mell that breathes a certain intimacy, in which good taste does not reign. I lit upon a big picture representing two thick booted legs in air, incomprehensible and mediocre from the point of view of art.[2] While I diverted myself with this prodigy, the concert was going on; great success for a gentleman who was playing on an accordion! Fancy his two arms approaching one another with " expression," and above them his face, across which played the sentiments he was communicating to his bellows. I can understand how one can play a hand-organ—there's nothing to do but to turn the crank; to acquire a skill. . . . on the accordion! But

---

[1] Lady Burdett-Coutts, created Baroness in 1871, heiress of Coutts, the great banker.
[2] The fine pictures were at the Burlington Exposition.

it was much relished and almost as well applauded as a squeaking trio, that was led by a boy with a falsetto voice. Come, no more music nor painting —stick to banking and try to brace up your politics.

The newspaper bulletins, set out on the sidewalk in the streets, under the wheels of the carriages, announce: *Red flag in Paris.* Really I can't torment myself by thinking about it. It seems as if we had but to lift a finger for the world to end.

LONDON, March 13, 1871.

Saturday, lunched at Morgan House. I 'swapped' stories of the siege against the tales of the marvellous adventures of the Prince de Joinville, at one and the same time Prince and Fanfan la Tulipe. He wouldn't have been the one to pass the day in camp the 18th of August.[1] Children and flowers everywhere—cats, horses, dogs; an elegant interior with all the English comforts brought together in a good taste that is French; affecting souvenirs on all the walls; and the Duchess charming. I laid a wager against her that the Princes would be either recognized, or be elected everywhere. I chuck my recollections in pell-mell—you must arrange them for yourself.

As I was going out I met the colony from Twickenham.[2] The talk was of France, her perils, and her future. Discussing these grave questions we traversed the *green* which leads to the Thames, got into a ferry-boat, and the dog threw himself into the water to follow us.

[1] An allusion to Bazaine.
[2] His Lordship the Compte de Paris and his family.

Yesterday, Sunday, lunched at Bushy Park. The Princess Marguerite is agreeable; the Comtesse d'Eu wears an expression of extraordinary kindness; the Comte d'Eu struggles with success against his deafness. He keeps himself well-informed, "up" in everything: one sees that he is a man of merit. Henri IV—I should say the Duc de Nemours, spoke to me at divers times of my father and of the lithographs of him; he showed us his family portraits, the collection of the Château d'Eu, with comment full of interest.

Paid a visit to the Athenæum Club. It is imposssible to live in England without tea, beer, hansoms, and clubs.

Be it said in passing, it is edifying to see how English society busies itself with our troubles. I have just returned from the Mansion House, where the Lord Mayor presided over a Committee of Relief. Sunday I spent at a sitting of the Marchioness of Lothians'[1] committee, where I found a gay girl who spoke French with an agreeable accent and was managing the affairs of three or four poor refugees (of her own sex) from France.——To-day we visited the Tower. I was much struck by the hat of the official cicerone; I should have said it was Anne Boleyn's execution.

WEDNESDAY MORNING, March 16, 1871.

It is snowing in great flakes, the spring showers of March. It can't be worse in any event at Oxford.

[1] C. H. Mahonesa, daughter of Lord Shrewsbury, dowager Marchioness in 1870, died in 1877.

Even if it were, we should leave for there; how could we countermand a *Rector Magnificus* and a *luncheon* that are awaiting us!

FRIDAY MORNING.

Yesterday the day was superb and I was very busy. Spent an hour and a quarter on the railway. The English landscape opened out before us in fine style—meadows, the Thames level with its banks, undulations of the land which added a touch of the picturesque (properly speaking, they are natural valleys or dells rather), lots of huge old trees, nobody in the fields, only steam engines at work, and the smoke of the locomotives rising above the farms, and coal everywhere. What would England be without the coal that multiplies her population a hundred-fold, and without the Straits which guarantee her from brigands? At intervals, red houses. Oxford! How it had snowed! The meadows were white, but as the sun rose, the snow melted, except in the shadow of the trees, and there was a singular picture of all the trees with their bare branches outlined in white against the greensward hard by. But don't let's lose time. We had dropped back into the Middle Ages. You might find in India, perhaps, a sacred village that had as completely preserved its peculiarities; the colleges here are all pious foundations, beginning as far back as the thirteenth or fourteenth century, that were surprised by the Reformation, which secularized and perpetuated them—singular mixture of the spirit of independence and of conservatism in this country. The edifices and their endowments have remained,

The buildings are doing all they can to hold out as long as the institutions, but the English stone shales off fearfully—I don't know which of them will be the first to go under. All the structures look utterly in ruins, which does no harm to the picturesqueness of it all; ivy climbs everywhere, mildew discolors the walls, stones are lacking, and it all works together to lend character to the thing and to dissimulate certain commonplaces and vulgarities.

The total effect is astonishing; twenty colleges in a town of no great importance, and nothing but the colleges, chapel, abbey, gardens, libraries, halls and their out-buildings,—all in English gothic, but of a period when it was natural. It abounds in charming 'bits', nothing very impressive in height, but rather in surface, and it stretches on indefinitely—there is lots of it. The streets are such as you see them in the Middle Ages at the theatre. You meet nobody in them but Fellows or Tutors or Rectors or Chancellors—there are titles no end, every college has its own, and the only thing that obtains throughout is the little, black, horizonal square, ill-balanced on the top of their skull-caps. This original head-dress is obligatory for the students, even after dark, so that one may know them for what they are and hand them over, in case of disturbance, to the University authorities, to whom they are exclusively responsible. They don't give much trouble, however; first because there are only twelve hundred of them, (we French would put up twenty thousand at Oxford); and then they are of good family—it takes not less than five or six thousand francs to spend six months, or seven barely, at Oxford. The English students do not need one's sympathy. They have to turn up at chapel at eight o'clock in the morning; afterward there are lessons till two, and then—boating for ever! *Au canot!* Everybody goes in their jackets to the Thames and the races begin; some of the students are on horseback. It appears that there are, all told, some thirty who contend for honors and fellowships; for there are students' colleges and fellows' colleges. As far as I can judge, there are five canonries. By means of celibacy, a university degree, and the favor of the founder, you enjoy in an Oxford college a good prebend, and do nothing for it. There is a college of the sort in which you may traverse the abbey, the park, the library, and meet nobody. But where are the students? There aren't any! There are two Fellows, simply; and room for two regiments. For the rest, at New College (*new* though great-grandfather to our Pont-Neuf) there are seventy students. I should have thought there would be a thousand. These young people live here, as you may see, in a somewhat liberal style, much at their case, with all the independence possible, as much expense as befits them, and space to let; every one of them *is somebody* and costs his family and the public dear.

It was the New College that I saw best, for we went back there to lunch. We went, according to an itinerary laid out by the Dean of Westminster, (he had smoothed the way for us—had sent word we were coming), from college to college and from the *Rector Magnificus* to the Librarian or the Vice-Chancellor. The 'official cap' of the New College (I really do not know the title of this benefactor of humanity), perceiving that the Vice-Chancellor was forgetting to invite us to break bread, came "to take possession of us again" at the inhospitable door of this personage, and shared his lunch with us—he had come away in the middle of it to find us. It was just a bit rash to invite four famished guests that way to take "pot-luck"—I was no end hungry: —but not at all, there was enough to feed a platoon in time of seige. Our benefactor himself helped us to plates, glasses, silver, from a sideboard: "Will you have mutton, veal, beef, some ham?" Stores truly Homeric; they needed only to be carved. Then there was a great cake, equally designed for an emergency, and capital with cunim, and beer, and sherry. Our hunger was satisfied in a trice; and we went away much touched by such simple, "canonical" hospitality.

But a truce to colleges: we took a carriage and drove in the cheery cold to Blenheim[1]; it was the castle known as Woodstock before it was given to the greediest of vanquishers, and the one most given to pillage. Still, there was a touch of Mars about him. The first glimpse of the place drew from us in chorus a cry of admiration: lake, meadows, woodlands, valleys—it was splendid. I hesitate to speak of the castle; it is immense, and in the country, at a distance, is most effective; but in proportion as you draw near, it becomes ridiculous.

[1] The castle of the Duke of Marlborough.

Still, it is as big as a palace of the first rank. From all the windows, a view worthy of Louis XIV.; inside, immense halls and some pictures that I did not have the time to examine in detail, but there was a Raphael, in his earliest manner, the *Virgin and Child* and *Two Saints*. It looked to me quite authentic and very beautiful. We had to beat a retreat without carrying it off. A monument to the memory of Marlborough gave me a mournful reminder of the magnificent monument of the Maréchal de Saxe at Strasburg. We crossed the park, putting the roes to flight and chasing the hares by stamping on the ground. The crows cawed us a good-bye, and we went back to Oxford to dine in the magnificent hall of the Randolph Inn, big as a railway station. At midnight we went to bed.

LONDON, March 19, Sunday,
Five o'clock, 1871.

Frightful day; we only have a word from Ponticoulant.[1] The only telegrams that have passed seem to announce that there has been a battle to-day.[2] I wanted to start home this evening; the Duc de Broglie detains me, not knowing whether he will not himself go and take a seat in the Assembly. What shall we do? I have spent my day with the commandant, Robert Le Fort,[3] who arrived yesterday. Shall we start home together? Will it be

[1] Comte de Pontécoulant, chief of the cabinet of M. Jules Favre, Minister of Foreign Affairs.
[2] The 18th of March, the sedition began at Paris that was to become the Commune.
[3] His Lordship the Duc de Chartres.

possible to get to you? Still another great torment has been reserved for me : to know that you are in danger and to be hesitating to attempt to rejoin you. I can only commend you all in this moment to God. George is with you—it is my sole argument for remaining here.

Extracts from the Notes.

On the morning of March 19th, the Duc de Chartres came to find me and to ask me, what the Duc de Broglie and I would do, if the day's despatches should confirm those of the night. " We should start home," I replied ; and in effect the Ambassador and I were on our way across the Channel the night of the 19th. The sea was absolutely calm, but the fog was so thick that the captain of the boat was unable to find his way, and had given orders to stop, and the fog-horn and bell were sending out signals of our presence across the darkness of the night and mist. A passenger standing on the bridge enveloped in furs, came to me and let drop a word in my ear, and then disappeared with a sign not to carry recognition further. It was Robert Le Fort, who was returning to his post.

It is not my intention here to pursue him on that painful voyage; I have spoken of him only to set in its proper light a generous imprudence of this prince, a soldier before everything. His public duty ended with the war with Germany ; the most evident political considerations united with the gentle inclinations of his own heart, as a father and a husband, to command him to remain by his own dear and charming fireside. Nevertheless he left home, and it took the pressing entreaties, nay, the injunctions even, of his friends to make him return to England. I say it knowingly, for it was upon me that the storm burst when I came to announce to MM. d'Haussonville and Bocher that the Duc de Chartres was waiting in a retreat, to me unknown, in the neighborhood of Versailles, for their advice on what there was for him to do. The Prince on starting back to England wrote me the following letter :

MANTEO, March 24, 1871.

"Dear Sir,—

"The telegraph has brought me nothing. Your note of Tuesday evening reached me this morning. I obey and shall be to-morrow with my wife. I give over all my projects—abandon the measures I was taking to get into the ranks of the National Guard for the preservation of order. The moment I ran the risk of hindering ulterior views, there was nothing left for me to do but to bow submission. For the rest, do not believe that I am indulging in self-pity; no true Frenchman, no generous heart, no officer who still preserves the sentiment of honor, finds time to-day to think of himself—the frightful state in which he sees his country is enough to poison all the time he can consecrate to reflection, to embitter his repose, to deprive the pastoral life I am going to lead of all its charm.

"The experience of the five days I have just spent in walking hereabouts and in the environs of

Paris, convinces me that personally I may do as I please; and it is only my respect for the advice of my friends that induces me to leave, and to break the chain so laboriously forged six months ago between my country and myself. I remain, however, always at their disposition. I possess the means to be of service; and if I am ever notified that it seems advisable for me to take part in the struggle, six days afterwards I shall be at a post of danger and in a uniform this time that shall be above suspicion.

"Pardon me for having again spoken to you about myself. Thanks for your having taken the trouble to write to me. Have the kindness to accept the assurance of my sincere friendship."

I set down also what I recollect of my impressions on arriving at Versailles. All, or almost all, of what constituted for the time being the government of France, had been gathered together at the Hôtel des Reservoirs about the endless long tables, where every one was left to get a seat when and how he might, in the strangest pell-mell of deputies, generals, ministers, and fashionable women. These last gave the tone to the assembly. The members laughed, joked, cried, were witty, drank, with the utmost vivacity. Nothing looked less like the sorry expedient of a raft after the shipwreck. I thought in spite of myself of those gay prisons in which the noblest blood of France once waited, at the time of the Convention, its summons before the revolutionary tribunal.

It is not my purpose to enter here into the details of my sojourn, divided, as it was, between Versailles, Paris, and Courbevoie, from the 20th of March to the 2d of April. I make a note only of the departure of my family from Paris. It was the day after the massacre at the Place Vendôme; I could hesitate no longer, I had to have done with it. A passage for carriages still remained open across the barricade of the Maillot gate. My poor father, quite ill already, got through in the Victoria that M. d'Haussonville had forgotten to remove from Paris, and that I, most happily for the owner, remorselessly *requisitioned*. That was the word and the custom at the time. I had *requisitioned* in the same way at Versailles my friend Eydin's house, in which I put up my family, and the Duc de Broglie and some of his people.

I had counted on having my family rest a bit at Courbevoie, at the house of our respected friend Mme. Laruse, before going on to Versailles; but their repose was troubled by the occupation of the communists. I had the next day to organize a fresh elopement. I reached Versailles this time with the coupé of another friend, M. Hennequin. As I was passing in front of the Communist post established at the head of the Neuilly bridge, certain street-arabs called: "Duck him!" and I might well in effect have finished my journey in the Seine, if I had not by a happy inspiration inquired my way (which I knew quite well), of the very person who seemed to me most ill-disposed. He became markedly polite and showed the coachman the way, and nobody after that thought of stopping us. The sorry garrison of Courbevoie passed its night in beating the call to arms, in sounding the alarm, and, above all, in imbibing. By daylight they were all knocked up with lack of sleep and the drink, and my family effected its departure without difficulty. Our joy was great, however, when we reached the first advanced sentinel of the Versailles forces, a municipal guard, between Puteaux and Saint-Cloud.

On the score of historical information, I note here the feeling of complete security that the officers of the band which was occupying Courbevoie displayed in relation to Mt. Valerien. When I called their attention to the fact that they were exposed to the fire of its cannon, they replied that they had a secret understanding with Mt. Valerien.

. . . .

The Duc de Broglie, being unable to leave again for London immediately, it was decided that I should precede him to assume the duties of the Embassy, and I left accordingly, the first of April, with letters accrediting me as Chargé d'Affairs.

I quitted Versailles early in the morning with the first of the reorganized regiments, who were going, the next day, to open fire on the communists at Asnières and Courbevoie, under the command of Gen. Montaudon. I had to pass by Saint-Germain and Pontoise, skirting the district visited by the shells of the insurgents, to gain Creil. On the third I arrived at London.

From the beginning of April on, till the last days of 1871, I was almost constantly in charge of the

Embassy, except during the short trips that the Duc de Broglie took to London in March, May, July, and November. Confined as I had up to that time been to the offices and special duties of the direction of commerce in the Department of Foreign Affairs, I made my début at one-and-the-same time in the position of representative of France abroad and in the management of political affairs. Possessed myself of nothing that could give me notoriety as a diplomatist, or that could supply the lack of it, I found myself in addition called upon to represent a nation, vanquished, crushed, whose very existence had become a problem—a government overwhelmed by the disasters and charges of the war and the invasion, and by the horrors of the most shameful civil war.

The English were much disposed to take pity on us. They showed us the measure of their sympathy in sending succor and provisions to the famished in Paris and in the districts left desolate by the war. The government had associated itself with this movement by the timid observations it had made to the vanquishers on the figure of the ransom they were exacting from us. But nobody was at that time tempted to go further in the imprudent step of compassion. Fear of Germany ruled the situation; people lowered their voices when they spoke Bismarck's name; and they had even gone the length of convincing themselves, by the logic of hope, that he would re-establish the equilibrium of Europe.

The bloody convulsions at Paris continually disturbed our neighbors, a little on their own account, because of the example; also, they were frankly eager to see the struggle come to an end, and they could imagine no more expeditious device for reestablishing order in France than the restoration of the Emperor, (who had again become their guest), by the aid of the Germans encamped about Paris and dominating the city by means of the forts they were occupying. They had no scruples against condemning us to this supreme degradation. They were full of contempt indeed for the Imperial Régime, but they were none the less so for the Dictatorship at Tours or Bordeaux; and they made no concealment of the fact that, in their opinion, the people of the Imperial Plebiscites and of the Revolution of the 4th of September had no right to show themselves difficult upon the character of their government. If they wished us a return of the Empire, it was simply that they did not deem us worthy of liberty nor capable of bearing the weight of it.

Hence arose the great popularity of Napoleon III, when after his defeat at Sedan he arrived in England. The crowd pressed about his path to give him an ovation; the police had been obliged to step in to protect the railings about his residence at Chislehurst against the invasion of his enthusiastic partisans. The Queen set the example, she had been the first to render, by her cordial visits, a public homage to the misfortunes of a Sovereign, whose hospitality she had accepted. The English princes, the diplomatic corps, vied with one another in external evidences of respect and deference. Of course the favor with which he was received was not all intended for the Emperor personally, nor as approval of his administration ; to a great many naïve people, he still stood for France, and they thought they were paying homage to our misfortunes by saluting the author of them or by receiving him with acclamations. I received the proof of it subsequently, when the more or less official bands played the "Jeune et beau Dunois" as an honor to the representatives of the Republic. The unreflecting infatuation of England for every sort of novelty must also be taken into account; glory (like shame) moves the mob. Notoriety of any kind is welcome there, is at a premium. The English are the greatest "flats" on earth.

Perpetually, on my arrival in England, France for the English, even for the English government, lay rather at Chislehurst than elsewhere, and her official representative was still the Marquis de la Valette rather than my quite obscure and wretched self. This notion was also shared by the greater part of the agents, the Empire had nominated, and I found traces of it even at the Embassy, where I found a good many other things to set to rights.

First there were the expenses that, by virtue of powers more or less regular given during the war, had under all the various administrations been incurred in the name of public safety. I had to put a stop to them, and to take steps, while there was still time, for auditing and allowing such payments as had been already made. The Embassy, taken by surprise, had patriotically accepted, under the pressure of necessity, the burden of accounts it was in no wise prepared for, nor able to determine the extent of in advance; but the war once at an end, it was necessary to return as quickly as might be to the beaten road. The concurrence of my comrades was not wanting to me; but the task was not the less heavy. Actions at law, the issue of which justified the promptitude of the measures taken on, the first days of my arrival put an end later to this painful liquidation.

Extracts from the Correspondence.

LONDON, Friday, April 6, 1871.

The newspapers which come in as I write inform me of the beginning of the pillage in Paris, of the sacking of our churches, of the arrest of our dear curé.[1] There is a general outcry here against the temporizing policy of M. Thiers, who is going to permit the shedding of innocent blood to avoid shedding guilty, and to avoid remaining face to face with a majority in the Chamber and with indignant France. I prefer to believe that he is awaiting the arrival of fresh troops, but the suspense is horrible, and the satisfaction I experience in thinking that I rescued you from that vortex of crime does not render me indifferent to the dangers of those who have had to remain behind. . . . Our dear curé, first: it is true, that personally he would not be sorry to suffer martyrdom at a time when the cross is trampled under foot.

[1] The Abbé Deguerry, curé of the Madeleine.

Would you believe that the Prince de Joinville, some days ago, just missed waking up in Paris? He had fallen asleep and passed unaware the last stop before the Saint-Lazare Station, and he had to jump off while the train was going.

I am taking lessons in speaking English. Their talk goes like an express train; there are twenty carriages and you see but one. It isn't easy to catch, on the wing.

LONDON, April 8, 1871.

Yesterday I exchanged a few words with the Directors of the Foreign Office and the Foreign Ministers. The meetings are sufficiently curious; everybody keeps a hand on himself and is on the *qui-vive*. Either I am greatly mistaken, or I left them convinced that they had a rather capable youth to deal with. The Turk, to whom no doubt somebody has said something or other about the relations of the Embassy with Twickenham, made me an Orleanist profession of faith. I seized the occasion to say: " God save the Princes from such a burden in a time like this. I love them personally too much to hope it for them for the rest, it is only the Republic that is equal to the days of June in 1848, or the siege of Paris in 1871."

This game of chess that one has to play every day is amusing enough at first. It will be an odd passage in my life. If I did not know you are at Versailles, what trouble I should be in!

April 18, 1871.

I have received from the Comte de Paris a letter

felicitating me on the great success obtained by my chief:[1] "They have found in him at last a political orator. I rejoice in it sincerely. I rejoice in it the more that I was fearing this début of his which had to be brilliant to meet the general expectation. It was perfect, and I am especially happy to see him attach his name to a liberal measure adopted under such circumstances. It is altogether a new thing in our parliamentary history, and gives me great hope.

I took pains to show myself at a rout given by the Lord Mayor at the Mansion House. In spite of the rigor of the times and of the humility commanded us, I took some satisfaction in representing my unhappy country at the palace of the city. It is a fine hall with Corinthian columns and Gothic windows; the band of the Parisian Guards, which took refuge in London after the cataclysm of the 18th, was there; also the Lord Mayor and the Sheriff with their bands, the gold-plate that has never been pillaged, lots of bare-headed Englishmen, and Englishwomen in dresses with trains. I made my entry with a number of "Very-glad's" and of hand-shakings with the Lord Mayor, with his wife, with his daughters, with whatever presented itself; Franqueville was doing the honors of my person. Lesseps turned up there quite à-propos to supply me with a comic incident. He took me for somebody else and led me to his wife. She was a bit surprised at first, and then grew voluble in admiration of my

[1] The Duc de Broglie, who reported a law on the offenses of the Press, had spoken on the 14th of April in favor of an amendment giving the law a more liberal construction.

beard, which had made me look strange to her. I replied that it was the siege that had made it grow, and this remark finally dissipated her remaining doubts. After some time, Lesseps, who began to suspect something, rejoined me and to repair his error asked me if I was with Mme X. *For shame!* I told Mme. de Staël the story and she laughed heartily.

Decidedly, Montaudon[1] has made a hit.

The London journals are asking me for his portrait and for a note on him. He is the hero of the day. Things have gone off on another tack here: "To the block with the insurgents." They are vanquished! I greatly hope their account will be settled, sword-in-hand. It is too late to admit a capitulation. They have got to be punished.

LONDON, April 21, 1871.

In the morning, toward six o'clock, I come down the stairway, to the great scandal of all the housemaids who are squatting on the steps or before the fireplace which they are polishing.

They all flee at sight of me, like frogs that leap into the water. The sense of inferiority in the women in service, their humility not only in the presence of their master but before all the males of the household, is one of the things that shock me the most. I arrive at the office of the Duke with the great oak wardrobes all about it, a sort of sombre hall with two big windows, in front of which the amazons

---

[1] General Montaudon, afterwards commander of an army corps and a Deputy.

defile at a hand-gallop from nine o'clock on, and the Horse Guards pass and repass, and the Grenadiers, also, dressed in white like scullions, with two pibrochs. It all goes on at the sky-line, almost above the line of vision, as in an aquarium. At eight o'clock the journals come; at half-past eight, the courier and your letter: it is the best minute of the day. Hour after hour the telegrams come in; when they relate to Jules Favre, my interest redoubles; and then the personnel, the visits, and the close of office-hours.

To-morrow I dine, the only one of my tribe, at Lord Granville's.[1] If my neighbors only speak French ! This same Granville played me a trick yesterday that might have given me trouble. At noon he sent the Duke word to come to him at three o'clock to exchange the ratifications of the agreement about the Black Sea. I replied to the bearer, by a note scribbled at the corner of a table, that the Duke was absent, etc. That evening the protocol reached me with my note inserted at full length. I do not know what effect it will produce in Europe, but, for myself, it turned me cold. Happily it is all right.

LONDON, April 24, 1871.

Yesterday I dined at Lord Granville's—a fine house, really elegant, and what is still better, a charming wife,[2] very beautiful, very fashionable, speaking French with a bit of an accent, just enough to lend color to her words. I was presented to all

---

[1] L. Leveson Gower, Earl Granville, born in 1815, Minister of Foreign Affairs; he died in 1891.
[2] Castalia Cambello, second wife of Lord Granville.

the guests one after another;—impossible to catch the name of any of them. They all talked French more or less: I was humiliated not to be able to return them a word in their own tongue. We seated ourselves at table and I found myself on the right of Lady Granville; I am not yet up to so much honor. The dinner was good, with some oddities, such as a dish of cheese to finish with after the ice-cream. At dessert, the ladies rose; I got ready to follow my beautiful neighbor; but not at all—I had to stay where I was and help pass and repass two small decanters of wine which were making the round of the table. That lasted happily but a half-hour, and at ten o'clock we entered the salon.

Had some good chat with Brunnow.[1] "England likes you." "She believes that we shall last more than a quarter of an hour," I replied. Some days before he had said to me, "England will be well disposed toward you, if you last more than a quarter of an hour."

LONDON, May 18, 1871.

I joined the Duc de Broglie at the Rothschilds'.[2] Magnificent place; here is gold well laid out, a luxury of high good taste. First, the stairway, with three rows of columns, a spacious structure, with the light falling from above, all that could be desired by a Guardi, and flowers, such as I had never dreamed of. A fine square brings you to a salon, which is somehow horribly *sterling* and ex-

---

[1] Baron de Brunnow, Ambassador of Russia, died in 1875.
[2] Lionel, Baron Rothschild, head of the Banking-house, died in 1879.

quisite, with old French hangings, 18th century embroidered silk, and some "old masters', Del Sarto, Murillo, Greuze, just enough to decorate the place without converting it into a gallery, all very comfortable. There were some ladies present: Mme. Alphonse,[1] a beauty of an odd sort, something of the race of Jacob in it; the Duchess of Manchester,[2] a beauty of the sort that is conventional in courts that go in for amusement; the beautiful Lady Granville; the Countess de Flandre,[3] quite royal—if you knew Latin, I should say, *Incessu patuit dea;* she is no bigger than she should be, but she does not make herself small. Those were the beauties in the salon. Add to these, the Baroness,[4] and her husband in a chair on rollers. Well, I succeeded somehow in saluting each of them; the Duke has given me his perch with a vengeance.

Guided by the Postmaster-General,[5] we visited together the central telegraph office: there we found five hundred young girls, who had all of them read their novel that morning and made their tea—they did not belong to the laboring class. They were transmitting messages to the four corners of the world with movements of feverish trepidation, talking the while. It is a market-place for words. We were accompanied in our visit by a small man, very

[1] Baroness Rothschild, daughter of Lionel.
[2] Louise, Countess d'Alten, married in 1852 to the Duke of Manchester, and remarried to the Duke of Devonshire.
[3] Marie, Princess of Hohenzollern, married to the Comte de Flandre.
[4] Baroness Rothschild, died in 1884.
[5] William Monsell, created Lord Emly in 1874.

simple, a bit pock-marked, lame, looking more like the descendant of some clergyman than the representative of an illustrious stock. He is the last offshoot of the Dukes of Norfolk.[1]

LONDON, May 19, 1871.

We have organized our ceremony for Saint-Cloud.[2] Gounod has arrived with the Curé. He is a queer chap, always half up in the clouds. We shall have a sermon, chanted prayers, a concert, a description of the ruins. This morning I obtained a permit from the Archbishop[3]—fine head, grand air, ascetic and highbred face ; he quite charmed me. . . .

I saw the Queen in her carriage—the Scotchman Brown on the box. She was going to the new colossal statue of Prince Albert, the statue that was chosen from among all the rest. The Prince must be greatly embarrassed by his pedestal, for he was a man *comme il faut*—and embarrassed still more by the temple they are raising to him, facing Albert Hall—temple, kiosque, pagoda, Byzantine phantasy. It is enough to make Wellington jealous—*he* has only two statues, the one with a three-cornered hat, and another at the opposite end of the park, with nothing on but a sword.

At the same time the national liquidation goes its

[1] Fifteenth Duke of Norfolk, H. Fitz Alan Howard, First Duke of England, hereditary Earl Marshal, born in 1847.

[2] Benefit concert to assist the curé of the town of Saint-Cloud, burned in 1871.

[3] Henry Edward Manning, Archbishop of Westminster in 1865 ; cardinal in 1875, died in 1892.

way; the ministry is nothing but a syndicate; it is unsettling everything. Some days since, Mr. Gladstone did not conceal his sympathy for woman's franchise; then, another minister almost gives over the Established Church. They are pulling up the piles, one after the other, from under the great island.

Extracts from the Notes.

While I was fencing with all these difficulties, the bloody struggle was going on at Paris and lengthening out, keeping me in an anguish that displayed itself in those about me by a veritable " every-fellow-for-himself." The Duc de Broglie came to relieve me toward the end of April; he brought me, along with his own approbation, the most explicit testimonials of satisfaction on the part of the government. The time did not lend itself to the dry restraint of regular diplomacy. Dating from the first steps that I made, M. Thiers and M. Jules Favre had felt in my measures and my language a breath of patriotism that belonged to the occasion.

The Duke was not to remain long in London. The 6th of May, I was charged with the painful duty of announcing to him that his son had been wounded before Paris. It was soon no longer possible to hide the gravity of the case from him, and he decided to leave at once for Versailles, the 20th of May. His departure was even so precipitate that he excused himself from assisting that day at the official banquet at the Foreign Office on the Queen's birthday. As it was indispensable that France should be represented there, I had to present myself, rigged out in the Duc de Broglie's uniform. The same carriage took us, me to the palace of Foreign Affairs, Whitehall, and him to Charing Cross Station. He was much depressed, and I scarcely less so. I needed all my courage to face for the first time, and under such circumstances and in such a garb, the eyes of the diplomatic corps.

I had till then avoided mingling with society more or less official; I had held myself apart, waiting till I should have something other than condolences to gain by coming forward. This reserve, which was abundantly justified by the state of my father's health and the loss it menaced me with, did not obstruct my introduction into the world of fashion, in which I was slowly to win my place. A representative in mourning befitted a France in mourning for two provinces and for the pick and choice of her children.

Never did the feeling of my isolation, of my impotence, of my insufficiency, weigh more heavily upon me than when I presented myself at the Foreign Office to confer with Lord Granville. Foreigners had lost all shame, some of them in the arrogance of parvenues, the rest in their abasement before the stronger. I remember the bitter reflection that rose in me, while I was waiting my turn for an audience in a room that opened on the inner court of the Foreign Office. The clock which was sounding, with a pitiless vibration, the hours, the halves, the quarters, seemed to me the voice of destiny crying to me: Room for the sound of limb—woe to the vanquished! Room for the nations who know how to control themselves—woe to the peoples touched with madness! . . .

Extracts from the Correspondence.

LONDON, MAY 21, 1871.
Sunday Evening.

. . . At seven o'clock we received Roger's [1] telegram announcing the entrance of our troops into Paris. Madame de Staël excused me, that I might go and announce the good news to the princes, who all gather on Sunday at the house of the Comte de Paris. Whip up, driver! . . . Everybody was there—a little surprised at my arrival. I gave them some better news of the Duc de Broglie's son, and handed the Comte de Paris the telegram in its envelope. The Comte read it. Imagine the sensation!—the messenger from Marathon was not better received; they wanted to hug me, and for my part they might have had their way, provided I did not have to begin with the aged Princesse de Salerne.

But to return to the Duke's departure. He left me in my harlequin's disguise at the door of the Foreign Office; I begin by reassuring you—I was the most beautiful of the lot! That is small praise, it is true, to the others; but can you conceive me rigged out like that in the midst of sixty diplomats and high dignitaries all of whom I should have known? Lord Granville only half listened to me;

[1] Comte de Pontécoulant, chief of the cabinet of M. Jules Favre.

Odo Russell,[1] a German rather than a Frenchman, had to accept me as his neighbor at table; farther off sat Hamilton Seymour, the shrewd diplomat who saw through Nicholas' game in 1854. Course succeeded course, the service all of silver, to the perpetual accompaniment of the military band. At dessert they drank the most frigidly comic toast in the world to Her Majesty the Queen. The ministry replied by a toast to the sovereigns and official heads of the friendly states and allies who were then and there so worthily represented. They drank once more, but the wine elicited nothing *spirituelle* from out of all those uniforms. After the wine I waylaid my friend Brunnow in his silver coat; I took him up at the word when he offered to lend me a hand; I begged him to present me to the score or so of ministers and ambassadors whom I had not met. We began with Bernstorff,[2] who wears the paternal air of a good German: I had to tell him how the Duke's son had been wounded; when he learned that it was done by the insurgents, he cried out with what was intended for politeness: "I am glad it was not done by us." I made the round of a dozen embroidered coats with the same story.

Lady Granville arrived, gracious and beautiful as always, and then the mob poured in. Toward half-past eleven, Prince Ladislas[3] and I fled while the

---

[1] Odo Russell, Ambassador to Germany, made Lord Ampthill, in 1881, died in 1884.

[2] Count Bernstorff, Ambassador of Germany, died in 1873.

[3] Prince L. Czartorisky, born in 1828, married to the Princesse Marguerite, daughter of the Duc de Nemours, died in 1894.

band was heralding the Prince of Wales with a *God Save the Queen*.

LONDON, May 23, 1871.

We are taking heart again about the Duke's son. We have just passed a delicious morning—Mme. de Staël herself was in raptures. I had brought Gounod with me, and he was sparkling. Finally he sat down to the piano, and gave us the third act of Othello, the symphony with choruses; I don't remember now whether he spoke them or played them. One of the '*D's*' in my piano was out of tune; as he took his leave, seeing the pleasure he had given us, he came back to me and said: " Have the *D*, fixed against I come again."

This is the reply Saint-Saëns sent to Gounod's letter asking him to play the organ—what do you think of it? " Accord in *ut*, accord in *sol*, i. e. perfect accord." [1]

That sort of thing charms Mme. de Staël—has quite turned her head. She's a saint—with Cardinal Manning's permission; she edifies me, makes me quite envy her. Immersed in affairs, my mind and life in full activity, my thoughts do not dwell, as hers do, upon God; I would they did.

LONDON, May 25, 1871.

Paris effaced in a single night from the map of the world![2] There's nothing left for it but to found

[1] A play (for which there is no equivalent in English) on the French phrase *être d'accord*, meaning, of persons, " All right, I agree " (Je suis d'accord), and of musical instruments, to be in tune. —(Translator's note.)
[2] News had just reached London of the fires lit by the Commune.

a new commonwealth (shall we even call it—
France?); but for such an undertaking—to support
misfortunes of such magnitude, there needs a
people in full vigor, with virgin forces and a violent
and audacious patriotism. I mean all those who are
responsible for our misfortunes; they ought to know
when to step aside and give place to the younger
generation—and to faith—which alone can save us.

Roger has sent me a succession of telegrams dated
from Mt. Valérien, one of them in some sort terribly
eloquent : " I dare no further, Colonel Lokner says,
question the horizon." A telegram reports that the
old Louvre will be saved. The pictures I know are
at Brest. If they leave us Sainte-Chapelle, with
Notre-Dame and Les Invalides, we might rebuild
Paris.

LONDON, May 26, 1871.

I've been on the jump since morning to get the
London firemen off. Mr. Gladstone spoke some
words of sympathy yesterday and I hastened to
thank him, and also Sir Robert Peel,[1] who had
pilloried the Commune with his customary vigor of
speech. I suggested to him the notion of sending
to Paris a detachment of the London fire-brigade
with their steam-pumps. He's a "hustler" as the
Yankees say: the sort we need to gather up our
scattered fragments. The idea took effect and
spread (it is no exaggeration) as if by electricity. We
took a hansom to the first fire-brigade station; to
hurry the thing an appointment was made with
Capt. Shaw somewhere along the route. It was all

[1] Brother of the present Speaker, eldest son of Sir Robert Peel.

settled—orders and instructions given, the ship chartered, M. Jules Favre notified at the same time as Lord Granville. . . .

LONDON, Friday Evening.

Orders countermanded, under the pretext that the fire has been mastered. I replied in vain: "What difference does that make?" It was in vain, I kept my minister's telegram in my pocket. Lord Lyons[1] had been notified, and Lord Granville had sent for me to come to the Foreign Office to advise me of the countermand that he had received and transmitted. I was not well received when I brought the order "to stop" to the firemen and volunteers. They had gone into it with a will. But they could not be more disappointed than I was. It was a precious opportunity to fraternize lost.

The night of the 23d and 24th of May, with its dismal glow, which was seen on all sides of Paris, reminds me of the night of the 24th of August, 1572. These are two crimes that belong together.

What has become of our dear priest? Pray heaven to spare him.

Extracts from the Notes.

. . . La Commune at an end, I felt public opinion fall away from us, at least that expressed by the press, which is not always to be confounded, however, with that which rules the masses. It was the moment when sympathy was taking a turn in favor

---

[1] British Ambassador to France; died in 1887.

of the Communists, whom every tide scattered on the English coast. It was forgotten that the blood they came stained with was that of their victims; it was the fashion to bewail their miserable fate. Lady Burdett-Coutts gave the signal, and at her own expense took charge of one of the first bands of disembarked; she even had one day the hardihood to ask me to take charge of them myself. Subscriptions were opened for them in the newspapers. Nothing gives a better idea of the stupidity of the opinion reigning at that moment in London than the question asked by a Lord (by courtesy),—that is to say, by the son of a peer. Some one was speaking to him of the wound the son of the Duc de Broglie got in the course of the recapture of Paris, and he inquired naïvely on which side he was. Of course the British government did not permit itself such a change of attitude, but Lord Granville's reserve redoubled. I thought I had advised the government for the best in engaging it to make no useless protests, to let the reaction in opinion come about spontaneously. And, if it decided on following up anybody, to launch the blow at some illustrious rascal like Felix Pyat. This was the advice of the Minister of the Interior, Mr. Bruce,[1] whose gorge rose against this inundation of blood-stained filth, and who did not admit that the law could extend its protection, under pretext of political exigency, to the most execrable of assassins. Still, in a matter of this sort, the honor of England was at the mercy of her judges, and the government had no desire to

[1] Created Lord Aberdare in 1873.

compromise itself by a movement of generous indignation. The Gladstone-Granville Cabinet did not show itself more courageous in the presence of the agitation of the radicals in favor of the Commune than in the presence of the prestige (not to employ another word) of the victories of Germany.

Extracts from the Correspondence.

LONDON, June 12, 1871.

This morning the Comte de Paris came to pay his official call at the Embassy. He is waiting for the Princess to be confined, and could not follow his brother and his uncles,[1] but was unwilling to postpone coming to take possession of the right which has finally been given him again.

He got out of a hansom, like the plainest of mortals, in a pouring rain. I hastened forward to receive him; a little more and the doorkeeper would have refused admittance to so unassuming a visitor. You perceive that the scene scarcely lends itself to historical painting of the sort at Versailles.

It was a solemn moment all the same, and for me a delicate one; I had to be on my guard that neither more nor less than the proper thing should be said to the Prince; more than all it was especially difficult to catch the exact shade of the terms, full of deference, but distinctly respectful, in which he should express himself in regard to M. Thiers. I

[1] The Chamber had repealed the laws exiling them, and M. Gavard had had the honor some days before of signing a passport for the other Princes.

was happily inspired with the idea of asking the Prince himself to take the pen and he wrote at my table the following dispatch : " The Comte de Paris came Saturday to Albert-Gate-House. He said to me, that the Embassy being French territory, he had hastened to knock at the door. For the rest the special object of his visit was to express to the official representative of his country the profound joy he feels at the recent decision of the National Assembly which opened to him the gates of the land that he has never ceased to love above all others. In particular he asked me to act as his spokesman to the chief of executive power and give him assurance of his respect."

The message was sent the same evening with the simple addition of S. A. R. Mgr. before the name of the Comte de Paris.

LONDON, June 15, 1871.

Many compliments about *my* dispatch, on the part of the duc De Broglie, as well as of M. Jules Favre who regretted however that I had added . . .

LONDON, June 27, 1871.

Yesterday evening I visited parliament. You outsiders think it exists; but it does not. I found one individual who gesticulated, making motions to waken another who slept on the bench opposite him. The conservative party was combating the great innovation, the secret ballot-bill, destined to fill this imprudent land with democracy brimming full. Nothing could be, I should say, more antagonistic to the English character and habits of thought: it is a slur cast on the civic courage of the electors, it is a step toward universal suffrage—nay, even toward allowing women to vote.

They were fifteen in all. Near half-past nine, a reinforcement of twenty arrived, who had been asleep; from time to time somebody woke up and cried: "*Hear, hear!*" The orator took fresh heart, and turned toward the benevolent auditors. Suddenly the sleepers leaped to their feet and removed their hats: the speaker had finished and they wished each of them to have their say and be done with it, so as to go home and get to bed. I began to understand that nobody comes but those who wish to speak.

LONDON, Sept. 5, 1871.

Mr. Gladstone has made a speech. In France we should call him a socialist and it may be should not be wrong. Another stampede among the horses in the camp at Aldershot. If the English have forgotten how to tie their horses, and can't sail up the mouth of the Thames without running aground, and can't open their mouths without cheering on the rich, there is material for a new book on England.

. . . .

I started off at nearly two o'clock; not having a church to visit in this country without a personal God and without art; I passed by the National Gallery, and stopped for some time before my beloved Italians; I amused myself by comparing the Madonna of Corregio and that of Raphael. I had some things to do; ascertained, by the way, that even the chief of police is in the country. And the robbers? . . . In public offices, as in the Board of Trade, there is absolutely no one, all the employees are off to the Continent for two months. There would not even have been a doorkeeper left but that we had announced a communication and some one had to receive it. At last I reached the Club;[1] it is really charming to find oneself in the midst of so many books; with all the means of occupying the mind and being alone! Here is Grote, Mommsen, the most beautiful editions of all the classics and of the books on the European galleries; only there are too many of them, they neutralize each other and puzzle the will, and I sit looking at them, unable to choose.

I took Denys[2] to Covent-Garden. The opera is converted into a sort of promenade concert. You should see the inventions in Musical art in this country: they put the gas out, light it again; fire off cannons (I mean literally); have horses stamping over the floor and outbursts of savage cries from different parts of the hall, and instantaneous changing of the orchestra from the pit to the gallery, and they call all this music. The audience is enchanted and the leader of the orchestra thinks he has outdone Wagner.

LONDON, September 20, 1871.

I was delighted at the Club yesterday to read M. Guizot's article. Have been turning over the old

[1] Athenæum.
[2] The Baron Denys Cochin, now Deputy.

Duc de Broglie's biographical notes. They bring him back very vividly to one. He was a politician of the school of St. Louis, and deserved to be his minister. The old man that I knew and whose memory I revere was certainly the young man who at twenty forgot that he was the head of the House of Broglie; he might well say it because every one believes him. . . .

To-morrow morning I am going to assist at the battle of Dorking;[1] planning the while my commercial dispatch. This new sport is all the rage. Every minute a new supplement of the newspapers appears to give the news of the battle; some of the military engaged are distinguishing themselves even. Our neighbors go from sublime to ridiculous.

WALMER CASTLE, [2] September 27, 1871.

I hardly know yet where I am, for I arrived in the night. I saw a portcullis, a lowered drawbridge, enormous walls, the most bizarre corridors, vaults, and at last a donjon where I am established like Foquet or Bolivar. Don't push the comparison too far.

I arrived at half-past seven; I was taken round and round, sometimes upstairs, sometimes down, without being blindfolded however, till I reached my hostess, who was reposing on a white sofa—white on white. How beautiful she is! and how amiable, in spite of

---

[1] The military manœuvres devised as a reply to a pamphlet entitled the Battle of Dorking. In this pamphlet an hostile army was supposed to attack London, and you are told of its success.

[2] Residence of Earl Granville, Lord Warden of the Cinque Ports.

a little coldness of manner which goes well with her brilliant complexion! I was presented to her mother (her eyes are buried in her head; she sees, however); and then to the charming Lady Georgiana Fullerton.[1] We dined without the beautiful Countess who remained where she was, stretched on her sofa. The talk was unimportant; everybody rose at the sacramental ceremony of passing the wine, and then we returned to the drawing-room. But I must tell you a little adventure I had on the way here! I met a lady and her daughter on the train; we had had a bit of an accident with the locomotive, and the mother was overcome with curiosity; she wanted to see what the trouble was, and I helped them off and on again; and presently they began to speak French and we understood at last what we were saying. They got out at the station before Deal.— Everybody here was on the *qui vive*: " Who can she be?" There is to be a wedding Tuesday in this neighborhood and the two ladies had come down to attend it. Every one was curious about them, they asked me who they are—cross-examined me. Finally the description they give me evoked an image: it was the two ladies—Lady Vernon and her daughter.

Meanwhile, the Minister of Foreign Affairs had relapsed into business—he opening boxes and sending telegrams, at the other end of the room where we were chatting. When he was done, he came over our way and told some funny stories and told them

[1] Daughter of the first Count Granville. Died in 1885. Authoress of some well-thought-of novels.

well. You could see that he is in the habit of telling stories, and that his auditors are in the habit of listening and applauding. Silence was restored when we played chess, and was only broken by the sound of the moves. We held our breath. I began like a greenhorn. Perhaps it was only a feint. My adversary was taken in the snare and played carelessly. I pulled myself together and he would have been most astonished but a telegram came and was passed to me.

It was of course from Lady Vernon—her thanks to M. Gavard. When Lord Granville had retired to his corner, instead of relapsing into business, he had written to his neighbors: " M. Gavard presents his respects to the ladies whom he was able to serve on the way down." This bit will give you an exact notion of the amiable character of Lord Granville and of his sociability. Immediately afterward every one went to bed. So here I am in my cavern. It is a regular Noah's Ark: contains some of everything—spiders, gnats. . . . The house, however, is as clean and comfortable and orderly as possible.

Sunday.—First, "luncheon," with all sorts of things to eat at half-past nine. I made the acquaintance of Lady Vita (Victoria-Alberta) a mischief with golden hair; my poor heart could not resist her— "my poor heart," I am afraid, may become a bit hackneyed with all its infatuations. I went to Mass at Deal with the Fullertons, in a little chapel where there were some Irish Soldiers. The poor priest bungled the High Mass with all its religious images; but he hopes to keep his congregation as long as the rival Establishment.

On our return I stopped a bit at the castle, thinking of the poor priest at every little opening in the picturesque view; the walls are covered with ivy in the foreground and overlap each other, and there are trees that stand out against them, and cannon peeping through the stones, and the sea at the horizon like a ribbon of silver. Ships pass and repass along the greatest ocean highway in existence. In my excursions about this great toy—this fortress fitted up by an upholsterer—I found the beautiful Countess lying at ease between two cannon, drinking in the breeze. She is a hyperborean beauty— one of the kind that does not flourish except in the rain and the wind and cold.

Her poor mother, Mrs. Campbell, is blind; I thought it was only an apparent infirmity, but no; she has not seen a ray of light for fifteen years. She lost her sight by reading to her husband at night. Now, however, she is so skilful that I lunched and dined with her, and I saw her at a game of chess without suspecting that she was blind.

Our *second* lunch we took at two o'clock, after which we walked over to the cliffs of Kingsdown. From time to time one could see France; between it and us lay the dangerous shifting sands of the channel. We recognized them by the way the waves broke. There, between the sands and us, was an immense fleet: I counted one hundred and twenty vessels. It reminded me of my walks along the sound or the straits of Messina. There are no doubt more vessels here than in front of Scylla, but where is the sun, where are the oranges, and the indefinite I know not what, that intoxicates, that creates memories, and leaves one agreeably melancholy?

A little person accompanied us on her pony; nothing could be more amusing than this little horsewoman, who chatted busily all the way. She is four years and a half old. On our return we found the beautiful Countess still reposing between the cannon. I kept her company until the cold drove me away. Afterwards I checkmated my minister in good earnest; I promised him his revenge; and then said good-night and *au revoir*.

LONDON, September 26, 1871.

I spent from eight o'clock this morning to five this afternoon at Shoeburyness,[1] immersed in artillery. What a Sabbath! It was very interesting; there was a special train; my place was next to General Storck (Under Secretary of the Minister of War), who presided at the fête: an Englishman without the prejudices of country. Our officers appeared very well; all eyes were on them, and in especial on Colonel Berge[2] who used to know George and saw him frequently at Metz. He is distinguished-looking. We fired some shots both on land and at sea, pierced armor a metre thick, admired the Moncrieff gun-carriage: a six-hundred-ton piece which turned somersaults in air at every shot and came back of itself to its original position. It is really very pretty

[1] At the mouth of the Thames, left bank.
[2] Baron Berge. He had been commandant of the army corps.

—too much so, no doubt, to be practical. We got some quite good shots at sea at eighteen hundred metres. If I had not been afraid of being indiscreet, I should have proposed moving the target five hundred metres nearer, or farther away. We should not have had, no doubt, such fine results.

LONDON, September 27, 1871.

God save us from a lonely old age! This morning I visited more than seven hundred old men—childless, unsurrounded by affection. They have food, lodging, such care as is necessary, and everything is very clean;—but it is horrible. To have lived so many years and have no fireside of your own, to leave behind you here below no hope, to be contracted to the little that is left of yourself, to your pains and misery! Mr. Vernon (Guardian of our parish, Belgrave Square and Grosvenor Square—the wealthiest in London, and comprising a hundred and fifty thousand souls) came for me this morning and took me to a workhouse for old men—hospice or hospital. There were also some children there, picked up in the streets; they stay there a short time, and then are distributed in certain proportions among the asylums out of town. The establishment is large and well kept; no bad smells anywhere. Though I did not come out of it especially cheerful. I made an appointment with my "Guardian" for the coming week, to visit the workhouses for sturdy vagabonds.

That is the great social and economical problem: humanity must be reconciled to facing enough in the way of irksomeness, so that the hundred and fifty thousand inhabitants of this parish will not demand the asylum of the workhouse. I should have found this visit less depressing if I had run across the white caps of the Sisters of Charity there, that is to say, the love of God, the volunteers in the service of the Divine Love, instead of the salaried functionaries in the service of humanity. Still, prayers are offered up there; there is a chapel, but one might call it a refectory and not be far out. My " Guardian " pleased me infinitely;[1] he is a brother-in-law of the Lady Vernon of the railway train.[2] Nothing could equal his kindness nor that of his young wife. These English astonish me; their charity for France is frantic, passionate, such as we ourselves unhappily do not all practice.

LONDON, October 7-9, 1871.

I learn that Léon Say[3] is going to come to a banquet at the Mansion House, on the eighteenth. Nothing could be more opportune than this visit, unless I have to take the field again because of M. Thiers' wish to "decorate" the Lord Mayor. The amenities of the first campaign, which brought on an exchange of remarks in Parliament, seem to be forgotten. M. de Flavigny had brought a fistful of "decorations" to some Irishmen who had deserved

[1] The Hon. William Vernon, younger son of the second Lord Vernon, married to Mlle. Boileau, who died in 1881. She was a grand-niece of Boileau.
[2] See above the letter of September twenty-seventh.
[3] M. Léon Say, then Préfet de la Seine, was coming to thank the English for help sent France during the war.

well of France during the war, but not so well of England. Three of them were engaged in the agitation for Home Rule. Lord Granville appreciated the efforts I then made to avoid for both governments a tiresome complication. The ill-omened names disappeared, and I remember a note that I received, while the mess was still undisposed of, suggesting that I substitute *china* for the decorations. It was his amiable lordship who gave me this discreet and charitable piece of advice. This time Lord Granville consents to shut his eyes, " since my government finds it agreeable to give foreign subjects decorations which they will not be authorized to wear."

LONDON, October 10, 1871.

Some friends took me yesterday to the church at Eaton Place, which was decorated for the harvest-home. Poor Mrs. Vernon was quite knocked up, tricking out a pulpit with fruits and festoons, sheaves and inscriptions in grains of wheat. It didn't prevent the church from looking like a cow-pen divided into stalls.

In the evening I saw another church which I shall designate by the name of its founder only, Mr. Beresford Hope. It is well enough built, in the Byzantine style, but the ornamentation is not happy. Two rows of colossal reed-pipes first struck me; they were the organs decked out with ribbons; nothing but the mottoes were lacking. They all sang out of tune, the men on the right, the women on the left, but they were very fervent and serious in this church, which one would have said was Catholic, for they had the word perpetually on their lips. They are "high church." The Pope is the only thing that holds them back.

Before dinner we visited the managing office of the Westminster workhouse and the place where the houseless are sheltered for the night. Fancy, in the first place, a whole land of authentic miracle behind the big buildings of the Westminster region; the depth of misery is cheek-by-jowl with the height of wealth. You have only the fair exterior, the seamy side lies behind. I do not say that the house of refuge where shelter is offered overnight, is seductive: twenty-four beds spread about the chamber of a ramshackle old house; still, it had been cleaned and the walls replastered, and it had all ceased smelling bad by the time we visited it. The guests sleep under covers made of leather (it is less encouraging to vermin); before going to bed they take a bath and put on a night-shirt; their clothes they leave behind. They are given a piece of bread and some oat-soup, and before leaving in the morning are obliged to break stone. The hospitality, it seems, is without limit, but the home is full in winter only.

LONDON, October 15, 1871.

This is one way of passing the night. After a day of writing, I was nodding with fatigue over my novel, Jane Eyre—it is so long! I wanted to profit by the happy moment and crept into bed; but good-night, sleep! I took refuge in codeine. The good effects of it had hardly began to become perceptible, when bang! bang! It was X—— in a white cravat ; the Prince Leuchtenberg had to have a signature : a secretary was waiting at the door. I signed and slept a bit. Bang ! bang ! It was a telegram. And so I reached three o'clock. Bang ! bang ! Another telegram, which brought me to five o'clock.

A letter from Say : we shall be inseparable. Called on the Lord Mayor, who makes us his guests, and on Lord Granville, who approves my toast to the Marchioness of Lothian, for I am to make a speech ! Can you imagine it ? and no chance to plead illness !

LONDON, October 18, 1871.

Yesterday passed off very well. At six o'clock I was at Say's, at the Mansion House. The first repast was enough to make Gargantua himself start back. The Dakin[1] household, in the midst of a service of gold, with lackeys in livery, under a ceiling of historic splendor, were sufficiently amusing—good, simple folk, with manners a bit common. Then we visited police stations, markets, schools. The middle-class school on Tabernacle Road, interested me most—eleven hundred children of from six to sixteen years old. They had them file out before us, in military style, keeping step. " By the left flank ! "—banners flying, trumpets blowing. First, in our honor, they gave the *Marseillaise ;* so be it— we bowed ; then the *Jeune et beau Dunois.* It never occurs to these conservative folk that we change our music too at each revolution.

I took Say afterward to Lord Granville's who, as

[1] Sir Thomas Dakin, Lord Mayor in 1871.

always, was most agreeable, but we accomplished nothing. Say is going to speak this evening and to go bail for us; he is the leader of the free-trade party in the Chambers, and very well-received here —they will believe him sooner than they will us. It is our last card.

Visited the French hospital, the church, the Sisters. All these good people were enchanted—nobody had ever thought of them before. The young Sister Superior was as interesting as could be when she and Say were recognizing each other.

Have been to another informal dinner, of forty places. The table groaned beneath the weight of gold and victuals. What abysses such stomachs must be! . . . The Lord Mayor wore his cross about his neck. They admired the model of our "late" Hotel de Ville. Then, after the dinner which lasted from half-past seven to half-past ten, a young clergyman came and warbled love songs. " Marvel," Montalembert says, " at the power of England; she is long-suffering! "

LONDON, October 19, 1871.

I have made my speech! . . . I spoke from beginning to end without a mistake—nay, with warmth even. It was not so difficult, after all. Really, I was quite calm; and nobody understood what I said, and everybody listened. It came off at the court of the King and Queen of Spades. The king and queen came in arm-in-arm, their high officers about them, one of them carrying a sword, the others carrying nothing. Then there was a mixture of music, prayers, talk, nut-cracking, in a magnificent hall. Finally, after the feast, which lasted hours, there came speech-making, which lasted hours. The toast-master succeeded the chaplain, and he stood behind the Lord Mayor, and presided over the ceremony. You should have heard the intonations of the speakers, you should have seen their solemnity of feature. In the midst of it all I spoke. Here is the end of my toast:

"I wish to speak also of the noble women who united to aid the French refugees in London. They procured them bread, clothes, employment, shelter; and when the houses provided for their reception no longer sufficed to hold them, took them, as you know, under their own roofs. They gave them more than mere material aid, they gave them what is more precious to an exile—consolation and encouragement, they stretched their arms out to them, they took them like friends to their own firesides. I wish to thank them deeply, from the bottom of my heart; and I ask your permission, my lord, to propose two toasts: To the generous women who organized at London the Ladies' Committee of Relief for the French refugee families, and who have directed it during these long months of the war with a solicitude that nothing has checked, with a devotion without bounds;—to the Marchioness of Lothian, and the august personages and noble ladies who shared her labors! To the members of the Committee of Relief for the French peasants and farmers, and to their president, Lord Vernon!"

This morning I went back to the Mansion House

to see the King of Spades dispense justice in his royal apparel. He did it in a room hard by his bedchamber; and then went to preside over his parliament: two hundred members, aldermen and sheriffs, all tricked out with wigs, halberds, swords, hammering the table, and *cheers*. Say's speech, the replies to it, and cheers, all went off nicely. As we were coming out we were shown the first charter of the liberties of the city, a bit of parchment from William the Conqueror, which they have since merely continued It was a most interesting visit.

LONDON, October 20, 1871.

The day ended as interestingly as it began. At six o'clock I went to find Say. They were still at table, and there was another little festival, and some more little toasts, one of which I offered when my turn came. Finally, the loving-cup made its round. The way of it is this : You rise and face one of your next neighbors, hold the lid while he (or she), also standing, drinks; then you exchange a compliment (if it happens to be with a pretty woman, so much the better), and face about and pass the cup and the ceremony on.

After dinner we went to the Fire-Brigade Station. When we had visited the establishment, the steam-engines, the harnessed horses, the men perpetually in waiting (the whole of it tucked away in English fashion, in an economy of space that is a miracle of good management), the signal was given. We held our watches in our hands. There was a rush of men, horses, engine ; they tore like mad up the black-paved lane, they went to the end of the street and came back—time, two minutes and a half. I complimented Captain Shaw. Then he led the way and we followed through a pelting rain, with the four Misses Dakin struggling along through the mud, in the dark, over all the nameless filth that finds its way by night into the city alleys. We reached the Thames. A boat, with steam up, was waiting for us. We stepped aboard, and suddenly, on every side, it poured forth jets of water that arched and fell into the middle of the Thames. It is your own fault here, if your house burns down. The "setting" was excellent; it was a place where the bridges cross; the trains came and went with a frightful noise, the night was dark, the rain was falling, it was all very picturesque. The Misses Dakin would have preferred going in a close carriage. One was waiting for us indeed, with its four lanterns and domestics armed with canes, and it was thus that Say was conducted to the railway station.

I finished my evening at the Vernons'. Nothing could equal the vivacity, the sprightliness, the frankness, the gayety of a lady I met there—the wife of Colonel Anson, M. P., an officer who was in the Crimean War. "Why do you like the French so much?" I asked her. "I don't know," she replied; "because they are so unhappy. And yet that cannot be; I loved them before they became so." She has recently returned from Strasburg, where she had gone simply to encourage the "honest" party and to annoy the Prussians.

LONDON, October 23, 1871.

I received to-night the following telegram : " My compliments on your toast.—Broglie." My friends in England like it, too.

To continue my journal : Saturday, went with the Vernons to Haymarket Theatre to see The Rivals. If the amiable Mrs. Anson had not accompanied us, I should have gone to sleep. Sheridan's art struck me as in its boyhood, the acting was crude, and the public, in the things that it admired, inept. I dare say the beauties of the piece escaped me. " Haven't you noticed my ring?" said my neighbor. " To be sure, the colors are a little loud. Look." It was an escutcheon in three colors, with France in relief on Alsace and Lorraine. She had bought it in Strasburg.

Yesterday I dined at the Rothschilds' villa—I don't know its name—out in the direction of Kew. The dinner was a surprise: only the family was present ; but such a chicken!—nothing but a chicken, but with the whole animal and vegetable kingdoms represented in the sauce! The Lord Mayor would have sucked his fingers. Stomachs that can face such dishes twice a day fill me with admiration. And such feeders! . . . And yet, really, in the midst of all this luxurious upholstering and pampering of the flesh, a great simplicity obtains. It is Alfred, the son, who fetches the wine from the cellar. (The cellar, to be sure, is like that of Frederick the Great, where he kept his treasure.) He brought up a lafitte and a sherry, that you find only at the villa of Lionel de Rothschild. The incontestable superiority of the wines here is in part due, it seems, to their being laid away in a cellar as isolated as an observatory, and to their being never moved nor jarred. Of course, you know, some one was good enough to forewarn me that their superiority *is* incontestable.

LONDON, October 29, 1871.

London fog! It is easy to understand how it should give occasion to myriad adventures and mistakes. I had to go to the Embassy through a fog so dark that from Piccadilly on we could go no faster than a walk, and had to give warning by loud cries that we were coming. I had been to see Mr. Gladstone on his way back from Greenwich, where he had made a speech to fifteen hundred people. His voice was gone. He had scored a great success, but I don't believe his ministry will stand. Mr. Disraeli grows every day, to my mind, more and more master of the situation. Gladstone is clever, and has a clever tongue, but for the present he has talked enough, and done enough, both for his own interest and England's.

I have not lost sight of my *work*—the founding of a sort of *Clearing-House* for the French charities in London. You don't know what I mean? Listen: I want to establish a sort of central committee for all the institutions which exist at present in individual isolation—for the Hospital, the Committee of Relief, the Sisters, the Leicester Church, the Embassy, the Consulate; and as a beginning, I want to have a sale, which will bring us in a lot of money.

We went with our young friends to the Prince of Wales' theatre. It is quite elegant—almost like a drawing-room. The piece was dull—a compound of flat plagiarisms put together without art. The acting capital, but the total effect sufficiently offensive ; not in the way of indecency as with us, but of triviality, and of a sort of failure in gentlemanly delicacy that we should not tolerate, in the representation of the father of one of the characters. We might shorten the skirts as much as you like; but render paternity and old age repulsive and ridiculous—no, we shouldn't be capable of that. They don't know where to stop, and fall presently to brutality. Still, it interested me much, nay, entertained me, even. I understood well enough.

LONDON, December 10, 1871.

He seems to be mending;[1] the bulletins have stopped two days now tolling his knell, and speak this evening of his being better. Hope is returning; though the anxiety is still widespread. England begins to perceive that she has not yet wholly shaken off her monarchic prejudices. The newspapers talk of nothing but the Prince's illness, and on all other topics suspend discussion. Crowds stand about Marlborough House[2] watching for the telegrams. Bulletins are posted almost hourly in all parts of the town, and reflected in manuscript copies here and there set up by the zeal of individ-

[1] The Prince of Wales was down with typhoid fever at Sandrigham.
[2] The Prince of Wales' palace in London.

uals. If the poor Prince recovers, it will all have been for England's good and for his own.

LONDON, December 19, 1871.

The Prince of Wales safe! Lord Granville invited me to "pot-luck." He added Arnal's witticism: " Perhaps you'd rather I didn't treat you like a friend!" The dinner was excellent, and interesting ; Goschen,[1] Hartington,[2] and Reeve[3] there.

I took my young friend yesterday to dinner at the Club,[4] and showed him its mysteries, its turns, and all its points. After which I conceived the fatal idea (or rather it was suggested to me) of taking him to the Alhambra. The house is fine no doubt, large, well-lit, or rather illuminated ; but for the rest, fancy a miscellaneous lot of so-called Colonels of the Horse-Guards for box-openers, women of the town in the body of the house and on the stage (the latter altogether naked), acrobats flying through the air, epileptics whose fits the public encourages by its applause, a brutal charivari, a veritable cumulate cacophony of strident sounds, and finally, in the midst of all of it, *God Save the Queen*, which they listen to standing and hats off. Is it art in its infancy or its decrepitude ? They

[1] Right Hon. Goschen, born in 1831 ; Privy Counsellor in 1865; First Lord of the Admiralty in 1871.
[2] Right Hon. Spencer Compton Cavendish, Marquis of Hartington, eldest son of the Duke of Devonshire, then Chief Secretary for Ireland.
[3] Henry Reeve, Registrar of the Privy Council, Associate Member of the Institute, Director of the *Edinburgh Review*.
[4] St. James Club.

have literally reached the point of putting epileptic fits on the stage to the accompaniment of the band. If you have seen it once, you will never want to see it again.

LONDON, December 22, 1871.

We reached the station yesterday at North Camp toward eleven o'clock.[1] A magnificent dragoon stepped forward with an envelope ; it was farther on, at another station, that our staff were waiting us; and there they were indeed—holding their horses by the bridles—some lancers and a glittering officer who came and gave us his hand like a Frenchman. We hastened to mount into the saddle, for the train was late and the troops had been under arms since half-past ten.

We went forward on a smart trot and reached the scene (a wide prospect) of the manœuvres. A fog hovered over it all, thick enough to soften everywhere the middle distance without totally obscuring it. The ground was undulating, broken by moors, bits of forest and hill, and scouts were out waiting for us in one place and another, to give us our direction and to hasten forward and announce our arrival. Through the fog we discovered a black line; it was a regiment of cavalry with helmets and scarlet uniforms, and we recognized the dragoons. The horsemen who had announced us came back at a gallop, and there was Lieutenant-General Sir Hope Grant, with his chevrons, won in the Crimea,

[1] To take part in a review of the camp at Aldershot,

in India, in China. The meeting occurred in the presence of our respective " staffs," who had the politeness not to laugh except in their sleeves. When we had shaken hands, we directed our horses toward the troops ranged in line of battle. Flags flying and *God Save the Queen* greeted us. We passed along the front rank and I was presented to the generals, one after another. I stopped and examined things with the attention that constitutes politeness in great men—here a bamboo-lance, there a modern or an old field-piece, a new knapsack that distributes the weight along the back and reins, a boot on trial. I had the courage to ask whether the flap was made right; an observation that ranked me at once among the fanatics in favor of the old-style ordnance.

Presently the troops filed out. There were seven thousand men—I do not guarantee that all of them had attained years of virility. Fine review order—performed their evolutions with the stiffness of automata. I was stationed by the general, surrounded by a respectful crowd, the band facing us. The officers saluted us. My faith! I bowed in return—they had been presented to me! It would have been more soldier-like to have left my hat on my head, but I am a President of the Republic—don't forget that. The general had the cavalry file by again on the trot, that I might remark the general effect of their appearance. It was capital. But I noticed there were but few officers present—half of them are away on leave. They are under no especial pressure in England ; provided they turn up in time for the war, or for the great manœuvres, they may pass the rest of the time on the Continent.

Then the battle began, the scouts thrown out in front. We gained a height already occupied by the artillery. Horizon of superb extent. The first discharge of artillery took us in the rear and was an agreeable surprise. The snap and splutter of the fusillade awoke an echo in a wood across the river in front of us. Our entire first line deployed for skirmishing; the second line advanced supporting it on the left, the reserve behind. The fusillade redoubled. We retired in good order; the artillery descended a rough slope, the horses squatting on their hams slid down with the piece on their backs; the officers set off at a gallop along the sharp declivity covered with heath and gorse. We fell back upon a second position which was well chosen. The cavalry, in ambuscade, appeared from behind a knoll and advanced across the plain; at three hundred metres the hussars and lancers charged the enemy at a gallop and threw themselves upon them. Their order was not good; there was a jam in the centre and a thinness in the wings—the lack of officers made itself felt. Happily there were still the dragoons in the second line; their charge was better; the enemy retired, our right advanced and outflanked them. With an admirable courage we moved forward everywhere in the teeth of the firing. We found the general in the midst of a cloud of smoke; the victory was ours and night was falling. *Cease firing!* The troops formed again and came back, with the bands playing national airs: *La Belle*

Hélène, Les Pompiers de Nanterre! It made me heavy-hearted—made me think of the wretched retreats of our own unhappy soldiers.

I returned with the general, who absolutely wanted me to declare that the Duc de Broglie is for monarchy. He is against the communists and their accomplices or their dupes. . . . We reached the *9th Queen's Royal Lancers' mess*—a sort of " box." My companion did not perceive that the lancer who hurried forward to relieve him of his horse was an officer; he was presented to him an instant afterward—it was Lord Beresford![1]

At the mess the cooking is a little too Indian or English, but the reception is cordial. Our hosts did not leave us till we were in the train on our way back.

LONDON, December 28, 1871.

There is in London a " Boxing-Day,"—the day after Christmas. And then there is Christmas itself, and it is not too much to call it a saturnalia. The morning papers all print articles a column and a half long, advising the people to beware of bringing on themselves an indigestion. It is meat-day.

Yesterday evening we went to the Lyceum Theatre, in the Strand. Always the same grossness in the execution, the same exaggeration in the by-play and the exclamations, the same heavy-handed indecency in place of sprightliness and pleasantry.

There is a total absence of everything that constitutes dramatic art—there is neither conception,

[1] Lord Beresford, W. Leslie De-la-Poer, son of the Marquis of Waterford.

nor continuity, nor verisimilitude. It is all as discordant as the colors they bring together in their toilets or as the edibles they mix in the same plate. In the " Bells," an adaptation of Chatrian's romance, they have hit on a device (by means of a dream represented on the stage) for being present at the murder, at the death of the victim, at the agony he suffers—not without an accompanying outcry of horror on the part of the dreamer; then they make him die a second time on the stage on his awakening, sparing none of the details that in my judgment are plain horror and sacrilege.

Afterward, a funny piece, out of *Pickwick Papers*, a story by Dickens: caricatures that depart so widely from the truth that they do not make one laugh. A caricature is droll only on the condition that it resembles its model; one has to feel the reality beneath it all before one's mirth is stirred. The authors and actors undertook to represent a sort of swindler, who persuaded an old maid to elope with him. He looked and acted like a pickpocket pure and simple; he was dressed like a beggar, without a shirt, and in a coat that looked as if he had found it kicking about the street. That is not the costume in which "Knights of Industry" present themselves and make their way. That sort of thing is for me too broad.

I have forgotten again and again to tell you a queer thing that happened to me when I was behind the scenes in one of the theatres in Whitechapel. A crowd had to be represented on the stage, and the best way to represent it, in the opinion of the management, was to send on the miscellaneous public and employees that were encumbering the side-scenes. It was in this way that I came to cross the stage on a run, representing realistically one of the rushes familiar to the bands of pickpockets who exploit the crowds of London.

LONDON, December 30, 1871.

We have passed a night of somewhat sombre interest in and about the London slums. Vernon went with us. The party began with a dinner in which we all figured as toughs. I fairly believe that, with my short-pipe in my button-hole instead of a flower, I took the prize.

Here is a report of our excursion:

From Belgrave Square to Whitechapel the way is long, but not sufficiently so for the contrast between these two parts of the world. You are acquainted with the part of London in which an income of a hundred thousand francs per year constitutes no more than a modest competence: come here with me and I will show you where shelter for the night can be had at threepence, and a week's lodging for fifteen-pence.

It was dark; a three-quarters of an hour rapid drive through the streets—sombre, endless, eternally alike, and we brought up in the midst of noise and light. We were in the district of the extremes of misery and debauchery. Our appointed meeting-place was a police-station.

A man whose nose somebody had just smashed with his fist (a policeman was washing the blood from his face), gave us a foretaste of the sort of place that we had entered. We visited the police cells; in one place we found a drunken man stretched on an inclined-plane skilfully adapted to conjure away the consequences of his disorder; in another place, a lot of unhappy wretches comfortably shut away till (sometime within four-and-twenty hours) they shall be produced before a magistrate. Two employees of unimpeachable bearing and politeness took us in hand to show us the way and to protect us in our excursion through the circles of hell.

A theatre stood at the door. Not less than three thousand spectators, of every color and of every odor, were shut into a house of *papier-mâché* that a match trampled under foot would have converted into a fine *auto-da-fé!* At the rate of threepence a head, the public is admitted to the enjoyment, for three or four hours, of a sort of Italian farce, which is neither more nor less brutal than those one pays ten shillings a place for at the best theatres. We visited in the same way, during the course of the evening up to eleven o'clock, four or five theatres or music-halls (and there were others that we passed by), and all were full. In all of them the *entrepreneur* makes a fortune. In Whitechapel, too, the people have money in their pockets. And they have a taste for the arts. There was one hall, or rather a barn, in which wax-figures, after the manner of those of Mme. Tussaut, were on exhibition, and where they magnetized; there you saw, side by side with the Queen and the Prince of Wales, the criminals and rascals of the day. All they have to do to keep abreast of the times is to put Cavour's wig on Benedetti, or Napoleon Third's on William. But how do all these people live? From the door of the theatre we went to the lodging-house quarter, by a number of obscure lanes, in which I stumbled more than once on the unevennesses of the way.

For three-pence you can buy a place to lie down for the night. In one place men only are admitted, in another women only; a bit further on they take in everybody—the whole family, the children, and the dog. You go first into a sort of common-room, with a great fire, in front of which some of the guests dress their sores, some broil their herrings. There are tables about the room and people sitting at them eating, or playing cards, or reading a newspaper, or (some women) working.

The employees are generally repulsive-looking: gin, misery, personal uncleanliness, and vice have set their mark upon the faces, and it is the fairer half of the human race that in especial turns one sick. Still their behavior is better than at Miracle Yard: gentlemen may come with impunity to fatten their curiosity on the spectacle of all this misery; people bow to them, say good-evening to them—no doubt in a measure because of the Police-Inspector, they all know, who accompanies them. He in his turn knows them, and whenever he stepped into a new place, he took care to say: "These are workingmen; these are vagabonds; these are robbers of the worst sort; there is a man just out of prison, there is another whom we have not yet succeeded in catching *en flagrant délit.*"

Every lodging-house has its line of patrons;

some of them are not disreputable. We visited one to which three hundred workingmen come every night for shelter, more than two-thirds of whom are *habitués*. They are not permitted indeed to take anything but their clothes with them into the dormitory; but lockers are provided in a room apart, which enable them to acquire property and to become almost indefinitely superior to the nomads who go away in the morning with no associations to bring them back.

There are in London fourteen thousand of these lodging-houses; they receive every night thirty thousand people. Thanks to the surveillance of the police, though the common-rooms are pestilential, the dormitories are relatively clean, the walls are rigorously whitewashed and the ventilation what it should be. Each bed has a regulation mattress and, in the fourpence houses, a blanket covered with inscriptions; you couldn't carry off a piece as big as your two hands without its everywhere testifying against you that it had been stolen from such and such a lodging-house. It seems that the proprietors of these places do not lose either their goods or their time. They showed us one of them who, after eighteen years of hospitality at threepence a night, has become the possessor of a nice place in the country and is willing to dispose of his beggarly clientage for three thousand pounds.

As our visit took place the day after Christmas, in all the halls, even those frequented by the least edifying classes, the walls were covered from top to bottom with holly, with sprigs of evergreen, and ornaments in paper; and in the midst of these festoons, and framed by them, were inscriptions—all of them Christian, and without admixture of politics, except for blessings on the Queen, the Prince of Wales and the Ministers. The proprietors and their wives even are not without responsibility for these pious invocations. In one of the lowest hovels we had the curiosity to ask who had presided over this decoration and who had paid for it—the expense being some fifty francs or thereabout; well, the proprietor had contributed twenty-seven francs, the beggars, vagabonds, street-vendors, and robbers, who composed the rest of the company, had handed in their pennies to make up the rest. There was something distinctively English even in the dregs here of society. But we had not yet touched the bottom; vice and misery had revelations still in store for us.

We went out into the deserted streets again where you meet nobody but stragglers now and then from some public-house, men or women, in either case equally drunk. We made our way toward the Thames, to St. George's in the East. It was nearly midnight. The narrow lanes were wide-awake, lit up by half-open doors. People were drinking, dancing: flags of all colors notified us that we were in the sailors' quarters. We pushed a door open and at the counter saw a modest-looking woman; the police who accompanied us assured us she is above reproach; that she should be so is made a condition precedent of granting her a license. She showed us the way to a dance-hall where the most frightful specimens of femininity were waiting to be invited to waltz. That evening there is not much dancing; it was Friday, and the sailor in all countries alike is out of money on the eve of his weekly pay-day. Often when we went in we found music only; they were places whose dance-licences had been revoked, on the ground that the dancing had degenerated into something else.

We rested a bit in one of these establishments in the presence of a savage who swallowed fire at our instance and gave it out again in tubes which came out of his intestinal furnace. What then were we yet to see? I spare you a description of the resorts to which the chorographers of the *Prussian Eagle* and *Fire-eater* retired, when the door of the house closed after them and their companions.

It was one o'clock in the morning; what could there be for us still to see? Our guides started on once more; we were lost in a labyrinth of sombre streets, eternally alike. The height of the houses and of the stories was singularly reduced, but the model was always the same, the depressing square box with holes in it, that from Baker Street to St. George's in the East constitutes the highest product of the English genius in the line of architecture. In place of open squares you find narrow courts entered by obscure passages. We went forward in the suspicious darkness. In front of a ruined, tumble-down house our guide stopped and called. A voice from the interior replied; and we entered a door and climbed with hands and feet a sort of rope-ladder that ended above in a hovel. A strong and peculiar odor mixed with the natural evil smell of the place fairly choked us as we entered. For the rest, the place was small and we went in one by one to the side of a couch that occupied the biggest part of it. By the glimmer of a sort of night-lamp we perceived what looked like the posts of an antique bed but they were badly out of line and seemed to be there only to bear witness to the misery and disorder of the place. Hard by the night-lamp, seated on some rags a woman smoked a cigarette and by her side against the wall lay a man wrapped up in what had been a blanket. His head, and such portion of his clothing as was visible, showed him to be a native of the land where opium is grown. His eyes were open but he saw nothing; his face wore an expression of complete beatitude; he gave no sign of life except that he breathed noisily, giving his hostess to understand that he wanted to smoke again. She carefully prepared a bamboo instrument, put one end of it into his mouth and lit the opium at the other end with the candle. The Hindu drew in two or three puffs and went off into another ecstasy. The old woman filled a pipe then for herself, and drew at it. She bore it better than the Hindu, who is a beginner. She told us that she has been for twenty years a victim of the vice by which she now earns her living. Opium is killing her, but she lit her pipe once more while we were talking to her. " How old should you say she is ? " one of our guides asked. We said " sixty." " She is barely thirty-five."

We saw a light next door and there we found a

full-blooded Chinaman on a divan. He was dressed though in rags and tatters, of a mode distinctively English and was employing a Christian tongue in the service of oriental corruption. At his elbow were a Chinese tray, a candle, a bamboo pipe and doses of opium of various prices from threepence up. This wretch supplies the black smoke to others still wretcheder than himself; the "joint" he keeps is a house of refuge open the whole night through, where one may purchase ecstasy at so much a penny and dream, in the midst of the most hideous dirt, of the paradise of Confucius or of the Fairies' Kingdom.

Opium smokers form but an odd chapter in the annals of misery in London. They amuse the curious, they lend themselves to romance. Turn the page and you enter on the chapter of misery pure and simple, the misery of unmitigated hunger and cold. Our little promenade in hell showed us nothing more horrible. We saw mud-houses and windows minus window-panes; we saw houses with their street-doors off their hinges. What good would a street-door do them? There was scarcely an obstacle of any kind opposed to our stepping right into the sleeping-rooms. We entered and surprised people in their beds—families who paid fifteen-pence a week for their shelter. "What! does anybody rent this garret?" I thought as I stuck my head into a sort of hovel; I couldn't have squeezed my body in. A woman squatting before the embers of a coal-fire rose from her bed—from some rags, that is, on which she slept—at the sound of an approach. Something black covered the floor about her; it looked like the contents of a rag-picker's basket. Under this ruined heap three children lay and slept through everything the sleep of the blessed. As we were going out, a door at one side opened and a wretched woman thrust out her head and hand; she was just out of jail and hoped to keep out.

We might have prolonged indefinitely this dismal round of lodgings at fifteen-pence a week; but the night was advancing and we wanted to reach the workhouse in Saint George's in the East before the occupants had left their beds. As we were setting out for it, we crossed a bridge over a canal coming out on the London Docks. Our guide called attention to a policeman on duty about midway across the bridge. "He is there," he said, "to keep women from throwing themselves off into the water." It is a favorite spot, it seems, with the victims of debauchery. Is it the drink in them that drives them to suicide, or the depression that follows drink? Almost every night there is an attempt at precisely this place and nowhere else. The quay rises high above the water and the current below is strong; the parapet once cleared, all is over—one is delivered from the past and from a still more frightful future. It is to prevent these unhappy creatures from seeking to discover, at the bottom of the water beneath, the oblivion they no longer find in the bottom of their glass, that a burly policeman, the father of a family, passes there eight hours a night. "What wages do you get, my man, for this unpleasant job?" "Twenty shillings a week. But I am only on duty every other night." That doesn't pay.

Finally we reached the workhouse. Our double knocks roused a guard, who took the time to put his uniform on before he opened the door. The workhouse is the last resort of those who have lost every penny they had in the world; if they had a farthing left in their pockets, they would not be admitted. On condition only of poverty absolute, they may knock at the door and it will be opened to them. A piece of bread and a bowl of soup, with bits of meat in it are waiting for them; but before they are admitted they have to submit to a bath. The new arrival's clothes are taken from him in a waiting-room and carried off to be fumigated, and others belonging to the house are given him in exchange. When he has dressed himself in them he climbs up to a dormitory where an iron bed with a barred mattress and a blanket is ready for him. The place is steam-heated; ventilators keep the air pure; the walls are whitewashed; the cleanness of the floor is above reproach. Some thirty men were sleeping peacefully when we were there—old men, young men, men in the full vigor of their life— among them more than one robber, I was told. When they "turn out" they are given a meal of the same sort as on their arrival the evening before. The establishment is admirable—"luxurious" I couldn't help calling it when I was being shown about it. Cleanliness and comfort such as that go beyond what mere charity obliges us to. But how does it happen that the patrons of the fourpence and the sixpence lodging-houses do not exchange their suspicious pallets for this gratuitous and comparatively sumptuous hospitality? There is a regulation: the exit is not free, there is a certain amount of work to be done in the morning before the guests are permitted to go their way—there are stones to break, or oakum to pick, or logs to split. It made me think of the dog that carried the mark on his neck of his master's collar.

As we were coming out we met a woman with two children at the door. She had come from Barnes, a neighboring town, and requested shelter for the night. She was very poorly dressed, much worse dressed than the children. Her appearance and the replies she gave to the inquiries put to her indicated that she was a respectable woman. The children said in answer to our questions that they had been to school and were beginning to learn to write. We wanted to give them some money, but were hastily warned not to do so. If any money should be found on her, she would not be received —such is the law. We bowed to the word which in England is supreme. May it ever preserve its magical power! Having breathed which prayer with a profound feeling of envy, we succeeded in making an arrangement with the guard to the effect that the money we had offered should be given to the children on their departure the following day. To avoid the law is in some sort to respect it.

It was after two o'clock and high time we turned back toward Belgrave Square. Rolling home in the cab I found myself stirred with pity at the spectacle of so much misery and depravity, and with admiration for the energy of the efforts made by English society to relieve its strayed and fallen members.

Extracts from the Notes.

At about this time I began to frequent the Athenæum, though I was not yet admitted to it on a permanent footing; it was not till later that I succeeded, by the aid of my friends, in avoiding or ignoring the regulation in force in that intellectual caravansary which excludes all resident diplomats, the heads of the respective embassies only excepted. Still I was even at that time aspiring to become acclimated to its chambers and to dwell there. It is the rendez-vous for intelligence of every sort, the confluence of all the sources of information. Men, books, papers, come here regularly from every parish. It isn't that there is a great deal of talk going on; quite the reverse—everybody is at home there—has his own little table to himself. He moves about a bit now and then from one table to another to exchange a few words in a low tone with some acquaintance; and then returns to his own place to read, and still to read, and then to write and write. A great part of the scribbling that floods England every morning is done there—articles for the newspapers, for the weekly, monthly, quarterly reviews. How many times—writing myself in my own retired spot—I've watched out of the corner of my eye this hive of thinkers—noted the mixture of opinions, the most amusing and instructive contrasts and juxtapositions in the world! Here, the law, the church at one side, the Bible minus the church hard by, or else Catholicism and Darwinism side by side, great explorers and members of the Royal Academy of Fine Arts, the House of Commons or the House of Lords and the Cabinet. All of them make their honey in the Athenæum—climb ladders to hunt out a book, descend again, exchange a word as they pass each other by, take tea on their writing-tables, drop letters in the box; and when the sign is given for collecting the mail, their activity redoubles. Few of them have gained the right to trouble the silence by talking aloud. My old friend, Abraham Hayward, the eldest surviving "British Essayist," notably possesses it. Towards four o'clock you see him appear in the great reading-room. His day's work is done, he goes from table to table trafficking in news and recruiting players for his whist-table. (One or two card-tables are tolerated in a room apart.) Toward seven o'clock he comes back again to pick up company for dinner. He has his especial table in one corner of the vast dining-room—it is often doubled and tripled by the neighboring tables being drawn up alongside of it. There is a good deal of talk and of loud laughter in that privileged corner—it is called the *Hayward Corner*. People sit at table there long after their more silent neighbors have disappeared. The conversation increases as the time goes on—the voices rise higher; the amiable and impassioned old gentleman's memory is inexhaustible, but he grows less and less indulgent for those who have crossed his path in the fields of literature, and he subjects English ears (always chaste in a public place) to a more and more severe ordeal. The talk, or rather the dissertation, sets out from literature and history, parliamentary and political reminiscences and anecdotes; but it declines in dignity as the bottles one after another are emptied; the supernatural is as little respected in royalty as in religion; and it becomes annoying to have to play chorus and one is glad to gain the door. If you turn back after dinner to the silence and solitude of the luminous vast reading-room on the first floor, you may find the indefatigable old gentleman still thumbing books, at midnight, and hunting for their *marrow*. I couldn't take my oath, however, that he has not snatched since dinner a wink or so of restorative sleep (there would be no lack of precedent for it), nay, that he has not troubled the silence of the temple even with his snores. You have to get used to it here; they sleep everywhere in England, and snore everywhere—on condition only that they don't prevent other people from hearing themselves speak. I have sometimes seen the secretary of the Club obliged to intervene to call a sleeper to order, or to moderation at least.

It was during days of idleness, of solitude, of spleen, that the Athenæum possessed for me an especial charm. Fancy a Sunday in London: there is a fog that, penetrates the very houses, and more than that, it is raining and the streets are dead. I reach the club without encountering a living soul; the club itself is deserted, I am remote from every one and everything. I cannot even send a letter to my family by the post. I install myself at a table in a retired spot in the library; I give myself up to a bitter sense of solitude and isolation. How many things have crossed my mind while I have sat staring mechanically at the Nelson on the top of Trafalgar Column, topping the neighboring roofs, or at the bust of Pope on the bracket opposite me! I have often passed hours in that way—day-dreaming —letting my thoughts wander along the streets to my domicile, or along the library shelves. And many times I have mentally run over the treasures that surrounded me without being able to make up my mind which of them to take down, waiting for chance or inspiration from on high to come to my assistance, and, the choice at last made, have drowned my cares in my book! I have not infrequently become so absorbed in my self-imposed task that I have lost all sense of the lapse of time; the dinner-hour would pass and I still turn the pages; my eyes would give out and I still wish to read; the long hours of the solitary day would prove too short. I had killed the time so effectively as to have forgotten the necessities of life, and have gone home finally to bed without my dinner, the mad desire to learn something having taken the place for the time being of the somewhat morbid enjoyment of the desolation about me.

THE YEAR, 1872.

Extracts from the Correspondence.

LONDON, January 6, 1872.

JUST returned from the opening of Parliament. It is a very unceremonious affair. Only the Lord-Chancellor and the clerks in wig and gown, and but fifteen peers were present. An aged Master of Ceremonies came officially to open the parliamentary "lock," and the members surged tumultuously up to the bar, close on the heels of the Speaker who wore a wig and alone was grave and solemn. There is always the same mixture here of dignity and buffoonery, ritual and go-as-you-please. The Queen's speech, read by the Chancellor who drawls, aims always to say as little as possible.

Yesterday a parliamentary evening-party at Mr. Gladstone's. The members of the cabinet had dined there in full dress. After dinner the Queen's speech was read and sent to the leaders of the opposition, who had met at the same hour at the table of Mr. Disraeli. That *is* "fair play." The house is agreeable enough : some works of art ; the candles set on top of the sideboards and bookcases alone took me a bit by surprise. I am beginning to be able in an English political salon to turn round and name the faces.

LONDON, January 18, 1872.

London is beginning to revive, windows are opening, carriages are being brought out, and a few invitations sent. Yesterday I took a drive through the City. It is the part of London I like best—the life and character of the land show themselves there. You ought to see the City, the streets, and banking-houses in the obscure daylight, in the midst of the fever of business: fog, jostling, mess, congestion of vehicles in the streets—it is horrible to see, to feel, to hear. You ought to go into the little lanes where the great tall houses are—the banking-houses through which all the gold on earth circulates in the course of the day without a single shilling remaining unaccounted for.

I went to pay a call on the old Baron[1] in his den in St. Swithin's Lane. Don't look for the Baron's office in one of the great thoroughfares that are easy to find. A long passage, a carriage would so completely block up that a man could barely squeeze by, brings you to an obscure solid old mansion. The lane reminds one of Venice; the solidity of the house and the inhospitable look of the neighborhood are Florentine, and the Baron also who spends his days there, belongs himself to the aristocracy of wealth that founded the grandeur of those two mediæval governments. Every day he sits at his table from eleven o'clock in the morning to seven in the afternoon. No chairs are provided for visitors: standing discourages long interviews, unless one sits on the table, as I did. Two or three offices to right

[1] Baron Lionel de Rothschild.

and left are occupied by his sons. The paralysis in his legs which keeps him fast in his rolling-chair is in sharp contrast with the activity of his mind which interrupts his conversation from minute to minute to reflect upon the state of the courts of Europe, and to give orders accordingly. The face is a fine one, but the impression of it that abides with one is that of something inexorable as a mathematical calculation. When I thanked him for the damages the railway company had awarded me for my lost travelling-bag, "Yes," he said, "they gave you three hundred francs." The amount came to him at once out of the billions he has dealt with since.

One of his sons, after offering me a glass of sherry, took me over the establishment. What discipline! A great hall with fifty or sixty employees in it, abstracting letters, all of them busy and silent. Nobody communicates with his neighbor. There is no chief, or at least no other chief than the Baron and the son who opens the letters and directly oversees the work. Although there is a French department, there is not a Frenchman in the house. There are a good many Germans. This preference is not an affair of sentiment; it must be that the French are a less safe investment. The employees are appointed for life when they have once passed the door. They begin at two thousand francs, and there is no upper limit. Their salary rises with their ability. From the Correspondence Department I was taken to that of "coupons," which they there detach, verify, and put up in packages. Thence to the counting-house; you cannot see it except from the inside : an iron structure three stories high, protected by walls nine feet thick. I do not know whether it is surrounded by a moat as some of the other monetary fortresses in the City are, but a portcullis, an iron door, cut us off from possible robbers. There was nothing lacking but a drawbridge. It is by gaslight that you visit this pawnshop for crowned heads. In passing, my eye caught a little leather valise with the name of M. Thiers on it : like the great strategist he is, he takes pains to secure his retreat. I do not blame him for it. . . . I took my leave much edified and rather envious. If the public business had been administered in that spirit we should not be where we are.

LONDON, February 16, 1872.

Yesterday evening we went to Parliament to the beautiful chamber of the peers. Although it is really new, there is about it a suggestion of antiquity; it possesses already the charm of reminiscence—a perfume of aristocracy. The Marquis of Salisbury has a fine voice, his delivery is easy and distinguished, he adjusts his efforts to the importance of the debate in hand—you feel that he could easily do better than he does, he is an orator. The cabinet has had a narrow escape: it expected to be censured by eighty votes: it had a majority of two. The vote cannot be reversed. It is its faults that save it. "It has set us in the mire," Lord Salisbury said, "for the credit of pulling us out again." When shall we possess this political right-handedness?

I have paid a visit to the Baronne de Rothschild. I found an unpretending ease in her manner and a total absence of anything approaching the characteristic haughtiness of the parvenue. I met Mr. Disraëli. He said but one thing worth repeating: as the reply of the United States was being announced as forthcoming in March: "Ay, the Ides of March." But what an old painted Jew! There was also Brunnow who said to me: "Either Bismarck did not know what a billion means or he never thought you could pay it." Nothing else happened. This evening we are going to hear a sermon by Cardinal Manning.

LONDON, February 24, 1872.

At the sermon in the *pro-cathedral* at Kensington, I was much struck by the archbishop's simple, sober, dignified delivery. The sermon was purely evangelical. Then I heard with Vernon one of the principal High-Church preachers, the Rev. Body. He possesses lungs—sounds the accent of controversy something too monotonously. Still, it was a good sermon—not a word in it that need be retrenched. And he invited us at the close to come to the sacristy and communicate our objections. I am quite proud—I did not lose a word.

I spent the remainder of the evening at the house of these excellent people. Nothing can equal their charity in their church, to the poor, and you see them now in the field for us. They are going to furnish the banquet[1] table with lords and colonels, and

[1] The annual banquet given by the French business men for the benefit of works of charity.

purpose giving a dinner to make us acquainted with them.

The whole town is covered with scaffoldings set up for the thanksgiving-celebration on the twenty-seventh: nothing else here is being attended to.[1]

The banquet on Monday will possess an additional interest because of the Duke de Broglie's speech.

LONDON, February 24, 1872.

An interesting evening at Lady Waldegrave's.[2] She knew acquaintances of mine and chatted with me a long while. She is a very clever person, and without betraying in her manner any consciousness of doing so, gave me a greal deal of precious information that will prove of use to the Embassy. I had a long talk afterwards with Fortescue about our affairs. With the diplomatists we dwelt on the pleasures and fatigues that await us Tuesday. There will be more than a million people along the

[1] The Prince of Wales's illness had preoccupied all England for some weeks to the exclusion of all else; he had really been thought (and with good reason) to be beyond hope. This ordeal reawakened in the hearts of the people an affection that they have avowed for him in spite of, or perhaps because of, his defects. He is a heavy drinker, a great eater, a man of pleasure, impecunious, but a "good fellow" with it all, obliging, and indisposed to trouble either the ministers or the Queen by meddling with the government or with party-politics. A great thanksgiving service was to take place on February twenty-seventh at St. Paul's. Up to the last moment there was some doubt whether the Queen would take the trouble to be present at this royal and national ceremony.

[2] Frances Braham, daughter of the actor. Married: 1st, to a Waldegrave of illegitimate birth; 2d, to Count Waldegrave; 3d, to Sir Harcourt; 4th, to the Hon. Chichester Fortescue, President of the Board of Trade. Died in 1879.

route. London is all covered with unpainted wooden scaffoldings to be rented at a pound a place. All business, all circulation, will be interrupted. We have no idea of so universal a movement from top to bottom of society.

Yesterday evening at eleven we arrived at Lady Cork's, wife of the Master of the Hounds. No better French is spoken anywhere. A large house, but such taste! One detail is enough: the mirrors are framed in festoons of bas-relief—arms, fruits, flowers, anything you like. When you look close, you find it is all of waxed leather. On all the furniture and over the doors were set lines of candles. All the seats had been removed from the rooms to gain space, and every one was forced to stand, so as to occupy less of it. The guests arrived, took the mistress of the house by the hand, maintained their upright position, and that was all of it. You couldn't see anything of the person in front of you but the neck and shoulders. If they were pretty, so much the better. There are many evening-parties here at which you don't succeed even in mounting the steps. If you are clever, you run from door to door; you elbow your way till you catch the eye of the reporter for the *Morning Post;* that done, the cup of pleasure has been drained.

Gladstone was there with his wife and daughter. As I was talking with the great man who has undergone such a fall in the public esteem, our conversation was interrupted by the press about us and we found ourselves face to face with "an old fairy"— the wife and devoted friend of Disraëli, Viscountess

Beaconsfield. They all talked together like the best of friends, though the two husbands the night before had launched at one another the most violent and bitterest strokes at their command. But that sort of thing can't last much longer even here. The unhappy Gladstone squirms like an enraged lion under the icy pleasantry that the leader of the conservative party with his sepulchral face pelts him with.

To-day we tried to go to St. Paul's to see the preparations. We had to turn back. In spite of the fact that it was Sunday, there was a solid crowd from Piccadilly to St. Paul's, the carriages so jammed that progress was impossible—they will be there still day after to-morrow. And all to look at the boards and scaffoldings in front of the houses. Such a national movement such an outburst of loyalty, such an uprising of the masses, was never before seen. The crowd will number millions.

LONDON, February 26, 1872.

This evening yet—that is to say, in an hour, the banquet will come off, and the speech. I am confident that the Duc de Broglie's tact and talent will be equal to the difficulties in the way of speaking at all in public on such an occasion.[1] To-morrow I

[1] The Duc de Broglie did preside, as M. Gavard expected, at the banquet at the French Hospital. It was the first time that a French ambassador had assisted at that ceremony. "Under the Empire," M. Gavard says, in his notes, "the French charities in London, the Relief Society and the Hospital, as well as the schools and the Refuge founded and directed by the Sisters of Charity at Leicester Place, were under a ban, because the Orleans Princes had from the

shall have to be up at daylight for the thanksgiving ceremony, in full uniform, in a carriage with eight springs, and valets in red and gold and yellow livery, and illuminations. It would tickle the Republic to see us pass by. It would be to meet myself in such a rig that would astonish me most. I have to school myself not to laugh when I see myself in such company, and have to school myself above all not to forget my lesson.

LONDON, February 27, 1872.

The weather was fine, the Queen came, and no accidents happened that I know of. *Rule Britannia!* At break of day we were on foot, we were not too much "guyed" on our way through the crowd. What a human flood as we drew near the City—as foul too as the waters of the Thames! No mob is

time of their foundation accorded them their active concurrence and generous assistance. This holding aloof moreover fell in perfectly with the tastes and habits of the members of the imperial diplomatic corps. The idea, unhappily enough, was that a Frenchman who leaves France has good reasons for not staying at home; the official representatives of France were imbued with it, and adopted it as a rule of conduct to ignore the French colony abroad. From the moment he arrived in London, the Duc de Broglie fell back on the earlier tradition and led the way for his successors by presiding with distinction at the annual banquet at the Hospital. A great deal might be said for an institution like this (annual dinner), which not only constitutes an advertisement for certain good people who find their profit in it, but presents one also with an opportunity to mix with them, to get them out of their ruts, to encourage them, enlighten them, assist them, give them a push forward. For my own part I did not relax my efforts to do so during my sojourn in England; and if I did not do more than I did the fault was a lack of time.

like an English mob; the signs of misery are so unmistakable. They are both violent and humble under the blows dealt by the police; and the ragbag reigns among them. Our national blouse is unknown in England; instead of this garment that hides things, they dress in the shabby remains of what once were coats, which reveal the filth and the nudity beneath. Such portion of the gathering as feared being *mobbed* had poured into the houses and scaffoldings. I never saw so many heads.

By eleven o'clock we were established in St. Paul's in a draught of cold air that *douched* us till two o'clock. At length the bells boomed like a volley of artillery, and the Queen arrived and came in. She was received with the royal silence that the sacredness of the place and the majesty of her office demanded—a real silence, not the natural silence of a void, but the silence of seventy thousand people who do not venture to breathe.

All the *royalties* filed up in a line in front of the public—the Queen, fat and short, in a street-dress, with a discontented-looking face; the Prince, with his already-recovered air of prosperity; and the Princess, as always, beautiful and charming. The music was grave, the sermon not too long. We got back in time to go to Hyde Park to see the return of the royal cortége in the midst of the deafening enthusiasm of the crowd.

But let us go back to our evening party [1] yesterday. It was a complete success. The Duc de Broglie received a most cordial reception, which, after

---

[1] The banquet above referred to.

he had spoken, became enthusiastic. There was a veritable uproar when he touched on this country, which for two hundred years has never once seen the law violated by the caprice of a Prince nor by the violence of the multitude. Each of his five toasts was a work of art. A tolerably exact summary of it is in to-day's *Times*. The difficulty of speaking of M. Thiers he very tactfully avoided by the aid of the Sèvres-vase sent for the lottery, and then he found an opportunity to speak of the noble use the Orleans Princes were making of such remnants of their wealth as spoliation had left them. Vernon was there, and brought with him Colonel Anson, who responded with much tact and warmth to the toast on the army—a loyal nature, simple and winning. We had also a Lord Eliott, ancient diplomat though himself still young, and a Frenchman in the turn of his tongue and his wit. He gallantly proposed the Duke's health.

LONDON, March, 1872.

The ceremony of the *levee* interested me much. All the diamonds in England filed before me, and trains to make a peacock jealous. The daylight and the current of cold air for the benefit of her Majesty were by no means favorable to the naked shoulders, nor to the color of the noses of their owners. The Queen was as gracious as she could be to Bernstorff,[1] and then! . . . we frantically ducked to her Majesty, and by a series of side-steps succeeded in regaining our places without turning our backs to the

[1] Count Bernstorff, German Ambassador.

enemy, and formed a row from which we looked down on the insignificant press of peers and barons of England filing by. It is a serious duty for every one, and for those who date their social existence from their presentation, a great day. I felt a certain sympathetic embarrassment for the first of them I saw drop on his knees to kiss the Queen's hand; and when a lady completed in the same way the reverence she was making, I was still more distressed; and then, when the Queen kissed the young ladies who were presented to her for the first time, I asked myself, what would have happened if the Queen had been a king? But how do I know I did not dream it all?

LONDON, March 3, 1872.

Was at a great dinner yesterday at the Rothschilds', where there was (what is rare in this country) an equal display of luxury and of good taste. We had the Duke of Cambridge[1] there; he chatted with me some time. Gave me good words on the French army, which had often been engaged three to one, and then he cited Bugeaud's saying about the English infantry: "*Happily*, it is not numerous." "*Un*happily," I replied; and we parted the best of friends.

We ate valiantly, and the wines were exquisite. Meyer de R. asked me at the end which had been, in my judgment, the best dish?

LONDON, March 14, 1872.

I have become one of the list of great people who

[1] Field Marshal, Commander-in-chief, born in 1819.

have appeared at Mr. Gladstone's and at Lady Margaret Beaumont's. I simply went in and came out again. At Gladstone's I picked up poor Musurus, who had just had a fall and broken his arm in three places. I put him into a carriage with a doctor. At Lady Margaret's I found the same set coming as I was to get their names inscribed on her list.

Immediately afterwards there was a *levée*. The Queen was more gracious to us than usual. She asked the Duc de Broglie for news of his son. Her daughter is quite handsome. The Duchess of Sutherland, who was covered with diamonds, stands daylight well. Here, once more, the diplomatic corps piled itself up in a heap; this time it was a brilliant Hungarian. He got mixed up with his boots, or his sabre, or his *attila*, and finally came down with a thud!

LONDON, March 16, 1872.

The Duc de Broglie shed tears and choked with sobs when he tried to speak of Cochin.[1] He had done so much, and yet so little! We were looking for so much from him that we forget he has left behind him a well-filled life. But he had many disappointments, and it is an ill chance that has closed his career. He too has been taken from us before his time—he, and Montalembert, and Perreyve, and P. Gatry, and P. Captier, who alone were able to turn the high-souled among us back to religion. What are the designs of God on our unhappy land? Whatever they may be, we must bow to them and pray. The poor Duke with death in his heart is

[1] M. Augustin Cochin, died Prefect of Versailles.

obliged to make ready for the fête to-morrow,[1] and to leave Tuesday for Windsor, instead of taking the road to the cemetery after the body of his friend.

For the dinner we had from hour to hour to send out fresh invitations in place of those that were met with "regrets." No Englishman who is at all strait-laced will consent to work his horses on Sunday even to meet a Royal Highness.

LONDON, March 18, 1872.

We played our part yesterday[2] to the accompaniment of the band. It went off nicely. The Duke of Cambridge at the appointed hour stepped out of his carriage upon the red carpet stretched across the sidewalk; red liveries, that might have made Louis XIV. or Babin envious, formed a line on either side from the steps; the Prince's people kept the crowd back with their sticks (I don't vouch for this detail, but it is part of the prescribed thing). All honor to the master of ceremonies who succeeded in having everybody take his proper place at table (this is for me); all honor to the cook who " What a pleasure," said an old diplomatic *fork*, "to be able to eat like this two hours à la française!" The strawberries at dessert did not cost less than three hundred and fifty francs. But the rarest treat was to see our young princess,[3] sparkling with diamonds, receiving perfectly at ease, as if she had done noth-

---
[1] The Duc de Broglie was to give a dinner the following day to the Duke of Cambridge.
[2] The dinner at the Embassy.
[3] Mlle. d'Armaillé, Princesse de Broglie.

ing else all her life, the homage of his Royal Highness on her right, and of the Prime-Minister on her left. She made head all evening against the assaults of the whole diplomatic corps, and that too with equal grace and modesty, a bit of a languishing air when she bowed to the contrary notwithstanding. And the ambassador was not the least happy person present. He forgot his grief, and admitted that it was a pleasure to have so fine a jewel to present. Nobody failed to come, not even the German ambassador; the trouble was rather that there were not invitations enough to go round. In effect, it was a complete success; it will be talked about, and that will do us no harm. As for myself, I spent the entire evening introducing people whose names I did not know.[1]

LONDON, March 22, 1872.

Heavy snow and thick fog. It froze and melted at the same time. The weather was frightful, but everybody was out in it. London poured out to Putney and the banks of the Thames by every road.[2] From Hammersmith on, to right and left, you saw nothing but umbrellas—except carriages, some with the horses taken out and sent to some place of shelter, some with horses still in, and the passengers on their seats, all waiting together motionless in the falling snow. With great difficulty and by the

[1] Soon after this entertainment, the Duc de Broglie left London for France. He had resolved to hand in his resignation in order to be free to devote his whole time to his duties as a Deputy. M. Gavard thus found himself once more in charge of the Embassy; a responsibility that lasted from March 24 to June 7, 1872.
[2] To witness a Cambridge-Oxford boat-race.

assistance of a mounted policeman who preceded us and jostled everybody out of our privileged way, we reached the *Cedars*, the property of Mr. Philips, a brewer, which lies at the very end of the racecourse. The tricolor floating at the side of the Queen's standard and those of the Prince of Wales and of Denmark announced to the populace that we had arrived. The house makes an effort at elegance and succeeds in being at least very comfortable and rich. It was abundantly supplied with ladies and 'swells.' Everybody ate to pass the time. People eat in this country as naturally as they twirl their thumbs elsewhere. The wait lasted two hours: everybody ate and drank for two hours by way of getting ready for the final luncheon. Negroes whose black was not proof against the rain executed musical and epileptic marches. The crowd laughed its loud laugh and forgot how slowly the time passed. It snowed incessantly. Suddenly everybody pushed everybody else and closed ranks; the signal had been given four miles away, and I braved the frost, too, with the rest of them and shinned up the garden, wall. The distant roar of a rising tide reached us, increased, drew nearer; hats were waved on the stockades and as the boats pulled up to the shore. As yet I did not see anything except some pigeons that were loosed; they soared away carrying the report of the race at four hundred three hundred and two hundred metres distance from the goal, to the four corners of Great Britain, nay, even to Greater Britain, for the telegraph wires were awaiting them. At last the first crew hove in sight; I fancied I saw a little line of light-blue on the water—it was Cambridge. The deep blue followed it three lengths behind, and was gaining evidently. The Oxford crew had been disorganized some days before by the illness of one of its oarsmen, who had to be replaced by a man not in training; and so the betting was two to one in favor of Cambridge. The light-blue came in first—but none too soon: it was but one length ahead. And then cheers, flourish of trumpets, and pigeons in more senses than one. But attention to the water! There were other, more formidable craft coming. It was the *City* that headed the little fleet of steamers; twenty of them followed her, whistling, pouring out smoke, blowing off steam, to try and avoid smashing the frail skiffs about them. Already the victors were returning in the midst of frantic cheers; it must be admitted, though, that the darkblues who followed them were not less cheered. A magnificent luncheon was awaiting them—victors and vanquished alike—at our host's. We were not able to wait for it, and launched ourselves into the chaos of vehicles with one, two, three, four, five horses. Our privilege went for nothing in a regular "block." We had to have patience. Our ears were greeted with the sound of a trumpet, with which the coachman of a four-horse omnibus whiled away his time by producing noises fit to make a dog howl. The coachman of a four-wheeler, with a typical rubicund face, made sententious little remarks with a truly magnificent indifference under the melting snow. Another person profited by the occasion to demand *a radical reformation of Parliament!*—and I distinguished by the intonations of a fourth that he was preaching his religion. I ought to add that nobody went back on his colors, and that the deep-blue Oxford ribbons had not disappeared from the whips, nor the button-holes, nor hats. From the top of society to the bottom everybody takes part in this contest; the wretchedest enter into it with as much passion as the blessed of the earth who go to see their sons, or the representatives and inheritors of their ancient university-rivalries, contend. It is not only in its political struggles, it is also in its games, in its national passions, that English society is divided, as has been said, not by horizontal but by vertical sections.

LONDON, March 23, 1872.

Sir Charles Dilke[1] being about to renew his attack on the Queen's civil list, I found a full house at Parliament. The members even flocked into the diplomatic gallery, where they were indistinguishable from the more polite gathering of their hosts, except by the privilege of wearing their hats and of shouting: "Hear! hear!" or other expression of their sentiments. It was a case of legitimate reciprocity—I have myself occupied the upper galleries reserved to the members of Parliament, but always with my hat off.

[1] One of the Members for Chelsea.
[2] "The sittings of Parliament during that session," writes M. Gavard in his notes, "took up a regular portion of my time. Whenever the bulletin-boards at the clubs announced an interesting sitting, I was as regular, either before dinner or afterwards, in my attendance as if the party whips had come to my house to rout me out."

Dilke had time to say all he wanted to; he talked an hour and a half without a pause, without a sigh, without an " Alas ! " or a " Halloo ! " from the House. It left it to Mr. Gladstone to express its sentiments. The placidity with which the chief of the cabinet had, during the adjournment, passed over the attacks directed against the Crown by the member for Chelsea before the Newcastle workmen, was no longer the fashion after the Prince of Wales's illness and the striking manifestations of loyalty on the part of the nation. Mr. Gladstone found accordingly a flood of eloquence in which to confound the imprudent aggressor against the Throne; he demmonstrated the errors the so-called instructor of the people had made in his figures, and brought out finally into sharp contrast this counting of pennies and farthings—this appeal to the smallest of our passions, and the grandeur of the institution, the services of which Sir Charles Dilke alone failed to recognize. The House went farther in its disapprobation; it lost, as it sometimes (not often) does, its patience. When Mr. Oberon Herbert,[1] brother of Lord Carnarvon, rose to second the motion of Sir Charles Dilke, it refused to hear him. The scene was perfectly comic; both sides struggled for more than an hour with an equal obstinacy. Mr. Herbert had barely uttered the sacramental word: " Mr. Speaker," before cries of: " Divide ! divide ! divide ! "—*Aux voix*, as we should say—were heard on all sides. Economizing accordingly his powers, and adapting his efforts to the length of the struggle

[1] Son of the third Earl Carnarvon.

he knew he was engaging in, the orator gave out his words syllable by syllable; each of them raises a tempest of cries; but as nobody can yell continuously without losing breath, and the instant the noise subsided, the imperturbable speaker, his hands in his pockets, pronounced another syllable and the tumult began again. The youngest members of the party being the ones who did the shouting, distinctive cries of animals soon became predominant in the chorus.

The Speaker assisted sadly at this "match," to which custom forbade him to put an end. When those who were making the interruption perceived that they could not tire out an adversary who drew on his resources so sparingly, they had recourse to divers legal ruses that are permissible. All at once a member rose and said with the utmost coolness that he did not believe there was a quorum present. He may affirm that there are not forty members present, in the face of more than five hundred of them who are suffocating with indignation and raising a rumpus that can be heard within the walls of Westminster No matter; what he says has to be verified—it is the custom. The Speaker rises and begins to count with his hat; but—a miracle!—everybody has disappeared—through the doors perhaps, or under the benches! Still, the matter is in doubt; there has to be a regular count. Thanks to the government, which must keep its seat, the forty are there. The crowd reappears like a resurrection of the dead and the fight begins all over again. At the end of some minutes recourse is had to the same expedient; the trick had been ill-done before, they hope to play it better. Vain hope!—the forty are still there. From that time on the victory of the unconquerable speaker is assured; the only concern now is to deprive him of the advantages that come from giving his words publicity. Some member accordingly rises and calls the Speaker's attention to the fact that there are strangers present; and the Speaker, who up to that moment had not observed our presence in the gallery and the presence of the journalists above his head, orders us to be asked to go out. The ladies, more fortunate than we, are permitted to remain because technically they are not in the hall, being separated from it by a screen. Thanks to this happy and transparent fiction they remained; and it was no doubt through them that the public learned this morning the issue of this Homeric struggle of one against many. It is true that the *one* had the right on his side.

LONDON, April 2, 1872.

The absence of the ministry and of all possible intermediaries, obliges me to sit with my hands folded. What a mistake it is to believe that England is a land of business! They are country people who come to town to rush through public affairs in the intervals of their hunting-parties and their sports. They maintain here only a temporary lodging and when they are in town are solely preoccupied with making the machine go faster, so that they may get back to their pleasures in the country. Also you ought to see how public business is done!

Here is a remark of my chancellor worthy of history. I had just reduced an expense: "That is a bad precedent," he said—"it is an economy."

We passed the day at Crystal Palace. It is the temple of vulgarity, the utter negation of every idea of art and of good taste. They have gathered together the cream of the masterpieces of the entire world, and made of them the most sickening collection conceivable; and more than that, to make them shine, they wash them at least once a year. They have so encumbered the gigantic structure that you might well think yourself in Madame Tussaud's bazar. It was "people's day"; the people had come to eat there—it seems the people eat better there than elsewhere. The public is worthy of the palace. How homely the race is, on holidays, when the Saxon strain comes to the surface! My young friend was much amused by it all, and in especial by a menagerie that we ran across between the Alhambra and an Egyptian temple. A black panther and a handsome lion, who wanted to eat their neighbor, a camel, excited our admiration.

LONDON, April 12, 1872.

Yesterday I wrote a long letter to the Minister, after my conversation with Lord Granville. Then I hastened back to Parliament, where I was much diverted by the spectacle of the *divisions*. When the House is in committee there is no Speaker, the mace is under the table, there are no long speeches, they vote often. One side cries: " Aye ! " the other follows with " No," which they call out all the louder because they are in a minority. As the result is regularly contested, the "ayes" go out at one door and the "noes" at another, and then the tellers presently return and bow, and I fancy announce the result together.

LONDON, April 25, 1872.

Yesterday at four o'clock we turned out in a costume neither one thing nor the other—black coats, colored cravats, and patterned pantaloons, but with *orders and decorations* on, and the ladies in toilet to match. We were going to Buckingham Palace; the guests numbered two or three hundred—*a select party*. Musicians in livery were stationed on the right—the conservatory, or its equivalent. They might have played whatever they liked, for there was nobody to hear them. In the central salon were a sentimental tenor, the piano, Mme. Schumann, the royal family seated in hierarchic order; it did not occur to any one to laugh. Vast sideboards stood in one or two adjoining rooms; the air is biting in this country, and you have to eat in self-defense.

The Queen moved about among the ranks of her subjects; the long habit of royalty has given her an air of dignity, but custom has done more for her than nature. Everybody stood with their heads bowed a bit, as in church; she stopped from time to time, and said a few words which will be treasured up and handed down from generation to generation. She held out her hand—not to me—that would have been an historical event—but with marked graciousness to a sort of pagoda at my side. I thought it was an old rajah of India—it was the Countess Beaconsfield. Behind her stood *Lothair, Conningsby*, the *Jew, Dizzy*, sepulchral as always in his old-fashioned costume of "Young England"; there is a suggestion of oriental tinsel in his painted face. He is not amusing except when he is baiting Gladstone.

The last effort of art after, or rather between, the two bands of music, was the introduction of two Scotch *pifferari*, armed with double or triple flutes. They blew on them fit to burst—the dogs are gifted in the matter of lungs. They came and went in great irregular strides, and blew eternally. It was as much as one's life was worth to listen to them.

We are going to witness the Queen of Prussia's visit next week. The prospect of meeting her is a painful one.

LONDON, May 2, 1872.

The telegraph informs us that M. Harcourt has been nominated.[1]

Colonel Anson is in a bad way; he has ruptured a blood-vessel in his chest; it looks as if there were small chance for his life. He is a splendid fellow— the best I have met in England—and congenial as can be. Mrs. Vernon stays continually with her friend. Vernon insists on taking his wife to Norway for the fishing. "The breezes," he says, "are so good for people with delicate chests."

Yesterday evening, *prima sera*, that is to say, at eleven o'clock, we went to Lady Jersey's—the

[1] The Duc de Broglie had handed in his resignation as ambassador; his place was filled by Comte Bernard d'Harcourt, of the ducal branch of that family.

daughter of Sir Robert Peel. There I met a lady who classified my acquaintances for me—into those who sing and those who dance. " Whom do you meet at her house ?—Nobody but the mob—you never see a Tory there !" " I saw Lord Derby there." " Do you call *him* a Tory?" For the rest: It is an odd sort of person that can visit Rome without finding herself edified—vexed that she met none but Piedmontese in society. One might have had some talk in this salon if there had been time, but we had to break off in the middle and hasten away to Gladstone's.

LONDON, May 9, 1872.

The King of Belgium presided at the banquet for the Royal Literary Fund. He acquitted himself of this task (a new one for a sovereign) with great good grace and with applause from an aristocratic and literary company, who were doubly flattered by the compliments they received as being from the mouth of royalty and in their own native tongue. The Belgian endowment necessarily defrayed the expense of the compliments and felicitations that were exchanged; but the name even of France did not figure in Mr. Disraëli's dissertation, nor in the reply made by the grandson of Louis-Philippe.

Musurus, who wishes to make himself agreeable at the Embassy, testified his surprise at not having met me at the banquet. I replied: "I cannot be surprised that France's representative was forgotten in making out the invitations, when France herself was forgotten at the banquet."

That was a witticism. So much the worse;

diplomatists ought not to pass for wits. But I was angry at the King of Belgium.

LONDON, May 14, 1872.

Yesterday evening I was presented to the Empress-Queen:[1] it took place in public at Prussia House. There was a crowd of kings and princes about her. A great silence fell when I appeared. The Queen, who talks capitally, does not pause even while her auditor is being changed; the conversation flows on from one to the other without period or comma. She expressed to me a keen regret at not having met the Duc de Broglie, whom she had long desired to know; she had been to Coppet expressly for that purpose. " Madam, I will convey your regrets to him." Then she complained of the bad weather and the rain. " Madam, the rain will smooth the sea for your Majesty's passage." Thus ended this memorable interview. That indeed was an occasion to beware of wit, and I conducted myself with accomplished stupidity.

The only amusing thing was a group of musicians at the foot of the stairs, who performed after the manner of a leaky tap: drop by drop, a distillation of discord.

LONDON, May 25, 1872.

Yesterday I bathed all day in verdure; nothing can equal the coolness, the brightness, the harmony of tone of the English landscape—product of the fog though it be, and in especial when it shines, as it sometimes does, beneath the sun. Everywhere

[1] The Empress of Germany came to make a visit to England.

you find trees of extraordinary age and vigor, with magnificent wide-sweeping branches, and underneath them a carpet of green—green on green; and the whole stretches away in gentle undulations on every side to the horizon, and at your feet flows the silver Thames. I was not more than twenty miles from London, from its smoke and noise—I should have thought it was two hundred. What repose! The trees and the air were full of bird-notes of all kinds—a pastoral symphony; few houses were in sight and fewer inhabitants. A great farm, that brings in twenty thousand francs a year, seems to run itself; a portable engine does all the work—labors, sows, mows, reaps, chops, beats, gathers in the crops. All they have to do is to change the accessories from time to time and let it go its way. The farmer is a respectable gentleman in a high-hat; his wife sits in the parlor with a flower-stand full of flowers before her window. Books from the circulating library lie on the table, a piano stands in the back of the room, and there are young misses in the family with rodent-teeth. I don't say that a bit more stubble, a few more familiar, disorderly chickens, and oxen in the yoke—a little less correctness and tidiness everywhere—would not have added to the picturesqueness of it all. Oh!—who will give me back the country in which the good Lord's beasts are at home!

My hosts, who are very agreeable, have taken refuge in a little "box" that they occupy some few days only in the year—a featureless little structure, composed of odds and ends, without antiquity or

character, and with a garden cut bodily out of the
fields which stretch away as for as the eye can
see. I found Hayward there—brevet-story-teller,
the middleman for all people interested in politics,
the diplomatist's Providence. Also Beaulieu,[1] who
read me the humorous letters he had written to
amuse the Prince of Wales; Lord Norreys[2] and
his wife (the husband changed his faith to marry
her); Borthwick[3] of the *Morning Post* (he married a
Clarendon and is a fine-looking fellow, open-minded,
cultivated, and agreeable); a certain Seymour, M. P.;
and I forget the others at table. I talked a good
deal with Fortescue about our common friends, the
Princes, whose portraits, it seems, are scattered up
and down his part of the country. *La Smalah* was
there also. He seemed to be more than a little annoyed at the position of the ministry. The Whigs,
the commissioners say, indisputably convict Gladstone of erroneous assertions. There never was such
fumbling in England nor such a disposition to continue in it. Gladstone had promised to stay and
keep a sharp lookout, and there he is in Wales.

LONDON, May 28, 1872.

The weather yesterday was fine, but there is nothing to rejoice the heart in seeing society turned up-
sidedown. It was a fête-day in all senses. Lots of
false noses and false beards were sold for those who

[1] Minister for Belgium.
[2] Future Earl Abingdon.
[3] Baronet in 1880 and M. P. Lady Borthwick was a sister, and a niece of Earl Clarendon.

for this once wanted to get drunk, but were ashamed of it. Everybody drank and ate till their cheeks puffed out. The great luxury is to eat in your carriage—to stuff yourself in the presence of the staring crowd, who gather up or steal the crumbs. The space left free by the horses and carriages is filled with flying sticks and arrows; so much the worse for you, if you run foul of one of their national games. As for shooting, they are obliged practice it in a big tube. There is less merit in hitting the mark, but it is not so dangerous. I say nothing of the horses and the betting. Perched up on the third story on the roof of the great tribunal, I got but a "bird's-eye" view, but the space set apart for the sport was even bigger than the crowd. In this rather brief account of Derby Day, I ought not to forget the myriads of tents that cover the plain and the hill—rags attached to four poles and flying in the wind. Beside them the raggedest and dirtiest outgrowths of the mud of London, calling out to all the passerby: "Accommodation, very good accommodation!"—the very triumph of English decency and you enter the appointed inclosure in the very midst of gentlemen and ladies at dinner on top of their coaches!

We started home before the end—it was one great orgie of drunkenness that we left behind.

LONDON, June 2, 1872.

The Washington treaty, I believe, is on the water, and the ministry at the bottom of the sea; but what chance is there of forming another? Mr. Disraëli aptly compared Gladstone and his colleagues on the government benches to a row of extinct volcanoes. The other side, however, are in no hurry. Lord Derby has formally declared that he and his friends are waiting for the country to make some more decisive sign ; he has no notion of putting himself at the mercy of the radicals, and of being obliged to do their will in order to keep himself in power. It is a pity that his bearing is so heavy and so odd—that his speech is so embarrassed and his words so far from " winged." One can imagine a country gentleman being like that, but not the son of Lord Derby. His programme of patient, effective opposition is a good deal more grateful to the party in office than to the conservatives.

Mr. Gladstone makes some of them uneasy by his daring spirit, by his enthusiasm and imprudences of speech ; he offends others by the haughtiness or the clumsiness of his proceedings and by the abuses of power in which he seems to delight. I ought to add that whenever I listen to him, I fall under the spell of his easy, rich, undulating eloquence, of his harmonious voice, of his beautiful clear enunciation, of his elocution and quick eye which roves among his auditors without his attention to what he is saying lapsing for a moment. But I find great difficulty in following his thought through all its wanderings, its incidents, its obscurities ; and I ask myself sometimes if he is always capable of following it himself.

Yesterday evening the " uniforms " dined.[1] Mine

[1] Dinner at Lord Granville's.

sat between that of the Minister of the Shah of Persia (who amused me by proving that with its obligatory ministry service and the poor-rates in England the Occident is becoming Mussulman!), and that of General Cust, the chamberlain, a very pleasant man well on in years, full of sympathy for France and appreciating at their just value the Comte de Paris and the Duc d'Aumale. A piece by Offenbach and the popping of corks embroidered our conversation. The dinner was not long. The beautiful Lady Castalia then appeared in all her brilliancy and grace and a draught of air was provided for her bare shoulders. During the evening Count Bernstorf honored me by hunting me out, and explained to me all his "decorations," one of which Bismarck is without. A friend in the Foreign Office showed me a secret stairway by which I was enabled to make my escape—the main stairway being occupied by the assaulting columns of the mob. It was thus made possible for me to reach Stafford House, the Duke of Sutherland's home, a little before midnight.

Ah! what a stairway! I did not have time to form an opinion on the architecture, but what plate! —it is more than royal! And with it all a duchess who must be more beautiful than the house she inhabits. The possessor of all these treasures when he mounts that stairway (it is wide enough to accommodate a battalion) may well think that all men are not equal. The great apartments were not open, so I did not see their three thousand pictures; but as far as I could judge at a glance there were below stairs some half-a-million francs' worth of daubs, portraits, water-colors, lithographs, ornamented with frames, of great value no doubt, but I could not see them distinctly and simply walked through, to arrive at Mr. Gladstone's at half-an-hour past midnight. What are we coming to! It was Sunday, and there were still twenty-odd people there—all diplomats it is true.[1]

Extracts from the Notes.

THE NEGOTIATION FOR THE TREATY OF COMMERCE.

Count Bernard d'Harcourt reached London the 7th of June to replace the Duc de Broglie. He left, dismissed, the 9th of August. On the morning of the day following M. Ozenne arrived with instructions from the president relative to opening negotiations at London, for a treaty of commerce. There had been some talk about it ever since the close of 1871. M. Thiers was tormented with the idea of freeing us from the odious treaties of 1860, and of creating at the same time, by a tax on raw materials, a source of income we needed to pay the interest on our ransom. The moment the chamber gave him the necessary authority, he did not hesitate to make use of it. March 15th, 1872, he announced that

[1] From June to October there is a break in the correspondence. M. Gavard's family being at that period with him, there was no occasion for him to write. From the month of August on, he was especially busied, as the reader will see, in negotiating a treaty of commerce, a ticklish affair that he had not lost sight of since his arrival in London.

the treaties would be in force but one year longer
—till, that is, March 15th, 1873. I shall not enter
into the details of the negotiations which followed,
except so far as may be necessary for a proper understanding of the comedy which was played between London and Paris in the months of August,
September and October, and in which I was one of
the principal actors. I call it a comedy, because all
our labors, though crowned for the moment with
success, bore no fruit, and because the only interesting thing about it all is the light it throws on certain characters.

There was no notion at first of giving me, any
more than the Duc de Broglie, a rôle to play; it was
M. Thiers's personal affair. Nobody else, we thought,
could bring it to a successful issue; he needed
nothing but a devoted instrument. M. Ozenne
accordingly arrived in London as a direct emanation from the brain of M. Thiers, with authority to
pass as well over the head of the ambassador at
London as over that of the Minister of Foreign
Affairs at Paris.

The instructions that M. Ozenne brought with
him were full of misconceptions. England was to
be asked to renew the treaty of 1860, augmenting
certain duties on the score of protecting home industries, and increasing the taxes relative to all
manufactured articles on the score of compensation
for the duties on raw materials; the new arrangement to take effect at once, before the legal expiration of the treaty in 1873.

I was well acquainted with the ground; I had

studied it long since, and I knew what we should have to contend with in the English Government: A strong disposition to preserve the treaties of 1860, and at the same time to permit us to straighten out our finances; but also a firm resolution not to run foul of the Cobden Club nor of its principles; so much for Mr. Gladstone. Lord Granville and Sir Charles Fortescue would be faithful besides to certain political considerations. It would be on the side of the Chancellor of the Exchequer[1] that we should have least to expect; hostile though he was on principle to treaties of commerce, a cold friend to France, and determined not to enter into new engagements that would hamper him in his projects. As to the country, it looked on the whole thing with great distrust, convinced that any proposition coming from MM. Thiers and Povyer-Quertier must mask some evil design. And against them we had only the great ship-owners in the great ports, who were desirous to regain the former privileges allowed by France to English vessels not trading "directly."

On the other hand, the delicate matters I had already been obliged to treat of had established a regular correspondence and a mutual confidence between M. de Rémusat and myself. I did not hesitate therefore to say to him: " If you want not to abolish but to preserve the treaty of 1860 and the principles on which it rests, facilitating for our government the collection of its new imports; if you want, in a word, certain purely fiscal modifica-

[1] Hon. R. Lowe.

tions, and if you are disposed at the same time to free the British marine from the sort of discrimination that it labors under at the present moment, I guarantee success for you. But if you have at heart secretly or overtly any protectionist project, you had better give it up." M. Rémusat immediately agreed with me; but it took more than one despatch and more than one trip on the part of M. Ozenne to induce the president to adopt these ideas.

At first it was felt that I was taking rather a high tone, for a chargé d'affaires *pro tem;* but before the end of a month I was complimented on the new turn I had given the negotiation. M. de Rémusat wrote me that the president had been much struck by my official and private correspondence, and had testified his satisfaction. From this moment on I received nothing but felicitations and encouragements to go ahead. I certainly had my day with M. Thiers during his sojourn at Trouville; rumors of it reached me from all sides; it was I who prevented the Emperor's descending upon France; it was I who hurried off Her Majesty's ships of war to the coast of the British channel to salute the president, etc.; and what was nearer the truth, it was I who managed the negotiation of the Treaty. Having succeeded in getting them to withdraw all pretensions to a protectionist amendment and to restrict the negotiation to the purely fiscal clauses, I undertook to have the question of principle separated from the question of its application.

I recognized perfectly the difficulty there would be in reaching an agreement on the determination of the taxes destined as compensation for the duties on raw materials only, in especial if interested parties were given time to express their opinions; nor was I unaware how long such an undertaking would naturally be in reaching a conclusion—loss of time meant to us loss of all that we were striving for. The nearer we approached March 15th, 1873, the less there was for England to concede to us, since at that time we should in any event recover our liberty. I threw my weight into the scales and showed M. Rémusat that we needed a renewal of the treaty, for our own sakes, and also for its moral effect on Europe, politically and commercially. Probably my reasons were found good, for, after having consented to the suspension of the protectionist clauses, they agreed also to disjoin the question of principle from the question of the application of the principle. It was understood that the treaty should consecrate the principle of compensating duties, reserving the determination of them to a meeting at Paris immediately after the completion of the signature.

The negotiation was not a month old before the necessity was felt of coming to my aid and of giving more weight to my words. I was officially designated as First Plenipotentiary of France, and my full powers were sent me the 13th of September at the same time with those of M. Ozenne. For me it was a great honor. M. de Rémusat confided to me one day that some one had said to him that the British government was waiting till we should send some considerable personage over to sign the treaty—more considerable even than the ambassador. It was nothing of the sort. Lord Granville, who appreciated my frankness and the spirit with which I had pushed the affair, was very happy publicly to testify his feeling about me, in signing the treaty with me; he has said so to me since and has repeated it publicly. The difficulty was about signing with M. Ozenne, whose hierarchic position in the French administration was not covered by his being a member of the diplomatic corps; still Lord Granville passed over that, and was gracious enough to say to me that it was for me to manage the signature to suit myself. I should give no just idea of the difficulties, not even of the mechanical difficulties, of the task I had undertaken, if I omitted to say that in the months of August, September and October there was nobody in London, and in especial no member of the Cabinet. It is true that Mr. Kennedy, whom Lord Granville had expressly designated as his middleman, was there; and I ought to say that it was to this appointment and to the intelligence and good-will of Mr. Kennedy that we in the main owed our success; but Mr. Kennedy's presence did not prevent my corresponding directly with the members of the Cabinet. My letters pursued Lord Granville to Walmer Castle, Mr. Gladstone to Hawarden, the Hon. Fortescue to Shewton-Mendip. Mr. Gladstone's replies were as cloudy, as obscure, as his drafts for treaties; those of Lord Granville were short but conclusive; and Fortescuc's and Lady Waldegrave's were veritably perfect; it was not for nothing that I had made use of the names of the Orleans' Princes to gain this confidence.

While we were thus making every effort to come to an agreement on the renewal of the treaty of 1860, the three Emperors met at Berlin, and the representatives of England, no more than those of France, had been invited to be present at this interview. I insisted at some length to Lord Granville that the absentees should profit by the occasion to come to an understanding with one another, and should unite two nations on the basis of material interest as a parallel to the embraces the three potentates were exchanging behind closed doors. I caused this thesis to be developed also in the newspapers, which bore their part in the negotiation. I was and I am convinced that, if one wants to manage any business properly in England, he must, at the same time that he addresses the government, negotiate directly with public opinion through the press and through members of Parliament or of the Chambers of Commerce, if there be at issue any question which concerns them. I have never neglected this device, and have always found the good of it, both in 1872 and later in 1875, with the Conservative Cabinet.

We have reached at last the critical period of the affair. The end of October was approaching and we had to come to some conclusion. Unhappily, the nearer we approached the limit of our time, the less distinctness there was in the directions that came from Paris. There was nothing but discussion at headquarters, which waxed all the hotter, that nobody dared go to the bottom of things and show the president that he was contradicting himself; he seemed to have forgotten the concessions that at the outset he had made. Poor M. Ozenne was at the end of his tether; he came back to me completely worn out. Happily, my letters proved a sufficient voucher of what had been said, and I went ahead with no other care than to conquer or to perish.

On the 24th of October I was of opinion that we had reached the psychological moment. On the one hand M. Ozenne had brought me from Paris an order to change our position, to bring to the front once more the stipulation for a time-limit that we had theretofore put aside, contrary to my advice. But it was too late to retrace our steps, even for the purpose of bettering the conditions of the treaty. I had observed that Lord Granville had been much shaken by its being found out in England that, with or without a treaty, we should not be able to discriminate against England, either as regards her marine or her commerce; I had been warned by a sure friend (Lady Waldegrave) that we must close the matter up promptly and give Lord Granville no pretext for backing out. A pretext for backing out was precisely what I should have given him, if I had followed my instructions and gone at the last moment to propose an alteration in the draft already made. The English Government would have been certain to suspect some hidden purpose on our part, and all the more so that there existed in reality nothing of the kind. The truth is, that the government at Paris had not taken account of the fact that the guaranty of favorable treatment secured indirectly for our treaty (because of the existing arrangement between England and Austria) precisely the same degree of permanence that I was ordered to secure for it directly by a special stipulation.

I announced at Paris that I had postponed communicating the new propositions, and I stated my reasons for doing so. Mr. Gladstone aspires to be the leader of the "free-trade" party, now that Cobden no longer holds that position; he considers himself the guardian of commercial liberty, not only in England, but everywhere. He feels therefore that he has made a great sacrifice in giving his approval to our proposition for a levy of "compensating" duties. From the moment that he agreed to allow those duties to be collected the enemies of the treaty on both sides of the Channel have left no stone unturned that could make him feel more keenly the responsibility he has incurred.

They have represented to him that without the treaty with England we could not hope for success in a single one of our negotiations with other powers; while, on the other hand, if we approach them with his approval the other powers cannot show themselves severer guardians of the principles of "free trade" than England has done. They reproached him with his assent as an act of foolishness and an abandonment of his principles. They say, in every conceivable form of expression, that he is preparing the way for the ultimate triumph of the economic theories that, but for his desertion, M. Thiers would have tried in vain to bring into recognition. Finally, I have reason to believe that a certain pressure now being brought to bear by foreign powers has not been without effect in lessening the good-will that England manifested so patently in our favor after the success of the loan and of the congress at Berlin. I am alarmed lest the prime minister, manifestly restless as he is, under the responsibility he assumed when he accepted our overture, should jump at the chance of distinguishing himself, considering it a safe course in Parliament to say that he had at first consented to the proposal and then withdrawn his consent before a too tardy acceptance. In the eyes of the world the treaty is an accomplished fact; the terms are known, and the two governments no longer try to hide their accord. If the thing falls through we cannot avoid misunderstandings, publicity, and indignant recriminations, which will have the worst possible effect on the relations of the two countries. Public opinion, which is ruled by commercial interests, will rise blindly, and, in the name of free trade, the government and the public will join in a regretable hostility to France and to the government of M. Thiers. It is to conjure away this result that I insisted on a return to the propositions to which I was authorized, on October 18th, to give in our assent.

I waited tranquilly for the effect of these observations. Telegrams began to arrive the night of the 26th. The president announced that he was sending M. Amé; the minister, too, had sent a courier with an envelope from the president. The next day, Monday, brought me nothing but the regrets of M. de Rémusat, who wondered if it would not have been better to carry on the negotiations at Paris. I repeated my messages. At three o'clock there came a telegram from the president: "I ordered M. Amé to leave yesterday evening, and am indignant that he has delayed his departure. In matters as grave as these one sacrifices one's personal affairs, at no matter what cost." Then he continued enjoining me to yield and sign. This injunction, along with other matters in cipher, was repeated a number of times. The English government was, for the rest, as determined as I was. At seven o'clock in the evening the courier arrived a good first. He brought a note from the president running: "Sign! Sign!" Also a letter from M. de Rémusat which was excellent, cordial, and unmistakably plain: "Put the thing through at any price, and good luck to you! I sympathize heartily with you in your anxiety." M. de Pontécoulant also had been charged to tell me that I was counted on to save the negotiation from falling through. At last, about nine o'clock, M. Amé appeared. He had lost his trunks, had secured no quarters at the hotel, and was no better informed than M. Ozenne in regard to the telegrams of the day. From this point on my sole anxiety was not to sign the papers on the 2d of November, which was All Souls' Day. M. Ozenne was ready to sign at any time, so as to have done with it, but happily, M. Thiers understood my feelings. We were, however, obliged to work continuously to be ready by the 5th. It was necessary, even at the Foreign Office, to work on Sunday to get the papers ready. Such a thing had never before been heard of, and the venerable Mr. March, chief of the special service (who violated the Sabbath), dying some weeks afterward, I was accused of being the cause of his decease.

On the 5th the treaty was signed at the Foreign Office at three o'clock. Lord Granville accompanied his signature with many gracious expressions, and in an official letter emphasized the amicable intentions which had moved his government to accept the new arrangement.

"For the one party," I wrote to M. de Rémusat "this is the treaty of 1860 renewed, surviving the Empire; for the other, it is an opportunity to apply the law in regard to raw materials." The same day I sent a dispatch which supplied the minister with an exposition of my motives. At his request I wrote out for him once more some arguments against the adversaries of the treaty: "It is important that our government should not misunderstand the magnitude of the sacrifice that the government of the Queen feels that it has made for us. It is only by being right on this point that we can estimate justly the amount of good-will to us which they have shown in agreeing to our propositions, and which Lord Granville expressed in a way not to be misunderstood when he wrote me the following: 'I can assure you that the Queen's government has given, by its assent in this matter, the gravest proof possible of its sincere desire (in the spirit of friendship toward France), to come to your aid in the present circumstances.' It cannot be to our interest to belittle such a testimonial."

M. de Rémusat had not misunderstood the bearing of England's action in the matter; he proved as much in a letter that he wrote me on the 7th of November : "I have received to-day," he said, "the text of the treaty and your dispatch of the 6th. ... I congratulate you on bringing to an issue a work in which you have taken so prominent a part. . . . The zeal and ability that you have shown in this difficult negotiation have been remarked by the President of the Republic, who asks me to express to you his intense satisfaction. As for myself, I can hardly express to you the value I set upon the service you have rendered the state." The rest was a review of the commercial and political importance of the treaty, etc., etc.

My task was done, my commission at an end, and I was in a hurry to return to Paris, where I was in demand in the discussion of questions of application, interpretation, etc.

It was at the time of this negotiation that I was in greatest favor with M. Thiers. He sang my praises so loudly,—a bit to enrage my superiors,— that I was thought to be destined to the most exalted station. The entire administration of France was put at my disposal. My influence was regarded as such by M. de Rémusat, that he sent for me at different times to come to Paris and make head against his terrible friend, who could hardly bear, or rather, would not listen to contradiction. The trouble was about the application of the treaty of the 5th of November. M. Thiers obstinately interpreted an important clause in a way quite subversive of the declarations of the ministers from the Tribune and of those who conducted the negotiations in England. The matter was discussed, in a sort of special council, at Versailles, at which I was present. M. de Rémusat gave me the floor, encouraging me by patting me on the back, to go ahead. One day, when I became too pressing, a regiment of cavalry happening to ride by, M. Thiers opened the window and had them pass in review at a distance, thus ending the discussion. At another time, when I was speaking with conviction and with *pièce de conviction*, he got up and went into his office to look for a box of chocolates. When he came back he filled my mouth with them, and thus once more ended the discussion.

I believe that the courage with which I defended my opinions did not displease him; the more so that I neglected no opportunity of redeeming my professional frankness by compliments which were the more graceful in that they were sincere. When the conversation touched on internal politics, or on people about whom we did not agree, I remembered the passing regiment, and in my turn opened the window to the *militeriana*. I had only to mention a subject to set him talking endlessly, and it was really a pleasure to hear him. I learned in this way one evening the history of all the transformations that the Roman army underwent. I had always thought of it as homogeneous from the time of

Romulus to the downfall of the Roman Empire; but it passed, it seems, through as many radical reforms as the French army has since there was a French army; in support of which very probable thesis M. Thiers abounded in arguments. From the army of Marius or of Cæsar we passed to Marius himself, to Cæsar and to Pompey. "Cæsar was an ignoramus; he knew nothing of the art of war, but he was a genius! Ah! genius makes up for everything." From the ancients we passed on to the moderns. "Turenne was the completest of warriors; in his person all the warlike virtues were united. As for Napoleon, he was a genius—a military genius such as Providence has but twice sent to this planet. What about our enemies? They have foresight. General von Moltke had universal foresight, but not genius. Which would one choose if one had to choose between the two? After some hesitation, M. Thiers voted for universal foresight. Perhaps he was thinking of himself when he gave this verdict. His talk was marvellously full of interesting details, and pithy, effective turns of phrase. It all came back to me some time afterward, when I heard M. Jules Simon deliver his eloquent speech against the nature and extent of the marshal's power.

The orator touching on general considerations and tracing the heroic portrait of the man of war, to contrast with it the figure of Napoleon III at Sedan; I recognized the thought and even the words, and told my neighbor that he was going to speak of Turenne. M. Jules Simon had at least as good a memory as I. The long-range practice from the battery at Montretout on another occasion stood me in good stead. As the conversation turned on questions that I did not wish to discuss with the president, I found it much more agreeable to listen to the history of the improvement he had brought about in military tactics. I remember in especial his vivid characterization of the " shell " as a loaded mine, that saunters through the air and holding its charge till it reaches the desired spot bursts, etc., etc.

But it is not my design to set down here all the treasures of learning, wit and eloquence he bribed me with from time to time ; I wanted simply to explain a bit my relations with him.

After the signing of the treaty of November, he conferred on me the commander's cross, and sent me to London with the same rank as before. I could ask nothing better. I had done M. Thiers' foreign policy good service ; I had contributed to procure for him the moral success which, at the close of 1872, after the notoriety given to this attempt to come into closer relations with England, he could not well have foregone ; I had helped him to anticipate, at the beginning of his economic campaign, a failure at London, which would not have given him time to withdraw gracefully from his financial projects. I had been therefore useful to him ; and he had recompensed my services by an official testimonial of his satisfaction. I regretted that our relations could not continue on the same footing ; but I had never had the least idea of following his lead

in politics. His political views were not mine—
never had been and never could be.

Extracts from the Correspondence.

LONDON, September 14, 1872.

Have been watching the manœuvring at Salisbury-field. That sort of thing here is simply a form of sport. They play at soldier from their playgrounds at school up to this great parade ground, where Mr. Cardwell [1] has succeeded in getting together thirty thousand men. The capital fact is the presence of this civilian minister, to-day, acting-chief of the army, taking his place at the side of the Prince who is the official chief, and enduring with a patience quite English, the little insults which neither the princes nor the representatives of the military aristocracy spare him. The presence of the minister signified that the army to-day belongs to the State, that the privileges of the aristocratic close corporation have given place to the law of the realm, the traditional routine to the reforms commanded by the new conditions of the art of war. I hesitate to compare Mr. Cardwell to Louvois, and the timid efforts of the one to the splendid creations of the other. But it is at least evident that the English minister of war, in his struggle to dispossess the aristocracy of its military appanage, has not been unconscious of the great French military reformer. And the comparison is far from displeasing to him I

[1] Viscount Cardwell in 1874; at the time referred to in the text, minister of war.

know, when it comes in the form of a delicate allusion. It is a far cry from the present state of things to the time when honorary commands might be offered to young men and refused by ambitious mammas on the ground that their sons were going in for merit.

LONDON, October 25, 1872.

There is no one in London to talk with about England's last misadventure in the San Juan Island affair.[1] At Geneva they levied a tribute on the English; at Berlin, they cut off a piece of her live flesh.

The *Times* said yesterday: "After all, if we do lose the Island which commands England's possessions on the Pacific Coast there will be economy in having one less garrison to keep up." They will be able to make many economies of this kind before long in Canada and elsewhere.

It was announced yesterday that the Russians had entered Khiva, and were approaching British India. The *Times* says, "So much the better—instead of having a turbulent and barbarous neighbor we will have a civilized one, and the benefits that come from intercourse with a great nation."

Yesterday's dinner at club was very interesting. Hayward, the celebrated Sumner,[2] of the American Senate, and Kingslake,[3] just back from

---

[1] Referring to the decision of the German Emperor in favor of the United States in the San Juan Island affair. The consequences were serious for British Columbia and for England's interests on the Pacific Coast. It was the result of Mr. Gladstone's faith in the panacea of arbitration.

[2] Senator Charles Sumner, a great orator.

[3] Kingslake, author of the History of the Crimean War.

Berlin, took a table together. Sumner quoted from memory and declaimed passages from all the great English orators. Hayward rivalled him, supplied him with missing words, recited in his turn, and ended by saying, " I have heard them all; Canning, Peel, Plunkett, and best of all, Brougham."

LONDON, November 10, 1872.

I attended yesterday a banquet at Guildhall. You will remember the immense hall. We were received in the new library, another structure of the same immensity. We had to walk between two rows of eager eyes, to the foot of the throne, where were seated the king and queen of spades.[1]

It was not until I was taking my place among these high dignitaries that I discovered that every one but myself was in uniform. Happily the other republican, the *chargé d'affaires* of the United States was also dressed in black. Republican manners, antique simplicity: I hope that this will stand me in good stead with Barthelemy-St.-Hilaire.

I do not believe any one noticed it in the midst of the crowd of twelve hundred guests. Suddenly the trumpet sounded,—it was some minister arriving in front of the building. Trumpets greeted him in every room till he reached the foot of the throne. It is a pity they were out of tune.

At last Granville appeared with the beautiful Castalia, a blaze of diamonds. The procession moved and we reached the banquet-hall full of tables. Making the circuit of them we passed in review

[1] The Lord Mayor and his Lady.

before the ranks. At the end of the route we met a minister of Honduras and of Spain. I breathed easy again. But for them I would have been the senior *chargés d'affaires* and would have had to do the talking.

At last we found our places. All the court took places; the toast-master, mounting a tribune back of the Lord-Mayor. The Squires, Sheriffs, Macebearers, and Chaplains to the right and left. A kind of grace was said, in a matter-of-fact way, of which the less said the better.

We took our seats opposite some tough cold chicken, which (to have done once for all with the menu) was the only dish I dared to touch.

The fête began at seven o'clock with *God save the Queen*. The music unfortunately was insignificant, they ought to have had a Prussian orchestra —Parlow's for example—and have played something in the style of Wagner. Nevertheless the effect of the hall was magnificent with Gog and Magog, the old stained-glass windows, the platform with the small arches, and the golden lights, the gigantic marble statues of Pitt and of the other pillars of English history. I saw two crimson-velvet chairs and was wondering to myself who they were for, when two cooks (they might have come out of Rabelais) with frightful cutlasses got into them. Whole beeves were put before them and they cut Pantaguelistic slices with an absolute ferocity. I think the beeves must have been make-believe for none of the slices came our way, but it was all picturesque to the last degree. Then the speaking began. "My Lords, and Ladies and Gentlemen, charge your glasses!" Toast followed toast in rapid succession. Nuts were being cracked everywhere, and at the bottom of the room, where nobody could hear anything and every one was bent on being heard, they let off fire-crackers. After the toasts, came the hurrahs at a signal from the baton of the "toast-master." There was a flourish of trumpets before and afterwards which was echoed from the table of honor in the zenith of the hall opposite, where the orchestra was perched.

Every class and institution of English society was toasted. The beneficiaries stood up to receive the compliment. It was really funny to see the woollen-wigs stand up in their red gowns. We were toasted too, as "Gentlemen of the Diplomatic Corps," but we all forgot to stand up,—my co-Republican, the Belgian, the Spaniard and the Honduras ministers. This unfortunate (the minister from Honduras) replied after refusing many times. He recited a little speech an hour long, improvised some years since. He had attached to it some sort of a panegyric, on Gladstone, and, in effect, he made an ass of himself.

A sheriff sitting behind me said in an undertone: "He would be more welcome if he could simply announce to the assembly that Honduras was going to pay her debt!"

All danger was not over for me, and my heart began to beat singularly when Granville came to the treaty of commerce—it was the back-bone of his argument. He began very gracefully by referring to "the most distinguished diplomatist," with whom he had signed the treaty four days before. (Cheers). It is all in the morning papers. It was my neighbors, the Misses Dakin, the co-Republican, and the Spaniard who did the applauding; as I said, it is all in the morning papers and if the French papers copy it pray heaven they won't forget the applause! I bowed my acknowledgments,—but think what a hole I was in! I had scarcely heard what Lord Granville said, so occupied was I preparing a reply. Fortunately, however, the toast-master did not ask me if I would reply, and so my anxiety began to relax.

All this lasted until eleven o'clock. What a splendid nation! The chief honors were for the new Lord Chancellor; then for Lord Granville,—his wife does him no harm.

I spare you the loving-cups, and the basin (pure gold) of rose-water; I've told you of that before.

A.D. 1873.

Extracts from the Correspondence.

LONDON, February 16, 1873.

The night of my arrival we had a memorable meeting in Parliament. Mr. Gladstone spoke for three hours in the House of Commons, and in a hall opposite Lord Selborne held an interested assembly for the same length of time. Mr. Gladstone was explaining, with infinite art and skill, his project for educational reform in Ireland—a beautiful topic—the march of liberalism. It is probable that he will go under with the question, and he knows it, but he wishes to round his career off with a flourish, and above all, to hand down the flourishing to his successors.

LONDON, February 27, 1873.

It is snowing, there is half a foot on the ground and a great deal more in the sky. This is the sort of weather for Longfellow's Jeremiads. It is hard for the poor people who have no fur wraps and who must pay fifty shillings for coal this year, as against twenty-five last year and fifteen the year before.

The old Dowager Duchess of Cleveland[1] is an original. I arrived at eight o'clock just; and a minute afterward the dinner was on the table, but

[1] Dowager Duchess of Cleveland, born in 1792.

the guests came straggling in one after the other. The dinner was amusing. The Duchess, who does not see very well, asked me what they were serving her, and I could not tell whether it was meat, vegetables or fish; but it was *skates in browned butter*, and quite in the proper order. At the close she asked for a special kind of knife to cut an apple. Lady Bentinck was there with her daughter, who is very beautiful, with blue eyes and blonde hair. Also my young friend Lord Beresford of the 9th Lancers (a regiment that has taken me into favor). After the ceremony of passing the wine, the Duchess sent us word that it was time to return to the drawing-room. Everything went by the clock.

I made haste to talk to my beautiful neighbor, as I wanted to know about this miss who was pink and white, tall, and well-dressed. She had just come in from the country that morning and was anxious to return for the hunt. Three times a week at least they are in the saddle, often from nine o'clock in the morning till night fall, and enjoy it hugely. They seldom overtake the fox, and indeed such can hardly be said to be their object, which is rather to ride as fast as possible and leap over all the obstacles in their way. Her father puts eight horses at her disposal, which she mounts indifferently. There are always from sixty to eighty people at the meet. When they let the fox loose all rush forward without regard for each other, and they trample over everything as naturally as you please. Rainy weather is the best for the sport. As for accidents; there are none. It is much easier than you think to leap hedges, ditches and walls. Thus the other day she sprang over a rather large ditch where the fox doubled on his tracks; as she was coming back she saw her little sister, eleven years old, who had followed her over, turn and jump the ditch as well as she could. She had an adventure lately that caused some excitement. Two months ago she was returning home with her father and they crossed an inundated plain. The water was up to the horses' breasts. Suddenly her horse disappeared in a ditch, she under him. As she knew how to swim, she soon reached a place where the water was up to her chin. Her father leapt from his horse and joined her; but there they were, stuck in the mud, unable to move. While a friend went to get them help, one of the horses struggled a bit and then sunk before their eyes. They shouted to a passing railway train, but in vain. At last helpers came with ropes and they were pulled out, after three-quarters-of-an hours' cold bath in the month of December. That evening she came into the drawing-room as pink and white as ever, and the second day went horseback riding and had no cold. While she was telling me this adventure, which interested her as much as it did me, I caught some significant looks from the mother. I felt that I was in the way of something and hastened to give up my place to a lieutenant, who is evidently a marriageable cousin. Decidedly the next time I go to talk with an English miss, I shall find out whether she is there for amusement only or for business.. I do not know what they were talking about, but from time to time the lieutenant whistled as naturally as if he were in his stables. It is all very odd.

LONDON, February 28, 1873.

The royal flag is floating over Buckingham Palace. It is a great event in London. I gave myself up to many reflections while crossing the park and watching this superstitious crowd who were awaiting the appearance of the sacred person. It is the supernatural in politics,—the element of stability and of safety amidst perpetual shift and change in English opinion and affairs.

LONDON, March 2, 1873.

Last evening I went to the 'Speaker's' house, a fine old mansion on the Thames, connected with the Parliament. The two principal rooms contain portraits of all the 'Speakers' since the first Parliament. I admired sincerely this continuous, unbroken testimony of respect for law and liberty. Some members of Parliament have made an appointment with me for to-morrow; there is to be the first great debate on the university. The government is much shaken. Fifteen days ago everybody was applauding Gladstone's speech, now no one wants the bill to pass. The Protestants refuse to share their revenues with the Catholics; and the Catholics do not want to share anything with the Protestants, but want the whole appropriation for themselves and the disinterested spectator does not understand a transaction which makes everybody discontented, and above all those who are to profit by it.

LONDON, March 31, 1873.

A very agreeable dinner,[1] with not too many people, in a partially disorganized house. I made the ac- acquaintance there of Mr. Motley, formerly United States minister, whose successor causes him to be regretted. He is an author and a well-mannered man, who does not find himself very comfortable in his great Republic. He has been here nineteen years. His daughter was present, too, and is as fond of Europe as he is. She was my neighbor, and talked very agreeably. She is neither beautiful nor ugly to look at. On the other side I had a Campbell,[2] who spoke to me frankly of the time when he was in the wine business at Bordeaux, then in tea at Liverpool; now he is partner in a big banking house in the city. He is the brother of the Marquis of Lorne. His wife is extremely pretty. When he presented me to her, after dinner, she pouted a bit engagingly, then, during the conversation, when she discovered that I was of the Embassy, her face changed suddenly; successes of that sort are always flattering. My second neighbor was the Marquis of Ripon.[3] He is very agreeable, not much inclined to radical reforms, although he is a member of the Reform Cabinet. The thing I like in all these ministers is their simplicity. Everybody is preparing to leave town for the Easter holidays.

[1] At Lord Granville's.
[2] Lord Archibald Campbell, son of the eighth Duke of Argyle; partner in the bank of Coutts and Co.; married in 1869 to Miss Callander.
[3] Earl Gray, created Marquis of Ripon in 1871. Viceroy to India in 1880. Catholic.

LONDON, April 13, 1873.

Comte von Beust presented me to Lady William,[1] mother of the three Russells; Duke of Bedford[2]; Lord Arthur, M. P.,[3] and Lord Odo,[4] an ambassador. I came here feeling a little like the shepherd who wanted to question the sphinx, uncertain of the fate that awaited him. Every one in London who flatters himself he knows how to talk, aspires to file before her. All are not admitted, and if but few are called, still fewer are chosen; it is not every one that would like to come back that can. This is where Beust lets off his newest puns and puts them into circulation. Did he fetch me with him as a compeer?

Lady William Russell has, in spite of her eighty years, a remarkable head and speaks in a tone of authority. She has seen a great deal of the world, kept her memories fresh and has ideas on all subjects. Wife of the minister to Portugal, at Berlin, and at the Congress of Vienna, she knows all Europe. She lives in a confusion of books and works of art of every description. You feel as if you were going along the passage-ways of a salesroom in reaching her corner by the fire, where she sits in her arm-chair. She has been an invalid for ten years, in bed all day, and only gets up to receive. This evening the Duke of Bedford was on duty,

[1] Elizabeth Rawdon, died in 1874.
[2] F. G. Hastings Russell, ninth Duke of Bedford, born in 1819; died in 1892.
[3] Lord Arthur Russell, M. P., died in 1892.
[4] Odo Russell, created Baron Ampthill in 1881; died in 1884.

for Lady William is never without one of her sons. The Duke possesses none of the attributes we should ascribe to one of the most titled and richest dukes of England. He is simple and courteous, and is an ordinary man in his appearance He was poor before the death of his cousin, who was a little mad. He managed his estates, and used to carry dolls to him to amuse him with. Who can be sure that this cousin was not secretly married ?

LONDON, April 17, 1873.

I spent a part of to-day at the Court of Common Pleas. When I saw the four judges in their wigs, I fairly groaned that I had not George's knack for sketching. One of them in especial. What a head he had! A perfect John Bull in a wig! And the rest were not much behind him. I got a good English lesson there without paying for it, and I will go often, varying the monotony by going from one room to another. The four principal courts of appeal are at Westminster itself; you entering by the large hall.

LONDON, April 21, 1873.

Dined at the Rothschilds', one of those dinners where you drink liquid gold. As for the table my impressions are summed up in a chicken soufflé à la Zingara; an old acquaintance that caught my eye from the moment we sat down. The dinner lasted fully two hours and a half without a break. I had taken the precaution to secure my old friend Hamilton Seymour as a neighbor. A great many stories and diplomatic anecdotes made the time pass.

On our returning to the drawing-room a young gentleman sang comic songs to us in many tongues. As he has no fortune, I was told he is paid for it. Afterwards another son of a lord imitated some actors for us; he did Mlle. Chaumont much too well to my mind. These children of Israel have lords now to marry their daughters and to amuse them! For the rest, they are very amiable and very charitable. I say charitable, having Mme. Lionel de Rothschild in mind. I know that she gives more than her money, which has no value to her, she gives her personal attention. She is interested in our bazar and has introduced me to a Catholic, Miss Gerard. Now that I know her I have one more saleswoman.

LONDON, April 30, 1873.

I am writing to you in Lord Granville's waiting-room, after a talk with the senior diplomatist of Europe. You do not get much out of that fine fellow, Brunnow: a malicious hint or two so delicately touched upon that it leaves you in doubt whether they were really touched upon or not. . . . He gave me, however, some good advice; he has registered his name for the king of Belgium at Buckingham Palace; and I am going to do the same. Before doing so, however, I must see Lord Granville and inspire him with some of my confidence about the condition of affairs in France.[1] I spent last night deciphering a telegram which filled me with a feeling of confidence which it is evidently

[1] M. Barodet had been nominated deputy of Paris, and the situation between the National Assembly and M. Thiers had become strained.

my duty to hand on to those about me here—as indeed I had been trying to do before the instructions of the president arrived; I had written as much yesterday to M. de Rémusat. I find that my premises are the same as those of the President; I wish I could be certain we shall reach the same conclusions.

Cham has sent a good water-color for the bazar. *Un chiffonnier ivre:*[1] "To think that if it weren't for those scamps at Versailles—*I* should be the ambassador at London!"—a subject chosen for the occasion. He might well have a chance to be the ambassador now.

LONDON, Monday, May 5, 1873.

Here is what happens when a successor of the dukes and peers, who formerly represented France abroad, goes to pay his respects to a king passing through the country.[2]

Just as he puts up his umbrella to go get a cab, an elegant *coupé* stops at his door—it is his tailor. It was impossible to refuse Mr. Cook the honor of saving me from the rain and to conduct me to Buckingham Palace. I shan't tell the Queen nor * * *! On the way the tailor gave me five pounds for the bazar,[3] and announced that his wife is going to make some purchases there. I got out of the *coupé* and found Solvyns,[4] who awaited me in the

---

[1] A drunken rag-picker.
[2] M. Gavard must have paid his respects to the king of Belgium, who was passing through London.
[3] Sale for the benefit of French works in London.
[4] Baron Solvyns, minister of Belgium, died in 1893.

first drawing-room, and presently I found myself in the presence of His Belgium Majesty : a personage with a big nose, big beard and drawling speech. By and by I joined in the conversation ; we talked about the Treaty of Commerce, about the personnel of the Embassy, about the elections, about his passage across the Channel. The Queen said that a bit of seasickness helped to make one appreciate the happiness of disembarking on the other side. I replied mechanically, " It is a bit of purgatory before the entrance into paradise." His Majesty did me the honor to understand and to strengthen my words by saying to me that it was about true. I found means to give him news of the Comte de Paris. After which I left, and no longer having my tailor at the door, I raised my umbrella and went out into the shower. Can anybody say after that that the old order of things has not passed away?

I spent part of my day listening to the Tichborne Case. How can such a trial be tolerated and so many months, and the lives of so many distinguished men be consumed in thrust and counter-thrust *à propos* of such rubbish !

It is a pretext for speculating and betting simply. Tichborne was turned loose as they turn loose a fox. Not that Tichborne himself resembles a fox ; he is more like an elephant. They have been obliged to cut out a circle in the table at which he sits cutting bits of paper and braiding baskets. The only thing that is comparable to the scandal itself is the smell of the place.

The English crowd has an odor of concentrated

misery that we never meet in France, even among the electors of Barodet.

LONDON, May 8, 1873.

A word of advice to those who believe that the English have a right to do as they like. I started to go to the *Court Theatre* to-night and found the doors closed. Lord Sydney, the grand chamberlain, was there last night and found the play unwholesome and has forbidden its being given. A good-natured actor had had the audacity to give a take-off on Gladstone and Lowe. The portrait of Gladstone was a great hit, so I am told. He was represented receiving an embassy from China which had come to ask him for Scotland. The Prime Minister reflected, then he said there were three courses open to him. The first was to hand Scotland over at once; the second was to wait a bit and then hand it over; the third (and this was the course he took) was to submit it to arbitration. It was cleverly done. I have just been to a "Drawing-Room." Had two hours of diamonds and trains of all colors. It is rather a fine sight to see so many millions sterling promenading about, with now and then a beautiful woman. The most agreeable was Lady Archibald Campbell, wife of the son of the Duke of Argyle. She is very pretty and well dressed. Solvyns got off a good thing: "England is the country where No. 2 goes to see No. 1 in order that he may brag of it at No. 3's."

LONDON, May 9, 1873.

A new Conservative election at Bath. It is an indication, a hint, but not too implicitly to be relied on in this country, where by-elections always go against the party in power. The country wants a bit of time to breathe, and moreover the Conservatives are powerfully organized. Ah! if we could only do as they do here; they have newspapers, associations of all kinds, pleasure-parties, and registering of electors. They are occupied with the elector all the time, they are always in communication with him; publicly in the meetings, and privately in the associations, workingmen's clubs, etc.

I finished my letter in the city. First I made a long stay at the "school-board." I continue to collect useful points on primary education in London. Then for two hours I went about in the numberless alleys of the city. It is a queer picture, this anthill. They have tortured space, without regard for looks or for the souls or the imaginations of the inhabitants. Everywhere you find buildings in black stone and only room enough left free for the people (whose eyes and senses generally, except their desire for money, they deaden), to move about in.

LONDON, May 13, 1873.

I have had an interesting day. The baroness[1] had given me a rendezvous at her Jewish school at Whitechapel. In going there you have to make your way through the alleys of the East End. You can study there the phenomena of spontaneous generation, and the germination of infusoria in the de-

[1] Baroness Rothschild.

composition of organic bodies. A bit depressed by the filth of the route, I reached the school. I visited first the kitchen, for the Jews who are impoverished and ill; it is a veritable school of cleanliness—a pearl in a dung-hill. They served a very appetizing lunch. In the schools I had the pleasure of seeing two thousand eight hundred little Israelites of both sexes and from all parts of the world. I should have recognized almost all of them by their faces—a fact which speaks well for the purity of the Jewish race in every quarter of the globe and in every social station—for the children that I saw were those of the poorer class only. They enter the school at three years of age, sometimes at two, almost naked, and they leave it, from eleven to thirteen, clothed from head to foot, reading and writing English well and able to decipher Hebrew. The thing, however, that I admire more than the school (which is certainly splendid) is the generosity that keeps it going. It is nothing like so difficult to find the school as it is to find Simone.[1] The manager of the institution, a veteran instructor, and proud as Lucifer, did not seem to be of this opinion when he said to me: "In my six classes I simply say some words, and make men out of animals; they bring me embryos simply which I supply with bodies and souls." And indeed from one room to another, as they grow older, you notice the improvement in cleanliness, in clothes, in intelligence, and in learning. When some girls were questioned on geography, one of the little witches replied

[1] Allusion to Count Musset.

that the Rhine separated France from Germany! Alas!

Madame Rothschild has sent me a lot of pretty prizes. She has a genius for charity.

LONDON, May 14, 1873.

The Queen will not be present at her concert this evening. She was at her *levee* the other day and presided half an hour, then she went to the Exposition to see an omelette made, and to listen to a lecture on omelettes. The English recognize the superiority of the French in things of that kind, and are trying hard to take it from them. They have associations, meetings, lectures, encouragements of the Queen, articles in the newspapers .... happy people!

Yesterday all London was in the park, ten thousand carriages to see forty " mail-coaches " make a " show " for the Queen of Belgium.

LONDON, May 19, 1873.

Last night I went to the Court Theatre with Conolly.[1] The first thing was a really primitive piece. It was the infancy of art. Everything came on at the right moment. It was expressly written for the occasion. Great care had been taken with the scenery—there was a garden on the Thames at Twickenham, the sign even of a neighboring public-house was exact, the people are in front of it, and the grass, reaching to the foot-lights, is so real you

---

[1] General Conolly, military attaché, died in 1885.

could eat it; daisies are growing in the grass and on an opposite hill,—they are so real you want to pick them. When the dialogue moves, the sun moves; he rises and sets; the moon in her turn rises too, and you see her reflection in the Thames; and then you hear the nightingales—it is charming. But what became of the piece? I have forgotten it. This is dramatic art! Everything is in the accessories and not in the plot. It is easier to make the sun and moon move and the birds sing than to make the actors talk or to animate them with a passion that would move the spectators. The evening ended with the farce of the "Happy Land"; a political caricature, rather broad; but the characters of the men were well enough drawn.

I forgot to mention another great resource of the dramatic authors in this country. They put colored glass (red, green or blue) in front of the footlights.

LONDON, May 20, 1873.

Yesterday we finished our sale with great success.[1] We shall have a thousand pounds. We shall make Sister Lucie's works live if we cannot make her live. Poor sainted woman! Her hands are skin and bone, and yet what energy she shows. The rush over, and the crowd parted, the Sisters arrived, busy as ants, to pick up and put things away. The auctioneer was a Colonel M. At the stroke of the clock he was on the platform. . . . It takes the English for perfect calm and self-possession in public. . . . It was really amusing.

[1] Sale of French works in London.

There has been a ball at court. There is always the same ceremony with the chamberlains in green. And *God Save the Queen* comes in everywhere, —the orchestra put one to sleep. Literally, toward one o'clock I was asleep standing bolt upright,—I was afraid I should fall all of a heap.

LONDON, May 24, 1873.

I received the *Times* at half-past seven, and read to many Parisians the address of the Duke (de Broglie). The question seems to me well put; the majority well rallied, and now (mid-day) M. Thiers has already finished speaking.[1] It is useless, however, to indulge in conjectures, I must wait the issue. That reminds me of the conclusion of my last conversation with M. Guizot; he said, "When M. Thiers gets into a fix, he will knock under." Since I am quoting from great men, Cochin repeated M. Thiers' remark, that the Duc de Broglie was the only person to whom he allowed perfect independence.

Yesterday I was restless and went to the spring exhibition. It was frightfully flat,—what a lot of time and color wasted. There were some new portraits—a *Miss Dorothy*, very simple; but well handled and elegant; and nothing else to speak of. The Marine pieces, for the most part, are well conceived. But when you have seen the public you understand the artists better. The public thinks only of the subject, and of whether it is "sensational" or "moral." If it is, they are satisfied, and show it by a little note in their catalogue, which, by the way,

[1] He refers to the debate following which M. Thiers left office.

they consult as often as they do the picture. There was one masterpiece there in two divisions: on one side the children before going to school, on the other side the same on leaving school. The first dirty, thin, and in rags; the others clean, large, plump, and comfortably clothed. Under the picture there was a Biblical inscription; above it was printed, " One Hundred Thousand Children in London without a School." For this conscientious public, this picture is the climax of art;—unless some one could paint a little onion so real it would make their eyes water.

They don't deal with the nude, they have no notion of design, there is neither blood nor life in their figures; when the colors on the canvas are not pallid they swear at each other; the composition is generally childish, and there is a total lack of atmosphere about or behind the personages depicted.

The great artist who paints portraits by special favor at fifty thousand francs apiece—nay, at seventy-five thousand if he throws in a pot of flowers—excels in painting wax-figures draped in gaudy dresses, and no one can surpass Tissot, our compatriot, in sticking them on screens. They love details here, blades of grass, wild flowers and leaves of trees. They display less feeling for the forest, the meadow, the total effect, the simple idea, the dominant thought, the mysterious something that was not in the model: *that* is a thing not understood anywhere, I am well aware, but less so here than in France. There is no statuary here; perhaps it is the fault of the climate! A *Bacchante printanière* by Carpeaux shines in this desert; also a terra-cotta, simple and touching in its reality (the mother and the child), by another Frenchman. Do you know M. Dalou in France?

And now this evening we must go from one reception to another without knowing quite who or what we represent. They are given in honor of the Queen's birthday.

LONDON, May 25, 1873.

I took courage yesterday from the account given of M. Thiers' speech. I had feared some clap-trap. At six o'clock, Rothschild allowed me the range of the Exchange, but that does not signify very much. Lord Granville came to the " Foreign Offices " at midnight to tell me that " Thiers was beaten by fourteen votes." I had arrived at about eleven o'clock, representing the government of M. Thiers. I replied to Lord Granville that I believed all would go well with the government. I had stayed as late as possible to get the news, and toward half-past twelve learned it from Lord Granville. Learned that I no longer represented the same government that I had on entering the Foreign Office; or, at least, that M. Thiers had been beaten and had resigned. I told him confidently that I had reason to believe that all would go well with the government I represented. We were inclined to look on the amusing side of the necessities and commonplaces of an official situation, and we parted with a burst of laughter that had nothing official about it.

I saw by this morning's *Observer* of the nomination of MacMahon. Lady G. Fullerton, who was there, was so happy she almost embraced me.

LONDON, May 26, 4 o'clock.

I have just returned from the *levee*. Every one is surprised that Paris has not been sacked. If I had been my own master I would have avoided being there to-day, in especial as I did not know what to reply to the questions.

(After May 24 M. Gavard was made chief of the Cabinet of the Duc de Broglie. He returned to London in December, when the Duke was no longer minister of foreign affairs, having been appointed minister of the interior. Comte Harcourt was no longer ambassador; he was replaced by the Duc of Bisaccia).

LONDON, December 10, 1873.

Had a capital passage. Stayed on the bridge all the way giving advice to the captain! The Dover-Chatham train, was cold and I found a "dark fog" on arriving in London. In crossing the fog I recognized my friend Dutreil.[1] We hailed each other, and then getting into a hansom rode slowly through the fog to Albert Gate, and here I am Minister of France in London. What a contrast! Day before yesterday I was at Versailles at the centre of things; here I am to-day at the end of a telegraph-wire in a depth of silence and fog. I used to like this fog and quiet; why is it that I cannot be contented now? Besides, this humidity and quietness is good for the nerves.

[1] M. Bernard Dutriel, then secretary to the Embassy; he is now senator; he became chief of the cabinet in place of M. Gavard.

LONDON, December 11, 1873.

Man cannot live by fog alone; it is a great pity in this country! I shall come to it by and by.

London is deserted—no one at the Foreign Office, no one anywhere. I have seen Beust, who despairs of having the new ambassador at his dinner. Bylandt,[1] is amiable as always; and Solvyns returned from Italy. He was in the midst of unpacking and full of enthusiasm about his luggage.

Lord Stanhope has been here lamenting what he regards as Bazaine's hard fate. His great argument is the letter of Frederick Charles, as if the conqueror could be got to declare that the man he vanquished was nothing but a clown, who surrendered his standards treasonably.

Brunnow shed tears of joy on seeing me again. He told me I owed my success here to Lord Granville, who had real affection for me; and that that was the reason he made things easy for me. I am struck by the strides the Duc de Broglie has made here in public opinion.

LONDON, December 15, 1873.

A great number of diplomatists, indeed, all the diplomatic corps, may come together in a salon without giving any one any pleasure. I am never so discouraged as at these family reunions. Last night it was at the Swedish Embassy. Every one accepted the invitation; they came like hungry wolves, but they took very little away with them. It is better to stay at home in front of an open fireplace,

[1] Count of Bylandt, Minister of Holland; died in 1893.

with a good lamp, with the shutters closed, and a sense that the cold and fog are prowling around outside.

Yesterday, in passing the Court of Appeals, I went in to listen, for practice in English, and what do you suppose I saw? The same judges, the same jury in the box, the same Tichborne, with the same stomach, in front of the same table as seven months ago!

I dined at "Hayward Corner." Toward nine o'clock our friend was tipsy. I stayed talking with an antiquarian, who was not so tipsy. We talked about an unknown letter (from Pompeii) which we had found at the library, in a rare edition of the papers of Sallust. Such are the distractions of bachelors. The letter itself did not amount to anything.

Ask Vaney[1] if *corum sepulcre* is a solecism. The question that is exciting this happy people just now, is whether or not the Dean of Westminster has made a grammatical error. Oxford opened the discussion, then came a reply, and then outsiders intervened. Poor Dean Stanley is likely to be convicted of having written theological Latin. It is hard on him. Who would suppose that theology would spoil his Latin?[2] It seems that *coram* cannot have the name of a thing for an object. Meurand[3] himself would perhaps have been caught there.

There is a new excitement here. Some people wanted to put a canopy over the high altar in the

---

[1] Advisor of the Court of Appeals at Paris; died in 1893.
[2] Mr. Stanley, Dean of Westminster, was thought rather sceptical.
[3] Director of Foreign Affairs.

church of St. Barnaby, Pimlico! The whole Church rose in arms. If the Pope himself had invaded England they would not have made more noise. Happy people!

This morning, as I was trying on my frock-coat, I told my tailor, the celebrated Cook, a lot of things, which he repeated ten minutes afterward to the Prince of Wales, whom he dresses, and chats with as he does with me!

LONDON, December 18, 1873,

The upholsterer of the Duc de Bisaccia is drawing up plans and taking measurements. He seems determined to do things on a grand scale. He does not spare materials. All trace of the past will disappear under the new draperies, mirrors and pictures. At this rate we might all of us outdo the Marquise.

My tailor did his commission very well. The Prince of Wales sent me word to make my arrangements with his aide-de-camp, General Knollys.

LONDON, December 21, 1873.

I've been to say good-bye to Beust. He vowed that if he was not always on the eve of departing, he could not endure the dreariness of the life here. If you do succeed in seeing any one in London it is only for an instant as you pass, and during the season you pass each other on the run. For a bit of talk you must go five or six hours on the train. It seems that Lord Granville returns this evening, but leaves again to-morrow evening for Walmer

Castle and when he reaches there, he will lift the drawbridge and shut down the portcullis. I shall see him to-morrow; it will be the last time for three weeks at least.

To divert my mind from my writing, I went for a few minutes to the Athenæum to fumble in the books. I was either too tired or too anxious to read them, but I took them down, turned them over, handled them. I have noticed that one always finds something one wants, even in that way.

LONDON, December 23, 1873.

There are times when I seriously ask myself whether this is the profession I have chosen. The satisfactions it procures me are so small and the deprivations so cruel. I keep repeating to myself that it won't last long. I had the pleasure of seeing last night a very coarse caricature of two French plays. One something like, *La Fille de l'Aveugle*, by Bayard, the other *Le chapeau de paille d'Italie*. There was too much respect shown to the authors to mention their names, but how they were mangled! All the fine things were left out; they do not understand them; and they were replaced by brutalities. They find a means here of being coarse without shocking their morals. We do just the contrary in France. One thing struck me: after the curtain went down on the poor piece entitled *Alone*, all the actors, as is the custom, came before the curtain, and the manager, Mrs. Lutton, was hissed. It was very unjust, as she was really the only one who showed passion, expression or charm in her acting. The hissing was done by but one man, and nobody cried " Put him out "—there were no protests made against him. Every one expresses his opinion freely here even in the theatre. One man may hiss while all the rest of the house is applauding.

I have been at last to hear some music in London. A woman played the trumpet ! Can you imagine it ? What a happy idea ! A rival virtuoso (also female) played the violin ; and a man brought tears to your eyes on the accordeon.

LONDON, December 25, 1873.

The fog is so dense and the streets so deserted, that I fancy it would be dangerous to be on them, so I have stayed rigorously shut up in my room, and have only put my nose out of doors to go to Mass. Which when all is said is solitude at its best.

About three-quarters of the English are drunk at this hour. These holidays are expensive for the poor families. I followed one in Hyde Park this morning. The father was carrying a heavy bundle, while the mother carried a nursing child, and then four other little ones followed as best they could. One of them coughed and cried fit to break your heart. They were all in rags that hardly covered the skin, but for all that they were evidently dressed in their best for a holiday. The way the toddlers followed their parents, with slackening steps, seemed to mark the solemnity of Christmas. The poor baby cried so hard that the father took it and gave his load to the oldest girl, and the little band continued. The girl, who staggered with the weight of the load, followed at a distance. I really wanted to help her! This wretched little group filed by beneath the windows of Dorchester House, only to pass a few steps further on to the house of Lord Dudley and the Grosvenor House. The contrast is perpetual here, and is a mystery in economics that I can never solve—so much charity and such frightful poverty!

LONDON, December 31, 1873.

I have gotten the necessary letters off, but the thing that wastes my time is the cargo that comes by each train—the squad of cooks, footmen, coachmen, horses and carriages. Where to lodge them? At the last minute a telegram comes—it has been delayed. I must rent stables and rooms, buy furniture, establish order in the house. Each new arrival wants a complete apartment.

Duc de Bisaccia will be here himself to-morrow. His splendid silver has arrived, and he sent word that all the servants must be powdered to receive him, —that would be all right if I am not to be requested to do the same.

The Queen will receive him at once at the Isle of Wight.

THE YEAR 1874.

Extracts from the Correspondence.

LONDON, January 2, 1874.

Last night there was a reception for the ambassador.[1] He is very pleasant. It ought to be not bad living with him. We agree perfectly about the work. . . .

LONDON, January 3, 1874.

The Duke has returned this morning from Osborne. Everything has turned out for the best. The Queen welcomed him as if he were *not* the ambassador of France. She chatted all the time about his parents, and of his children. It is certainly better for an ambassador to be the son-in-law of Prince de Polignac, and of the Prince de Ligne, the son or heir of a great name, than " Monsieur So-and-so." I am convinced that he has made a capital beginning. The account of the visit to Osborne I prepared myself. It is written in a tone of deliberate understatement, but nothing has been left out—everything is stated with scrupulous exactitude. Ten to one such and such a person, who shall be nameless, could not make the Queen or Lord Granville talk to such good effect. The Duke has evidently succeeded ; his proceedings have done him no

[1] Duc de la Rochefoucauld Bisaccia.

harm; he has squandered money in profusion which will do him good below stairs,—reputation often mounts from below upward.

LONDON, January 4, 1874.

The Tichborne case still continues. We are at the one hundred-and-fiftieth hearing. Yesterday the chief-justice and foreman of the jury lost their patience. It is now nearly a year that these twelve unhappy jurymen have been in the box; taken away from their own duties to judge a man whose culpability is as evident as can be,—but English law does not admit evidence without proof. Yesterday the "learned counsellor," for so they call the miserable lawyer who dared organize and plead this attempt at robbery, with infamous slander, contested the deposition of a colonel who declares he saw the tattooing on the arm of young Tichborne; and there is no trace of it on the present "claimant." He saw it when he was bled. The lawyer denied that he could have seen the tattooing unless he could demonstrate that it was daylight. The chief-justice interrupted him by saying that it must have been light enough to see the tattooing since the surgeon saw the vein. The lawyer replied that it was no doubt an imprudent surgeon. "Whether he was good or bad you can't make us believe he could bleed any one without seeing the vein." The lawyer replied, "It is your business to prove that it was light, and so long as you cannot demonstrate that it was light, I maintain that it was dark," etc. The foreman at last grew impatient.

It was an edifying spectacle; from beginning to end it is nothing but a contest between barristers. It was really characteristic. The whole aim of the lawyers is to drag the thing out as long as possible till some juror dies: then it will be necessary to begin over again for the third time. In English jurisprudence you may undertake to do anything, even to prove that a hippopotamus is a gazelle. All you need do is to organize a corporation to outwit the law. You may buy shares here in judicial enterprises to set aside succession to property no less than in associations for stealing diamonds.

LONDON, January 7, 1874.

Last night while at dinner we received a telegram for my chief, congratulating him and thanking him for his despatch. . . . I was not mistaken then. He seemed to me, however, determined not to force his success. Till now he has been occupied with his upholsterer, and from early morning he has been here wandering about the house, upstairs and down, measuring, arranging and ordering. . . .

I spent the evening with Lady Russell. It is really touching to see this old lady surrounded by her sons. She knows that I have a dear mother, and that I suffer in being separated from her. She charged me to say to Duc de Bisaccia that the Queen was much pleased with him, that he stands for all that she most admires. That is an agreeable commission.

LONDON, January 11, 1874.

We are going to have a John Russell meeting in

favor of Bismarck, and the persecution of the church, and an anti-Catholic meeting.

There will be some heads broken, and it will be a re-opening of the religious quarrels in this country. This Johnny has lived too long. Is there not among his papers a certain letter which commenced the Schleswig-Holstein affair?

The unveiling of a statue of the Prince Consort took place to-day ; this time on a horse in a gallop. The climate here makes statuary impossible, neither metal nor marble can stand the soot and the rain. When they show you a statue here you feel an irresistible desire to send for a chimney-sweep. We mixed a little in the " mob,"—among the ragamuffins of London, who are without equal anywhere else. The " policemen " were stamping among them as if they were so many ants.

This morning I saw the Archbishop.[1] He possesses the grand air and an ascetic figure which go well with an Archbishop.

January 18, 1874.

Lord Clarendon wishes to invite me with Borthwick to the Grove ; it is an old castle full of Van Dycks, and surrounded by the oldest and most celebrated manors of England, and only three-quarters of an hour from London. I must give you a notion of how Lord Clarendon spends his time. The first incident of the morning was his coming in from the hunt on horseback, a lackey leading the horse. He wanted to change horses in a muddy

[1] Cardinal Manning.

stableyard without getting down into it, and so he leaped to the other horse. It moved a bit and my lord fell in the mud; he cleaned himself off as best he could and remounted, when suddenly he was thrown over his horse's head. He was taken to the house and did not gain consciousness till some time after reaching it. As they have to nurse him a bit, to-morrow they will go shooting; but the day after they will be on horseback again. His lordship was late at dinner, and came in supported by two domestics, his legs having gone back on him after another fall. On his return to the city, however, he will become once more a serious lord, in running for a membership of the cabinet.

Lady Clarendon is one of four countesses. It seems that her mother spent her life repeating: "Four daughters, four countesses; four countesses, four daughters." No one knows which phrase was on her lips when she died.

The senior Russell has consented to be ill so as not to preside at the "meeting" in favor of Bismarck; but he will write. To make up for it the *entrepreneur* of the Tichborne case, the "Honorable" Whaley (Honorable!) will be present and give the meeting its proper stamp.

I intended going to-day to a "High Church" where they are teaching the faithful to make the sign of the cross. Every Sunday, so one of the devotees told me, they have a new innovation. Last Sunday the sexton was in a robe and this Sunday they are to learn to make the sign of the cross.

LONDON, January 26, 1874.

Parliament is dissolved,—eight days ago no one could have foretold it. Its term was a year longer, and the circumstances under which the new year opened, led no one to suppose that the Liberal government wished to shorten the session.

The announcement of the dissolution was the signal for universal disorder. You saw nothing but candidates crossing London, leaving wives, children and luggage on the way to reach their respective constituencies in time. Least to be envied of all were the would-be candidates on the lookout for a possible constituency and the constituencies on the lookout for possible candidates. The result will show which party is most hurt by the confusion. The secrecy with which the dissolution had been prepared,[1] the suddenness of the decision, the manner in which the public was informed, all concur to give this grave measure the air of a stroke of party politics. It is difficult, nevertheless, to forget that the personal intervention of the Prime Minister shows again some tendencies to break noticeably with English parliamentary traditions, and to approach the democratic conception of an appeal to the people.

In the Liberal clubs, as well as among the Conservatives, the opinion still prevails that the cabinet will succeed, though serious losses are looked for owing to the divisions which are day by day becoming more manifest in ministerial ranks.

[1] After his interview with the Queen, Mr. Gladstone did not notify his colleagues till the 19th of January; and on the following day the public was informed by his address to the electors of Greenwich.

LONDON, February 3, 1874.

Enticed by the recollection of the sensation Sir Charles Dilke has created from time to time in Parliament, I have followed him during this electoral period; a little, I must say, with the feeling of the Englishman who followed Van Amburg in the hope of seeing him devoured some day by his lions. I hasten to say that my evil hopes were disappointed. There was not the least scandal, not a word that might not have come from the most loyal subject of her Majesty; not a proposition that might not have been found in an address by Mr. Gladstone. They were dissertations upon various reforms, desirable and not desirable, set forth in language unfailingly precise and easy, a little too prolix in my judgment, but never enough so to try the patience of his auditory.

There was a large meeting at Chelsea last night. But first I must tell you a bit about the constituency of Chelsea. The district numbers twenty-four thousand electors, and reaches from one extremity to the other of the West End of London. It sends two members to Parliament. There are thirteen "polling-places," each candidate must have a central agent in each of these subdivisions, which necessitates renting a house for the purpose, and personal employees and agents of all degrees from the chief down (who receives not less than five or six thousand francs) to the sandwich man, who walks the streets all day with the names of the candidates on his belly and back. Naturally, to share the enormous expense of an election like that the candidates go into partnership. The Association extends even beyond mere questions of expense, for it is evident in the election at Chelsea that the two "baronets" are going shares also on their constituents. Sir Charles Dilke is the leader of the extreme radicals; Sir Henry Hoare persuades over to the common cause the voice of the liberals, who feel the need of reform but who do not want to kill the goose with the golden eggs.

The "sandwich men," independently of the announcements posted on the walls, had been announcing all day the grand meeting to take place in the general quarters of the associated candidates of the two ministerial factions. When the night came all the quarter was lit up. Outside the hall the public that had been unable to gain admission, stationed themselves in front of the glass doors where they could see the faces of the two "baronets" to whom they were invited to give their votes. Twelve hundred people had taken possession of the hall and were waiting for the candidates, which did not prevent five hundred more from squeezing into the hall. The crowd poured in at every door like streams of lava; they advanced slowly, insensibly, irresistibly; people were lifted off their feet in the jam, to the height of the gallery. I can see still the impassive face of a thick-set cabman who allowed himself to drift gently on at an elevation above the seats and the spectators who filled them. At the beginning of the meeting he was at the entrance of the hall, at the close of it he was in the middle, held up off of the floor by the crowd. The crush was not brought about without some noise, some blows, some interruptions of the meeting. I admired, however, the parliamentary manners of the mob, which found means to hear, and the talent of the orators, who made them listen. Sir Charles Dilke had the tact to bring his wife along. She is an Englishwoman, with a nose with a rising inflection, fresh coloring, bright eyes and a gracious smile. Dilke sat at the right of the chairman, Sir Henry Hoare at the left. After the formal introducton by the president, the first of the baronets began speaking and continued for more than an hour without hesitation or stopping for breath; there was not a period, nor a comma in the entire address. He hardly gave the audience time to cheer: but he sat down finally in the midst of cheers and applause, hats waving and tossed in the air, and pamphlets flying on all sides.

Sir Henry Hoare followed him;—a less fluent orator, but more animated. He seemed sometimes to hold his audience more closely, but at other times they grew restless. When he spoke of the third competitor, who, it seemed, had only introduced his candidature to divide the liberal party, he made them roar like caged lions. Some isolated protestations, in favor of the unhappy candidate, were immediately drowned in the shouting. The assembly seemed really on the point of splitting when Sir H. Hoare courageously gave his opinion on foreign politics. Mr. Gladstone, in his various addresses, had reduced (unfortunately) the English policy to defending only her Insular interests. Sir H. Hoare, in his turn spoke of the something wanting in Mr.

Gladstone's judgments on the outside influence of a great nation, and declared that for a country, as for an individual, their interests are inseparable from their honor. Some cries of " Long live Bismarck " were heard from the back of the hall, applause and grumbling replied to them, and it was evident that the audience was divided and restless; a good many were silent. The orator began again, and I give you a *résumé* of what he said: " Yes, gentlemen, I am for the liberty of the Catholics, because I am for the liberty of the Protestants. I believe the clergymen should teach and speak according to their consciences, because I want to speak according to mine. Yes, gentlemen, I am for France, because she has been brutally dismembered ; I am against those who have wrenched Alsace and Lorraine from her. I am against the man who wishes to hinder that great country from taking her place again among nations ; and against him who wishes to lay down the law for the press even beyond the German frontier. I am against the meetings which sympathize with the oppressors, against the oppressed. And if these declarations shut the doors of Parliament against me, and lose me your votes, I shall be proud not to have merited them." This courageous and eloquent speech carried away the audience, and the orator was recompensed by applause which followed him into the street.[1]

[1] M. Gavard adds, in his notes, that Sir Charles Dilke alone was elected; he passed with the conservative candidate who took 700 or 800 votes from Sir H. Hoare on account of his courageous declaration against the Conquests of Prussia. Meanwhile it produced for

The manner of my introduction into the large hall of the "vestry" of Chelsea is not a thing to be proud of. On my arrival I was ushered into a private parlor where the candidates and the patrons had gathered waiting for the opening hour. When the time came, as a stranger of distinction, I was given the honor of escorting Lady Charles Dilke, who was the only lady present. An unforeseen honor! It brought my heart up into my mouth, but it was not a case for hesitation, and I entered first, with Lady Dilke on my arm, welcomed by a burst of applause such as I do not flatter myself I can ever provoke again in my life. The candidates and their patrons followed in procession. The reporters were anxious to know who I was, wanted my name to publish the next day for all England to read. Happily Sir H. Hoare, perceiving the danger I was in, put them on the wrong scent as to my identity. Thus I escaped a misadventure which might have put an end to my diplomatic career; for, frankly, it was highly improper for me to be there on the platform, in the midst of politicians of known hostility to the crown.

LONDON, February 4, 1874.

Yesterday we had Mr. Gladstone to dinner. He was awaiting the result of the election at Greenwich.

him a compensation of which he was not insensible. His speech was published in many Parisian journals, a fact which decided a committee of the *Jockey Club* to present a very honorable address to the former member for Chelsea, who is still one of the most Parisian, and (in polite circles) one of the most popular of Englishmen.

He was magnificently tranquil, either as being certain of success or as affecting the resignation of a sage who is not unwilling to return to his favorite studies. This is the eighteenth time he has been before the electors, and he told me it was the last. He was charming, or at least he possesses always the art of charming me; with his openness of mind and his inexhaustible store of recollections. We passed in review about all the reforms that "the crotchet-mongers"[1] are peddling nowadays from "meeting" to "meeting." Gladstone seems to feel a sincere attraction toward everything that appeals to him as being generous. I repeat it, he is a charmer, though not, perhaps, a very reassuring one. During the evening he received the notice of the re-election of his son by a small majority. He had requested not to be wakened when the notice of his own fate arrived. His awakening could not have been very agreeable; he had passed with a small majority, second on the list, and all the morning's news was bad for the government.

Conversation continued till very late. He converted me a little to woman's suffrage, of which he is a partisan. So is his rival, the conservative leader.

LONDON, February 6, 1874.

"Great victory of the conservatives! Two more in Westminster." That is the cry on the streets as I write. The government has no longer a majority. I must hasten to show myself and offer my con-

---

[1] People who carry to extremes ideas that are foolish and absurd.

dolences to Lord Granville. It is a case of necessity.

To-morrow, perhaps we shall have no ministry, and I shall find myself between two saddles. It is probable that the cabinet will send in its resignation here in five or six days,—about the fourteenth. Then we shall see Lord Derby Minister of Foreign Affairs; Mr. Disraëli Prime Minister, Chancellor of the Exchequer, etc.

LONDON, February 14, 1874.

The result of the election is known to-day. It gives a majority of 350 votes to the conservatives as against 300. Their advantage is the more considerable, in that they reckon in with the minority the new members for Ireland, to the number of forty or thereabouts, who represent really nothing but an uprising against the maintenance of the union.

The composition of the new cabinet is generally approved. I am struck by the readiness with which the defeated party, in the newspapers and everywhere, accept the change in government. The conservatives, on the other hand, recognize such facts as have been accomplished. They seem to have no idea of using their return to power as a means of repealing the bills they opposed while in the opposition, and their adversaries declare that since the country does not care for additional reforms, it is natural that the reform ministry should retire and give place to a government in accord with the wishes of the nation. The strength of the new government lies not less in the unity existing in its own ranks than in the divisions in the ranks of the opposition. The breaking up of the liberal party is becoming more and more marked. Gladstone is the only one who will give any trouble. If his mind was open to reforms in general when he was in power, what will it be when he is in the opposition? Being no longer obliged to be a statesman, he will play the buffoon to the height of his bent.

The day of the election at Chelsea, Lady Dilke drove about with yellow ribbons, and bows of the same color, on her horses. It is the Radical color; she did not know that some one had pasted a conservative placard on the back of her carriage, saying: *Plump for Gordon.*

LONDON, February 16, 1874.

I am writing to you by the light, or rather by the frightful glare of a fire that threatens to destroy a large quarter of the city before daylight. The " Pantechnicon " which is the main store-house for furniture, carriages and objects of art, is burned. The heavy walls about the Embassy, which ought to protect it against the contagion from the neighboring houses, has saved the stables from the fire, if not from water. When I arrived they were moving things out by the windows; they were dragging out the carriages of state and distributing the horses in stables some distance away. If they had been my horses, or if the coachman had listened to me, he would have put them still farther away, for no one can tell when or where the fire will stop. We are at present protected by an immense crater that lies between us and the flames. There is still fire in the bottom of it, but as the walls are still standing, it is no more dangerous than a great brasier. Unhappily the flame has leaped the street and the fire is speading on the other side. Sheets of flame stretch up into the night and are beaten down upon the neighboring roofs by the wind. Nobody knows where the conflagration will stop. Captive fire fights against fire in revolt: you hear the pump and piston everywhere. The struggle goes on in the midst of a great silence, broken only by the tumbling walls and the whistles of command. I can see the firemen, as they come over the roofs, turn their faces from the fire, and the unhappy inhabitants pouring water on their windows and extinguishing the fire wherever it caught. The flames are reflected from all the windows in the houses opposite so that you can hardly tell whether they are on fire or not. The wind carries along with the smoke quantities of sparks over Wilton Place, near Grosvenor Gardens. All London is on the scene: crowds of women, oyster and orange vendors, musicians—all round the barricade made by the policemen it was like a fair. The "mob" is dispersing now, but I stay in my observatory alone, watching the fire. The smoke keeps me from seeing whether it is approaching or growing more distant.

LONDON, Saturday, February 15, 1874.

I send you a copy of the *Times*, which seems to have been much better informed than I, although I was on the scene. It is reported that there have been invaluable collections lost. Send your pictures to England to save them from incendiaries! There was a collection of Wallaces and some others, some one said, from France. The loss is said to be seventy-five millions. That *was* a bonfire!

Gladstone announces that he is going to return to his beloved studies, and has already brought out a refutation in three points of a book by Strauss; but in the meantime he seems in no hurry to retire.

LONDON, February 18, 1874.

I am writing to you in Lord Granville's antechamber. I came to pay him a farewell call.[1] I sincerely regret his fall from office. I doubt if I shall ever have, with another minister, the relations I have had with him. He said he hoped we should see each other now more frequently, and told me the story of an ambassador who was in too big a hurry to bid the fallen minister adieu.

LONDON, February 21, 1874.

The new ministers return from Windsor with the sacks, seals, keys and staves, all the accessories of the cabinet. Everybody is satisfied with the choice. . . . It is their own fault if they do not stay in office a long time.

Let us hope that Derby[2] will know better, in the present state of Europe, than to tread in the footsteps of Lord Palmerston. I shall have no end of trouble making my way with all these new men: I will do what I can.

[1] Lord Granville was leaving the ministry after the elections.
[2] Lord Derby was Minister of Foreign Affairs in the new cabinet of Mr. Disraëli.

LONDON, February 25, 1874.

To give you the order of my day, I went to the Foreign Office yesterday in uniform. The first incident was the German ambassador's arrival in citizen's clothes; he asked if there was time for him to go put on his uniform, and seemed astonished when he was told there was, but he went away to dress. The roll-call began next, and my turn came before all the other ministers; this was a fresh surprise. Then Lord Derby detained me for twenty minutes instead of five; surprise the third. I believe it was due really to chance, and a bit perhaps to awkwardness, or to forgetfulness. Still, I very much prefer to be on the right side of any such little mistake. As for Lord Derby, one cannot say too much upon the awkwardness of his first appearance. He snatched up a pair of new gloves and held them in his hands while he stood in an " impossible " position and greeted us with a muscular bow. We sat down and talked, and he was soon at his ease. He speaks French fluently—some few blunders—but really without hesitation. I did not try to force his hand on foreign politics and he did not volunteer anything. But I questioned him on home politics. Talking confidentially and on his own subject, he spoke willingly and for a long time. Too long for the other members of the diplomatic corps, who were waiting. On the whole, I think that a member of the old cabinet would have held the same language. He spoke of the momentary withdrawal of Mr. Gladstone, of his motives, of the necessity of change of ministry from time to time, in order that public men may see the questions before the country from more than one side. He spoke of the new House, and gave me his opinion on it. The members, he said, are rather old, very respectable, and very rich; but it will be rather dull because of the lack of young men. I told him that his description made me envious. He is more confident than I am over the intervention of the unionists. On leaving him I made an appointment to-morrow before the "drawing-room" for my chief.

LONDON, March 21, 1874.

A day is empty indeed in which one has nothing better to do than pay visits. When the Eternal asks you: "What have you done with your time?" it is no sufficient answer to reply: "Paid visits!"

Mr. Gladstone left the Baroness Rothschild's when I arrived. He complained of the ingratitude of the Irish, and he is not wrong, or rather he has made the mistake of counting on people like that at all. He awaits the judgment of history, but he exasperates his partisans by not telling them what he wants to do. It is the same as when he was in power. A lady who was there was guilty of the indiscretion of asking if he would remain after Easter. He replied in one of his vague sentences, of which he possesses the secret. He had hardly gone when Disraëli appeared, as always, like Banquo's ghost. I had had the pleasure of meeting him. He does not recognize me in uniform nor in citizen's clothes. But he tried to be polite when he heard my name, and he spoke kindly of my chief, whom I had presented to him yesterday. Fancy a Primer Minister having so much leisure in France! I saw Lord Sydney, the retiring chamberlain, once more (we are intimate friends now), and Lord Lennox and Beust, all of them at Baroness Rothschilds'. As she was offering me a cake, she stopped, not daring to call it by its name; it was a "Bismarck." Thereupon there was some joking with Beust to the effect that it would explode. "Eat it, man." "But no—I'm not burning for revenge." "Don't be afraid of being the first to begin; he has done it already. Look at his cheek—he's lost his color," etc. As you may imagine, it was not I that was poking fun at the "Bismarck pudding."

LONDON, March 26, 1874.

I was at dinner yesterday with the Marquis of Salisbury.[1] The house is a vast mansion half-finished; you reach the private apartments (I suppose you call them private) through long halls. The dinner at least was private. Lord Salisbury has a kindly face, pleasant look, and generally unassuming air; but his large figure and his head bowed down by the weight of his brain reminded me of poor Verdet. This is the spirited and ironic orator! My first impression of him is pleasing. We had a most interesting conversation about English institutions. Singularly enough for a man in his position and with his talents he gives his interlocutor a chance to be an interlocutor.

[1] R. A. Talbot Gascoigne Cecil, at first Viscount of Cranborne, born in 1830, married, in 1850, the oldest daughter of Sir Anderson. He was third Marquis of Salisbury in 1868. He was a member of the new cabinet.

I profited by the opportunity to draw a comparison between England, with her social divisions and hierarchies, and a ship with air-tight compartments. Then we spoke of India, and he explained very clearly about the exportation of grain during the famine. The marchioness is not young, but she seems intelligent, very agreeable, very tory, and not too certain about the future, in spite of the Conservatives' five-years' lease of power.

I talked a long time with Lord Carnarvon [1] about "Trades-Unions." I attacked them with some spirit, and he made little effort to defend them. We talked too, with Lord Eustache Cecil [2] (Secretary of War) about the English army. He claims that they have at their disposition sixty thousand fighting-men; I doubt if there are more than thirty thousand; there were only a thousand whites at most at Coomassie, etc. The two daughters of the house were there; they seem entirely dominated by their intelligence. I can understand why it is people say that this family is all men.

LONDON, March 29, 1874.

Lord Cardwell [3] was at the Duke of Bedford's yesterday. He took precedence of Mr. Gladstone, his superior in office. It was a bit formal. Frederick Peel,[4] a Liberal "whip," who was my neighbor, explained the organization of his staff—a whole

[1] Fourth Earl Carnarvon, Secretary of State for the Colonies.
[2] Son of the second Marquis of Salisbury.
[3] Minister of War until 1874, then created Viscount Cardwell.
[4] The Honorable Frederick Peel, now Speaker of the House of Commons.

corps of subordinates ready to jump into " hansoms " at the first signal. Every member of Parliament is obliged to tell, on leaving his home, where he may be found. If a discussion arises or a division occurs, that was not foreseen, the bells of Parliament and telegrams to the clubs are not enough; somebody must go in search of the missing members and bring them back. The discipline is severe! After dinner I approached Gladstone. He leaves to-morrow for three months' vacation, and day after to-morrow he will take up his pen again. He has a work ready on Homer, the tale of Troy, etc., which is probably about the same sort of thing as his other writings. He rents his London house. This retirement is not without its dignity. What a pity I am not a literary hack! a preparer of memoirs! These conversations with historical personages of England would be invaluable. He told me that this session would pass without discussion, and that things would move on unchanged so long as England remains satisfied with the present state of affairs. Somebody had been speaking previously about the movement of the workingmen in the country districts. The Duke of Bedford seemed to me not to relish the vague remarks of his former leader, who is not a landowner, and aspires to become once more the "people's William." What struck me most in the fallen statesman was how sensitive he seems to be to what he calls the popular gratitude. It seems to me, if I had brought about as many reforms as Gladstone has, gratitude on the part of the public is the last thing I should think of.

LONDON, March 31, 1874.

I left at ten o'clock for Windsor. The Queen reviewed the troops returning from the Ashantee war. At one o'clock we entered on the Royal lawn, with our post à la Daumont and the classic gray hats of the postilions. There were twelve hundred men in the army. There was no need for any more to go to burn a bamboo village on the equator. It is very meritorious to have calculated beforehand precisely the number of Englishmen necessary, to have provisioned them, to have got them there, and brought them back again on the day and hour set, after the fever and before the rains. The commissary which came last deserves perhaps the greatest share of the applause. The Lords and Commons were waiting in their galleries; we on top of our carriages, and the populace where it could. At last the Queen appeared with her roan horses, her magnificent Horseguards and Brown. All quite in the traditional style, except perhaps for the Highlander on the box.

The troops looked as if they had just stepped out of their "barracks"; there wasn't an Ashantee to be seen in their train—not even a little one. There has been no stinginess about the recognition accorded to Sir Garnet Wolseley. He has been made a Baronet, a General and Quartermaster under the orders of the Duke of Cambridge, has an income of one thousand five hundred pounds sterling, has received the order of St. Michael, K.C.B., C.B., a vote of gratitude from both Houses in speeches in which Gladstone and Disraëli vied with each other. Why do not all these colonels with which "Greater Britain" swarms engage (on their own responsibility if need be) in like and equally profitable expeditions. It all passed off with measured slowness. Furious cheerings went up when either the Queen or the troops came in sight of the public or of the Houses of Parliament. The clown's part in the show was taken by the nanny-goat given by the Queen to a regiment of which it constitutes the " Mascot." Its predecessor in office had died during the campaign, and the new incumbent had not yet become familiar with military discipline, and in default of training had to be carried.

LONDON, April 11, 1874.

The Duc de Bisaccia begs me to preside at the banquet.[1] So be it! I have only a dozen days to prepare my *extempore* speeches, and to consider who will reply to them. I have to find an unhackneyed witticism for each of my toasts: the Queen, the "Royal Family," the Army, the Patrons of the Hospital, and Thanks. I must not forget to add the Marshal—which is rather a new departure, but at present our rallying-point. In effect it is a good deal like the trip from China, one is delighted when it is over with!

Lord Derby has much more sprightliness and intelligence in conversation than I supposed. As I was pleading the cause of our dramatic authors, he said: "Why, if you should deprive our English playwrights of French plays what *would* become of them!" It was rather nice and encouraging.

[1] Banquet of French Charitable Societies.

LONDON, April 17, 1874.

I saw Livingstone buried at Westminster. It was a moving spectacle when you remembered the corpse had been brought out of Central Africa by the natives that had served under him. The embalming must have been of the crudest. Fortunately (as it turned out), he had once, in a fight with a lion, had his arm put out of joint at the shoulder, and had been obliged to reset it himself; he did it so imperfectly it always showed, and it was by this deformity that he was recognized. At the funeral there was a negro-boy who had interred the entrails of the great traveller under a tree, and marked the tree with an inscription, and said prayers at the grave from the English liturgy. The remains will repose under the pavement of Westminster, in front of the Pitt monument.

Spring burst forth this morning; the leaves hastening to make up for lost time. It would be charming to sit in the woods and listen to the golden oriole and the other songsters of the season. I care very little for the city except in bad weather.

LONDON, April 23, 1874.

Yesterday evening there was a large party at the "Foreign Office." The effect on the staircase was fine. It is to our ambassadress and her diamonds that our success is due. I have, by the way, announced our coming ball. We have already the approval of the Prince of Wales. Lady Derby was there, she is simple and charming, and Lady Granville who is beautiful always, but conversation with her never goes beyond a shake of the hand.

I took Lady Waldegrave's little Jewess a promenade. Then I discovered I had forgotten all my decorations. Unpardonable! But what can you expect of an orator![1] you must not forget that I rehearse my speeches incessantly, and that the people—at home—must take me for a madman or a ventriloquist.

I am a little embarrassed about the dinner on Sunday at Dilkes, especially if I do not find Rochefort there!

LONDON, April 28, 1874.

It was a complete success![2] There were one hundred and eighty guests at table and everybody was satisfied. I believe the receipts are very satisfactory. No one was absent. It was near nine o'clock when the speech-making began. The guests were seated at table at seven o'clock. I had all my speeches written out and in my pocket, but I did not disturb them; the sight of them would have worried and annoyed me. After the toastmaster had had the glasses filled and announced in a resounding voice (like the *tuba mirum*) that the " chairman " would speak, I had to stand up amidst "cheers," and turned upon the assembly an eye much calmer than myself. I said a few words of apology for the absence of the Duke, then toasted the Queen and the Princes. I got through with

[1] Allusion to the speeches that M. Gavard expected to deliver at the banquet of the French charitable societies.
[2] Still excited over the banquet.

these commonplaces calmly enough, and the public were agreeably surprised. The "cheers" were a matter of course; no matter what I had said they would have been forthcoming. After the three hurrahs, a new proclamation of the toast-master and up I was again; "My Lords and Gentlemen." This time it was for France and the Marshal. This was my own particular toast, the one I had inserted on my own responsibility, and it was a success. It took the room by storm. I proposed it with warmth. I had calculated my words well. From all sides my friends made me cabalistic signs to say that it was a success. "To France! To the Marshal-President of the Republic! To the soldier who has deserved well of his country on every field of battle! To the good man to whom is due the rare honor (in the midst of parties which unhappily divide us) of reuniting all of us in a common sentiment of respect, of confidence, and of gratitude—to Marshal MacMahon!" Thereupon the orchestra played the "Daughter of the Regiment." Behold me on my feet again with another toast, to the "Army and Navy!" First I said a few words of Anson, the valiant colonel who said such cordial words to us last year, but who is in Provence for the good of his health (the compliment was sent to him by telegram at once); then a compliment and a joke on Lord Eliot that we had cooked up together the year before; then a compliment to General Ady who was present. Finally I touched on the Coomassie expedition. Great applause, and while the orchestra played, my friends hurried up to tell me what a success it had all been. They seemed really quite satisfied. General Ady replied in a serious strain, speaking about the Crimea. I had carefully avoided mentioning it. It was one of the difficulties of my position, as I could say nothing that might displease Russia. Then Véron[1] spoke for the Navy and English fleet which never fights but in the interest of justice and civilization. Three cheers!

This brought me to my most difficult toast, the "evening toast." In the first place it was the longest; and then, I had determined to break in it with the traditional thing and to give some advice. I began well: I spoke of France, of the Sisters of Charity, of the teachings of the Mother Superior: I made an allusion to the Duc de Broglie, passed our works of charity in review, closed with some words of counsel on the subject of the maintenance of a good understanding between all those who were engaged in these Christian Endeavors. At one place in the toast I was obliged to stop; as I was passing from one work of charity to another I felt that I had forgotten something, and finding that I was becoming confused, instead of beating about the bush I stood silent until I had regained my self-possession. As a last word: "I ought to have stopped long ago, but if I should make an end without having referred to the Princes and Princesses of the House of Orleans, your very walls would accuse me of ingratitude." This peroration provoked an outburst of satisfaction.

[1] Military attaché of the Embassy, at present admiral and senator.

Ouf! I was done. And behold, Wolowski was on his feet, proposing my health, pouring out a flood of compliments, speaking of the ancient friendship between us, of Alsace and Lorraine, of the budget. Happily he had a horrible cold; if it had not been for that we should have been there yet. When he sat down there was a fresh surprise, "the toastmaster" announced that *I* would reply to him. And *I* had thought I was done and hadn't another line of MS. in my pocket. I replied that it was very evident that M. Wolowski had come there this evening in a charitable mood, and had made me the beneficiary of it. Then I gave my thanks to the assembly. I couldn't, you know, take up his reference to Alsace and Lorraine. Then there was also a toast with compliments of Eliot and two or three more.

At eleven o'clock I sprang into my brougham to go to Lord Salisbury's. The noise of my success had preceded me; the Duc de Bisaccia seemed sincerely pleased with me.—The place was full of people and of lights.—Lady Derby told me of the conflict at dinner between the Countess Marie Munster and the Baroness Rothschild. It was the old question of precedence between the daughters of the ambassador and the wife of the minister.

Salisbury had been so imprudent as to offer his arm to the Countess Munster. Nothing but the question of the dukes and the *légitimés* has ever raised such a storm. But it lacked a Saint Simon to make it truly interesting.

I met one of my young friends, Lady Ella Russell; she is the daughter of the Duke of Bedford. Her father is a Bedford, she is a Russell, and her brother a Tavistock. There, can you solve that!

How Wolowski does know his England! He only came to spend five or six days here, and he brought a whole array of decorations to wear.

LONDON, April 29, 1874.

Dined yesterday at Dilke's. Happily, Sir L. Malet was there, who is certainly one of my friends. When at the close of the dinner some one joked about the Bible, Lady Dilke gave the signal to leave the table. Curious people! Lady Dilke calls herself a tory, she is older than her husband, but is agreeable, and intensely vivacious. She is a great friend of Gambetta's, who sends her bouquets of flowers. It seems that he is very generous; no doubt it is since the war. She is also an admirer of Schoelcher and in everything a tory. She is a friend of Mme. Weldon, but never wants to see her again, because Mme. Weldon formed the habit of borrowing money of her. There was also present a Theatre-manager, a semi-communist, who said unpleasant things about the French embassy. I was obliged to mention my title in order to call him to order. Dilke himself, it seems, is a man of great acquirements and talent. It is said that in ten years (he is only thirty now) he will be one of the leaders of the liberal party.

Nothing is impossible in this absurd country.

LONDON, April 30, 1874.

Decazes congratulates the Duc de Bisaccia on the ball he is to give, and he is right. The situation has changed here; everybody seeks for an invitation, and in spite of yourself, you can't help believing in the existence of a country when you are begging favors of its official representative. All the princes are coming to the ball, so there will be two suppers set in the upper apartments; so as to give the august personages plenty of room and keep them from eating one another.

One thing that I have remarked in knocking about in society here, is the indecency (the word is not too strong when you are speaking of the younger generation), in the relations between men and women. Society is upside down. As the men have everything, fortune and titles, and the women nothing; it is the women that have to run after the men. The men take things easy and treat the women as inferiors.

LONDON, May 7, 1874.

We are absorbed in the preparations for our fête. The most serious thing is the report that the Duchess of Cambridge is dying. If so, good-bye to the princes. Morier, the British ambassador to Munich, says that if she dies she will show her lack of *savoir vivre*. The witticism is possibly an old one. The invitations are all the rage. Meanwhile the invitations crowd on us too, but I fancy they will cease when the senders give up hope of getting one of ours. Some people ask me if I cannot get them invitations, others thank me for things I have not done. Last evening those who have been invited were twitting those who have not. To give a ball is the height of diplomacy; the Duke's horses and his invitations do more than he and I together.

LONDON, May 9, 1874.

The place was a fairy-land of princes, of liveries, flowers, diamonds, emeralds, pearls, duchesses, lights and music as in the 'thousand and one nights.' It was a fairy-land, too, for the organs of digestion! When I saw five hundred persons in solid column assault the supper, (which passed insensibly into a breakfast—it lasted till six o'clock in the morning), I seemed to see droves of cattle and hogs coming up a back staircase to precipitate themselves into these English stomachs! I escaped from the party at four o'clock. Birds were singing and cocks crowing. I heard the last strains of the orchestra as I left. The morning air reminded me of the country.

It was a complete success. The embassy was buried in flowers. The panniers hung on the walls (an idea of the Duke's) were beautiful. The idea will be adopted by every house in London that can stand the expense. The princes began to arrive at eleven o'clock, headed by the Duke of Edinburgh. Every one rushed to the foot of the staircase to receive him. My admiration for my friend X—— made me forget all about princes. What a rare combination of vivacity and ease she has! She is to the manner born, is as much at home in society as a fish in water. The same ceremony was gone through for each of the princes, including the Duç de Nemours. He told me he was charmed with the dinner [1] and with the fête. He stayed till half-past three, dancing with the "Royalties." The Duchess of Edinburgh is truly beautiful and *striking*, as they say in this country. She was dressed in red and the Duchesse de Bisaccia in white; they were, I fancy, the most beautiful women there. The guests were numerous, but we could not have done with fewer; we needed, in especial, all the duchesses available with their diamonds. The Buccleugh collar drew my attention to one dear old lady whom I had forgotten. What did I do in the midst of all these beauties and royalties? I made myself as useful as possible. In the first place, I looked out for Lady Derby; then I promenaded with her daughter, the Countess of Galloway, a very agreeable person, who must have perceived that I found her charming. Then with the Duchess of Bedford and her daughters, on whom I kept an eye while the mother was dining. At one o'clock a supper, of forty-eight covers, was served on the upper floor. There was great difficulty in getting the right people into the right places, and in keeping the wrong people out. There was a little gnashing of teeth,—but every one was at last served. The beautiful Castalia,[2] simple and good-natured as always, was laughing at the mistakes in my successive invitations and at the satisfaction my errors had given her husband. We had had a correspondence that had given Granville an opportunity to indite some witty letters in reply. Lord Vernon

[1] He had dined two days before at the Embassy.
[2] Lady Granville.

and her daughter, my friend Wood,[1] and Lady Agnes, and Mrs. Holford and Eveline were there; I am much interested in this young girl,—she is so frank and naïvely happy. Lady Rosamond Churchill was very gracious and happy in the pleasure she gave; she is more amiable than her mother the Duchess of Marlborough. I found Lady Barington again, she is distinguished-looking and must have been beautiful once. Then there were the beauties, Miss Gérard and Mme. Murietta; a fire the night before had burned all the latter's clothes, except the dress she wore, which did not interfere in the least with her dancing gayly till the rising of the lark. And just now I've seen all these beautiful women repairing the fatigues of the night with a little gallop in Rotten-Row.

LONDON, May 14, 1874.

The Emperor of Russia only arrived last night. The delay was no doubt voluntary. It is said that he does not like to go where a crowd awaits him. About to-morrow no one knows yet whether the rank and file of the diplomatic corps are included among those to be received by the Czar, nor whether we shall have to wear "breeches" (*culottes*) to the ball at Stafford House? These are the matters with which we are preoccupied. It is really a bit absurd for a representative of France abroad to be obliged to give such attention to his *culottes* at a time when he may at any moment find himself representing a government *sans-culottes!*

[1] Lord Halifax.

LONDON, May 16, 1874.

This has been a day to remember. We started at noon for Buckingham Palace.

The diplomatic corps lined up, dressed to the right, each embassy headed by its chief.

After some waiting, the Emperor [1] entered very stiffly, followed by Brunnow, who was left to find his way as best he could. If he hadn't been already as old as could be, he would have aged ten years since yesterday. The Czar's countenance is handsome. He was courteous to Musurus, showed marked coldness to Count de Beust, was friendly with Count Munster, (shook hands with him), and more than friendly with the German Embassy, recognizing each of the secretaries. To our ambassador he showed little more than simple good-will, explaining in a low tone the necessity of a visit on his part to Chiselhurst and dropping a few gracious words about the Marshal. As he was leaving he added, in a voice this time that every one could hear: "In especial say to him that *I* am in favor of law and order." It was something too strongly accented, and though the Duke is as much (if not more) in favor of law and order as his interlocutor, he was a bit offended. The incident will of course find its way to the Continent. I noticed after this interview a severity on the part of the Emperor toward poor Brunnow. Brunnow had of course allowed the Emperor, in his trip through the diplomatic corps, to pay more attention than was quite befit-

---

[1] Alexander II.

ting to the Nicaraguan representative whose reputation leaves much to be desired; and the Emperor in consequence overlooks his ambassador and appeals for information to Count Schouvaloff, who follows him about.

Extracts from the Notes.

My mother and sister having joined me, I have no record (in the way of letters,) of the last festivities during my stay at London : notably a ball improvised for Ascot, at the place and in the stead of the Prince of Wales. The day before, flowers, illuminations, musicians, service, supper, and even a flooring for the ball-room were sent down by post. An affair that was at the time not less talked about was a certain reception given to the volunteers on their return from Havre, at which the ambassador consented to distribute medals in the midst of the popping of champagne corks. The "volunteers" came full-armed and brought their wives; and from that time on the Duke could not leave the embassy without a crowd about his carriage to see him get in. . . . Generous, loyal, chivalrous, more than chivalrous, the Duc de Bisaccia, much to my regret, wished to go to Paris with the Duchesse to the Grand-Prix. He left as an ambassador and came back minus that dignity.

The Comte de Jarnac is to succeed Duc de Bisaccia. Under the Monarchy of July, as First Secretary and *Chargé d'Affaires*, he had already played an important diplomatic rôle. His nomination relegated me to the position of a fifth wheel. I knew all the dangers and inconveniences of this situation. I did not, however, hesitate to recommend the appointment of Comte de Jarnac ; I had taken special care to write and to speak to this effect to the ministry every time that the succession had been open since my arrival in England. It was, at least for the good of the public, the happiest choice that could have been made. The Comte de Jarnac was really a born diplomat ; he was devoted, body and soul, his whole life through, to his career. He married, he assumed the management of a considerable property in Ireland, he was not without success in literature. But from first to last he was a diplomatist and a diplomatist only.

I counted at first on easing the difficulties of my position by frequent absences. I took my mother and sister back to France the 3d of September, 1874, and returned to London the 15th of November. I went to Paris again for the month of February, 1875. So that during the Comte de Jarnac's administration I passed at most three months in London.

If this period was not entirely unobscured by clouds, my loyalty on the one hand, and on the other a great kindliness on the part of my chief, and also his high intelligence, dissipated them as soon as they were formed.

M. de Jarnac showed a bit of sensitiveness and restlessness in his official relations. I saw there was a tension coming in his relations with Lord Derby, and that his fancy was creating one for him in his relations with the French minister. How uneasy I have seen him on account of his having, in his private correspondence, presumed to mark a shade of difference between his own notions and those of Duc Decazes, on the nature of the relations to be maintained with Mr. Disraëli's cabinet! He had undertaken to renew the former close alliance. In his proceedings, in his illusions, there was a bit too much of the traditions of a former time; and there was something old-fashioned in the turns of his official despatches, in the importance he attached to small things, but it must be said that he looked upon the official despatch as a necessary evil. He reproached me amicably, for putting so much into mine; he felt that one could be certain that a despatch is the surest medium for carrying dangerous information to the ears that have no right to hear it. Mistrustful, accordingly, of official correspondence he puts nothing in his own despatches but odds-and-ends or general reflections, that when one reads them afterwards are scarcely intelligible. He reserved everything for his private correspondence, and then indeed, he wrote it down with an unparalleled fulness and exactitude. The courage to contradict a minister he did not lack; in spite of his soft phrases, or rather by virtue of them, M. Jarnac was quite capable, when he felt it was his duty to do so, of making a resistance to the very Princes to whose cause he had devoted his life.

No one could be more circumspect than he in dealing with persons in authority, but there was a chasm between circumspection on his part and anything like compliance. Underneath all his certainty he knew how to lose his temper in case of need; and I remember having seen him, in the last days of his life, at logger-heads with John Lemoinne who had set down wittily enough in an article in the *Debats* precisely what we needed to do to estrange the English government from us. In his legitimate anger the Comte de Jarnac altogether lost control of himself—he raised his voice and stamped his foot; a little more, and he would have taken vicarious revenge on the incorrigible joker, and used me as the substitute.

Extracts from the Correspondence.

LONDON, October 9, 1874.

I ran across Count Schouvaloff [1] at the Countess's tea. He acts as if he were bent more than any other one thing on emancipating himself from any lurking kindness for Germany and the Germans. He fell brusquely upon Bismarck *à-propos* of D'Armin; he puts no faith in the embezzlement—it is purely, he thinks, a scheme for revenge, a stroke (I had almost said a stab in the dark), to injure him with the Emperor, and to get him out of the way as a possible successor. Then he criticised his colleagues from Prussia to London, past and present. Not knowing whether his purpose in all this might not be to draw me out I spoke favorably of Munster. Schouvaloff is not, however, a diplomatist of the school of Brunnow. He speaks in complimentary terms of his predecessor.

[1] He had been ambassador to Russia. Died in 1889.

To-day there has been nothing but a visit to the good Georgiana to report.[1] She told me that it was the conversion of the Marquis of Ripon that had enraged Gladstone, and caused him to write the pamphlet in which he insults the Catholics and outrages all the defenders of the Established Church. He acts as if he had taken an oath to quarrel with his whole party.

LONDON, October 26, 1874.

This morning as I was starting to mass, William Guizot arrived. He came to borrow a shirt from me, having lost his luggage *en route*. He breakfasted with Jarnac, and we spent a large part of the day, chatting about his father. It is to be wished that such respect for the memory of one's father should be more universal. I seemed to be listening to M. Guizot himself when his son repeated some of his talk. . . . He told me of his father's last hours. He slept a great deal and complained of it. "I am sleepy," he said, "I struggle against this eternal sleepiness, but otherwise I do not suffer." When he could not longer read he fell back upon his memory and used to recite poetry endlessly. When he could not recall a line, he would become uneasy, and repeat the preceding line over and over again ; to relieve him the missing verse had to be found and William was called to supply it. The eve of his death, he halted on a verse of which I am not sure ; something however as follows :

[1] Lady G. Fullerton.

Il avait le cœur grand, l'esprit beau. . . .
Le roi. . . .

The *lacunæ* in which he could not fill out. They called William who recognized it as the last of a poem addressed by Molière to a father who had lost his son.[1] In his weakness M. Guizot had confused it with a triade of Corneille's in *Nicomède*, where the same thought occurs. It ends in this way:

*Attale a le cœur grand, l'esprit grand, l'âme grande,
Et toutes les grandeurs dont se fait un grand roi.*

As soon as William had cleared up the mystery his father continued tranquilly with *Nicomède*. It was a favorite piece with M. Guizot; he used to recite it often to his children. As to the lines from Molière it was William who had impressed them upon his father's memory on an occasion in the Sorbonne. William was mounting the platform to give " Les Fourberies de Scapin," when the death of the Duc de Broglie was reported to him. He announced it and closed by the citation from Molière, saying, " These are lines that apply as well to the Duke as to ' La Mothe Le Vayer.' "

M. Guizot died very quietly, fell asleep without any one seeing him go. It was a fit ending of his life.

We spoke of his history of France, which he began

---

[1] " A Monsieur La Mothe Le Vayer ":
*Il avait le cœur, l'esprit beau, l'âme belle,
Et ce sont des sujets à toujours le pleurer.*

at twenty-three. Three volumes are published. He left the notes, which complete the fourth volume and bring the history down to 1789, to his daughter Henriette.[1] The volume will appear soon.

Henriette is the head of the family. " I can neither do anything, nor decide anything without her advice, she is the oldest son!"

I am sorry not to be able to repeat the rest that he told me; among other things, he mentioned an impromptu speech his father delivered at Nîmes. It was in a popular assembly, in response to an old man who came to remind him of his mother's charities in Nîmes.

It was a masterpiece of tact, caution and profound feeling. Then we ran over twenty of his speeches, William reciting them as soon as I could give him the clue from my confused memories.

He is to be here for a fortnight making some researches in the British Museum. I will get him an invitation to the Athenæum ; do you know I should never weary of this prodigious dictionary !

I finished my day with Jarnac, at Gunnersbury, at the Rothschilds. You go there, to be sure, through closely built-up streets, but you are in the country when you arrive—their park is a " country" in itself—an endless succession of meadows, ponds, ancient trees, greenhouses and herds.

We strolled about among these marvels, following the Baron on his pony. He cannot walk any more,

[1] Oldest daughter of M. Guizot, Mme. Conrad de Witt.

but he can keep his balance. The outing really did him good; but he does not allow himself to take it but Saturdays and Sundays. The rest of the week he is in the City, superintending his business. This place is altogether too beautiful, it attaches one too closely to the things of this world; it is better to live in furnished lodgings such as those from which I am writing you to-night! Be it said in passing that the church across the way is terribly ritualistic; superb music is wafted to me across the street and through my closed windows.

LONDON, October 28, 1874.

I had a very curious conversation with Schouvaloff. One of his secretaries urged me to go see him some morning. The talk was very unguarded—very blunt. He told me that on arriving at St. Petersburg M. Thiers had said, "I am ashamed to represent the Republic, it is the greatest sacrifice I could make for my country—I, the advocate *par excellence* of constitutional monarchy." Then Schouvaloff spoke of the Duc de Broglie. "He is the only statesman you have. He commands my greatest admiration. He is the only one who has made head against demagogism." Then he told me that he had just received the card of a certain "Monsieur, half marshal, half convict, M. Bazaine." Then he spoke of the Empress Eugénie who it seems has made a "dead set" at the Czarina, by dint of going to visit her, etc.

M. de Jarnac has requested me to put our conversation into a despatch.

LONDON, November 2, 1874.

The dinner with Schouvaloff was full of interest. He is a good talker, nay, even a good story-teller, is a wit, is agreeable, is seducing. Is he a person of solid abilities? No one could tell that after a single interview.

He entertained us at first by recounting his expenses, and telling how he had been robbed of five hundred pounds sterling on his arrival in London. He said that he met a German diplomat in the train from Paris, and found after talking to him that it was the first secretary of the German Embassy at Madrid who was on his way with despatches, Baron de —— He was going to England to see his sister. He gave him some curious and precise information about Spain, and also about Bismarck and Count D'Armin. It almost made one exclaim, the resemblance was so perfect. No one but an intimate friend of Bismarck could have been so accurate. On the way to the boat, at the station, they recognized each other again and shook hands. The Count received his visit in London. He was authorized by Bismarck to put him on the track of a large manufactory of Russian counterfeit banknotes. You could have the information for 500 pounds sterling without any risks, to be paid afterward. The money must be deposited at a banker's who would not surrender it except on the Count's signature. As the Baron, first secretary, was on the point of taking his leave, the check was handed to him . . . and he left as he said he would. It must be rather embarrassing for an ancient director of the Russian police to be tricked like that. He was really artless, and confessed, notwithstanding his freedom of speech, the effect the name of Bismarck, when properly employed, has on him. The joke is that it was probably an agent of Bismarck acting under his orders to teach him a lesson in modesty.

It was during dinner that he told us this adventure, and he did it with a good grace. Afterward I saw him and said to him : " There is only one man who could have carried off that farce and he lives at Clapham." "That is precisely the name of the station," replied Schouvaloff. For my part, I am convinced that it was one of the agents of a company of international forgers which has been in existence for some years, which mystified the Emperor and M. Thiers, and has made offers to us. Their stories are always so perfect, and betray such an intimate acquaintance with state secrets, that one is almost forced to suppose they get their information from Berlin. " I shall put the police on the scent," said the Count. I fancy that on reflection he will be more afraid of discovering the thief than of letting him escape.

Afterward he told us of his journey with the Emperor in the Caucasus. The journey was in the night-time but it was light as day. Over a distance of twenty leagues the forest was illuminated right and left. The memory of it stays with the narrator like a nightmare, as you can readily understand. Then he described their escort of three hundred cavalrymen rushing along at full speed.

Every now and then a horseman would catch up a woman from the ground without stopping and seat her in front of him on his saddle, toss her back to earth again when he was weary of her—only to begin all over again this eternal " Merry go round," with the next woman on the route that should catch his eye, etc.

He said it was folly to spend so much in men and money to conquer a country which brings in nothing. He is wrong. In less than fifty years, when Switzerland has had her day, every one will go to Circassia to play at " Merry go round " with the women. It seems, too, that there are as many glaciers there as heart could wish.

After dinner we had a more serious talk. He said that Germany is not so strong as before the war, and that her unity is at the mercy of Russia. He bases this opinion on the fact that she must keep at least 400,000 men in garrison about Metz to hold Alsace and France in check. That is true; but seems rather calculated to induce Germany to pick a quarrel with us again and to dispose of us for good.

He gave also a capital take-off of a Prussian municipal council. He described them as gathering together for official business. The Mayor or Magistrate dresses his people up in line. " No. 2, put in your belly! No. 5, advance!" Eyes right! eyes front! forward march!" to the chamber where their deliberations are held.

LONDON, November 8, 1874.

The difference has been explained to me (by the daughter of my landlady), between the church across the street and the one she attends in Piccadilly. There is singing in both, sacerdotal vestments in both; but across the way the priest turns toward the altar during the consecration, and in Piccadilly he turns toward the public. She could not tell me the reasons for it! "Across the street they make the sign of the cross, and they hide a rosary under their robes; and what is worse than all, they confess to the young " clergyman " who are likely at any time to marry into their families. It is horrible! If our priests were like yours, I should not be so scandalized at it." There is some truth in this reflection.

The truth is, the ritualists turn toward the altar because they believe that something happens on the altar and not simply in the souls of the spectators. They believe in the miracle, the mystery, in the divine action of the sacrament. They are eager to be Christians. I realize that it is much easier, but more dangerous, to believe that everything happens in the soul of the faithful.

Since you are fond of clever sayings, here is a good citation from Pitt. They are his last words in public, at a banquet given by the Lord-Mayor. Pitt had been toasted as the saviour of his country. "Do not say that a man has been the saviour of England; she has saved herself by her efforts and has saved her neighbors by her example." Then he sat down. Equally brief and eloquent.

HATFIELD-HOUSE,[1] November 21, 1874.

I reached "King's Cross Station" at half-past five. There I found Lord Carnarvon and helped him expedite the sending of a belated despatch to China, which reached its destination about the same time as we reached ours. A carriage was waiting for us at the station at Hatfield and took us up by the same steep uncomfortable road. As we approached the "house," the windows all caught the moonlight and flashed back at us a weird, colorless flame. You enter by a guard-room with forty suits of armor standing sentinel, then through a grand hall surrounded by books, where there was a fireplace with great logs burning. I found myself among acquaintances; in an Elizabethan castle; there was Lord Lyons with Sheffield, Lady Stafford Northcote and her second daughter, and the Marchioness and her sister. We passed down a gallery fully as long as the *Gallery des Glaces* at Versailles.

The Marquis came from London with Sir Stafford Northcote. We went up to our rooms; the staircase was winding and of wood. I half expected to meet James the First. This relic of the sixteenth century landed us among chambers with little diamond-paned windows, but for the rest supplied with all the comfort of the nineteenth century. Big open fireplaces, cabinets of all kinds, comprising— yes—the one we have so much trouble in finding at night in our hovels in France. It almost makes one

[1] Residence of the Marquis of Salisbury.

willing to be ill. All my things were ready and I dressed. Fortunately I found Sheffield on the staircase; without him I should have been lost in the numerous "halls." To reach the dining-room we passed by the gallery of a private chapel. Finally, we found ourselves in the small dining-room, the one with the old wainscoting. The dinner was excellent. The musicians played softly during the whole time. When dessert was served the children appeared; the two daughters stood by the Marquis and the two sons by the side of Lady Salisbury. One of them was Lord Cranborne. When I think that this young scamp of twelve is heir of this castle and of so many others, I am overcome with respect for him! After dinner, we went into other salons; everywhere open fires, lights, an air of vastness and all this for about ten people. A man must indeed be out of sorts with the world who could not grow fond of life under these conditions.

In a corner of my room, a programme for the day was posted. "Chapel at nine o'clock." What shall I do? Breakfast at ten; then hunt; then dinner at one o'clock; tea at five; and then dine again at eight! How can people live by candlelight in these great rooms? No wonder they see ghosts.

After dinner we were in a room too large for conversation, so we promenaded in groups and lost each other. The women and children at last surrounded Stafford Northcote. He does not preach to them as in Parliament, but tells them stories, or rather, funny dialogues. I lost all, or nearly all, of what he said. I could not follow it.

HATFIELD, November 21, 1874.

This has been one of those beautiful days in late autumn that are not uncommon in this rich English country. I have followed the hunt all morning, across the ferns, stopping in admiration before the prehistoric oaks. The end of the year has yellowed their crests. The sun shed a golden light on the low-lands. I was more interested in inanimate nature than in pheasants. We set out in two divisions facing one another, with the game between : it ended in a general massacre. The three members of the Cabinet took part in it ; the Marquis of Salisbury seemed a bit preoccupied. . . . I followed Sheffield, who is a capital shot. It was shooting enough just to watch him. I feel no desire myself to shed blood, not even that of the lower animals.

We began the day with prayer in the chapel, the guests were in the gallery, the family and servants below. The chaplain said prayers, and we chanted a psalm, the organ accompanying. At ten o'clock we met at breakfast. I was near Lyons, who is always pleasant. Some neighbors arrived booted for the chase. There was no time for serious chat the whole day through.

As we were coming back the castle stood out in black against a clear sky; it was magnificent. I shall make no effort to describe it to you—in the compass of a letter. On the way back we came across the stump of the Elizabeth oak, carefully puttied and encased. It was under this oak that Elizabeth was told of the death of her beloved sister, which made her queen. As we three stood together there —one of us among the greatest of the peers of the realm—I asked myself which of us runs the best chance of one day becoming king. I fancy I do. Which only shows the difference between this favored land and our unhappy revolutionary France.

HATFIELD, November 22, 1874.

There is a superb white frost this morning, and a great expanse of sky and landscape in view from my window. Yesterday evening the Jarnacs arrived.

We dined in the large hall with the gallery on the second floor. My neighbor was a very young man: I asked him if he was at the University; as it turns out he is a member of Parliament, very young, however, and at no pains to dissemble his age. He is the nephew of the Marquis, a Mr. Balfour,[1] I believe. At the close of the dinner, Lord Cranborne sat down between us. I had retained him for the "pass-wine," and he did the honors. He said : " I shall be an ambassador, my brother a general, the other an admiral, and the last a bishop." After dinner I chatted with the young mathematician ; he delights me much with his frank look and lively intellect. Stafford Northcote began his Devonshire dialogues again, which were a bit dreary. Then he played some card-tricks. I did not make a point of recollecting all the "good things" (à la Greville,[2] as

[1] The Right Honorable A. J. Balfour, First Lord of the Treasury under the last ministry, and at present leader of the Conservative party in the House of Commons.
[2] An allusion to the Greville Mémoirs.

the Marquis of Salisbury would put it), that were said.

I had a charming walk this morning over the frosty ground. Ferns and boughs were clothed in white that glistened in the sunshine. We found the rest of the household at breakfast on our return. Then there were prayers. It is one o'clock and another meal to eat! I can't, simply: I ate a pheasant's wing this morning, and can do no more. Don't copy my letters; there is nothing in them worth while.

THE YEAR 1875.

Extracts from the Correspondence.

WOBURN-ABBEY,[1] January 3, 1875.

IT is a mistake, I think, to feel that the power of the clergy lies in its wealth; the contrary is true. When a cleric is rich, he is an object of prey to the rest of mankind, and to find a pretext for devouring him they change a word in his *credo* and oblige him to choose between his riches and his faith ; or it may be they despoil him simply, without giving him any choice in the matter, and hang him, as they did the last Bishop of Woburn, to a tree in his own park. They show the tree still—" the Abbot's tree." If I had been told he was still swinging on its branches I should have believed it, my imagination was so worked upon by this vast domain, with its centenary shaded lanes which I passed through for the first time in the moonlight.

Nothing seems to have been changed in the cloister with its quadrangular court bordered on all four sides by a gallery. The immense building is

---

[1] Residence of the Duke of Bedford. Henry VIII. gave him a baronetcy in 1538, and the Abbey of Tavistock. Edward VI. created him Earl of Bedford in 1550, and gave him Woburn. The duchy dates from 1694.

divided off into vast cells. I occupy one with a canopy-bed. Was it here three hundred years ago when monks prayed and studied in the building—came here in their quest for heaven? The bell which calls me to dinner called them to morning prayers. Put not your trust, however, too implicitly in my first impressions; they were received, you remember, by moonlight; to-morrow may bring forth something quite different.

WOBURN-ABBEY, January 4, 1875.

I was decidedly the victim of my imagination last night. The ancient Benedictine Abbey does not exist by daylight. What I took for one, is a castle deliberately constructed down in a hole, in the taste of Escurial, and about as cheerful. . . .

Singular idea to have surrounded this monastery castle by a glacis which rises nearly to a level with its roof. The embankments are laid out in the form of a fortification such as Vauban might have planned. There is something grand in the total effect, because of the scale on which it is all laid out; but it lacks art. The house is partly shut in by immense out-buildings, that cut off the horizon—a semicircle of stables, barns, tennis-courts and what not. Inside there is a great square court, green with turf, but nothing about it to inspire gayety; and round about the court there are interminable portrait galleries. On the whole it is severe, monotonous and melancholy.

Last night I entered, without suspecting it, on the second floor, and as we went downstairs to dinner,

I thought the table was spread in the cellar of the convent. The mistake was mine, we dined in a dining-room on the first floor. The house is built on a hill-side,—one end is a story higher than the other. You spend your time in this vast structure in walking about from one room to another so as a little to utilize the space.

The danger is of losing oneself in the endless waxed halls (they all look alike), and of passing the door you are hunting for. You learn, finally, to guide yourself by the portraits hung along the walls of the interior gallery. I spend most of my time in the library, in the midst of old books, which I have rummaged among a good deal in search for a history of the Russells. The history of that family since the times of Henry VIII. is in a measure the history of England. Unhappily the origin of all these splendid fortunes is always the same—the confiscation of church property, and Royal donations; and it often involves also the hanging of the last abbot, as at Woburn.

Every day we dine in a different dining-room. Yesterday it was downstairs, under the gaze of ten portraits (full length) by Van Dyck. We were in ordinary dinner-dress. There was nothing to dazzle one but the plate, that flashed back the light in the centre of the hall, and the deep-blue Sèvres service (or rather an infinitesimal part of it) which was a "diplomatic" gift to the Duke at the time of the treaty in 1763. After dinner and wine we went up again to a beautiful drawing-room two stories high with a magnificent portrait by Reynolds over the fireplace of a certain Marchioness of Tavistock. A Tavistock is a Russell who is waiting for the Bedford dukedom. As it was all very informal, the evening closed early, after a little talk and some billiards in a hall near by.

One has to get up early to be in time for breakfast. With much circumnavigation this morning I did find the breakfast-room at last. It was in the hall that contains the four-and-twenty Canaletti. The sun poured into the room (for the winter seems past) and played over the '*Canal Grande,*' the '*Rialto,*' '*San Marco*' and '*tutti quanti*'; and lit up the contours of two vile Sèvres vases that are worth two hundred and fifty thousand francs.

After breakfast I visited, with the Duke, the apartments reserved for Royalty. They contain many historical portraits, three or four by Van Dyck, Reynolds and Gainsborough; almost all pictures of members of the family. One in special was of a former possessor of the dukedom: in calling my attention to it the present Duke said: "He was in his day the eldest son; fortunately he died young for he was a gambler." The "fortunately" was significant in the mouth of an heir. The Duke handed me over to Lord Arthur with whom I visited the grounds a bit. The park is layed out on a grand scale, there are meadows without end, and fine old trees. Deer and partridges swarm about the castle. Hunger and fear of the foxes keep them close to human habitations. Here in England the fox reigns supreme. He eats young swans, chicks, eggs, even fowl kept up in coops. Complain to the neighboring squire and he does nothing—the thief is privileged to die by the pack-hounds only.

On my first round with Lord Russell this morning I visited the sculpture gallery. It contains some few antiques and a great many imitations and English things. In one corner there was a little sanctuary to Charles James Fox, with a bust of him in an arched niche. I have seen many such in " Whig " houses. Poor Fox was perspiring sadly in the general thaw. It looks as if things in general might be melting on this low ground. Through a covered gallery that almost encircled the house, we went to the " dairy "— a Chinese dairy; but I abstain from speaking of it— it was all so damp the bare thought of it gives me a chill.

At "luncheon" I caused a scandal by my abstinence. They had noticed already how little I had eaten that morning. What should I say—except that I had not yet had time to digest my breakfast. It was a pity not to do honor to a repast of which the *chef* had furnished me with the *menu* when I paid him a visit in his stronghold—the kitchen, or rather the laboratory—a great hall two stories high, in which there were wood-fires, coal-fires, flaming gas, and not an odor, nor, so far as it was avoidable, an offensive detail. But you should have been with me when I penetrated into an adjoining room and found the French "artist" in the midst of his books—Monsieur X—— who put his hand to the sauce-pan for the first time in 1821 when Napoleon was dying. The good man talked of the present century with a melancholy air, of the decadence of his art. He warmed up a bit in the course of telling me that he has been fortunate enough to succeed at last in solving the mushroom problem.

"Is it satisfactory?" I asked. "Yes, the Mushroom-soup," he answered—"*purée de champignon*"; and as he spoke he cast his eyes upon the papers that littered his table—the algebraic formulæ no doubt. Then we visited the china-closet. We were shown the porcelain service, given by Louis XV., all in the famous blue Sèvres, there are from three to four hundred pieces of it. After "luncheon" we visited conservatories without number. There is one for every month in the year. Peaches and grapes are in season the year round. The "farm" (where I saw great basins full of milk with cream on the top and great basins full of milk still foaming and warm— all of it for the "House") is a model of cleanliness. There are also large shops on the estate—the Duke has undertaken to supply all the stores needed by the establishment and in the management of the farms. The running expenses of his country places amount to 250,000 francs. Fortune seems to have taken a delight in lavishing favors on the present Duke, and at a touch of her wand endowed him with a duchy, a marquisate, vast estates, more than six millions a year in ground rents, the ownership of a quarter of London. And he has remained, in spite of all this splendor, what he was before it came—a younger son in a great family, satisfied with a younger son's competence. Practically he is the administrator, simply, of this great fortune, which accident has brought to him. He is simple, sober, perfectly natural and independent, in the midst of this luxury of which he has no right to divest himself, and which he passes on to his guest. His son, too, is unassuming, as silent at the table as before he became the Marquis of Tavistock. There are also two daughters. The elder is noticably solicitous to escape attention. She has a dowry, however, and the second son, Lord Herbrand,[1] also will have an " estate." The Duke said to me : " If any one tells you I am a miser, say to him that I am economizing for my daughters' dowries and to purchase an estate for my younger son." The young ladies are simpler in taste than the " Nobodies " of London. They have never been on the Continent ! They do not ride horseback !

WOBURN-ABBEY, January 5, 1875.

This morning I visited, with the Duke, the schools, and the cottages rented to working men at the rate of one shilling threepence a week. The climax of these splendid charities is the workhouse, maintained jointly by sixteen parishes—an almshouse and a refuge. It represents the minimum guaranteed to every inhabitant of Britain overtaken by distress or old age, no matter who he is nor what he may have done. The landed proprietor or proprietors in the country have to supply the poor, for as long a time as they may demand it, with the necessaries of life. The only limit to the obligation to give is the need of the claimant—a dangerous principle anywhere—but what shall one say of it

[1] Present Duke of Bedford.

here where the house in question is less than half filled?

We had three "radicals" from the neighborhood in to "luncheon," one of them with spectacles on and prominent incisors—a veritable rodent; another an insinuating reverend, a veritable fox. It is from no lack of good will on their part, in my judgment, that they do not dismember "his grace." As the Duke is a liberal he has to listen to them and play the host.

This morning I read the history of Henry VIII. in a big folio. Such a story needs a volume of that size. What a scoundrel he was (he had many natural charms), and what scoundrels there were all about, to abet his hypocrisies, and self-indulgences, and passions. I really believe we are better than that. The history of his mistresses would be to the last degree funny, if every chapter did not end in blood. During the day I followed the hunt: always and everywhere the same massacre of pheasants with their beautiful plumage, and of hares that squeal. What a pity the sport is so cruel! I almost killed a fox! If somebody had not knocked up my gun, the Duke's standing in the county would have been ruined.

This evening we dined once more in the Van Dyck room—Van Dyck to the right, to the left, on every side—vessels of gold on the sideboard, a piece among the rest by Benvenuto Cellini. After dinner we spent some time in the drawing-room that contains the beautiful portrait by Reynolds. We were between two immense open fireplaces—caught between two fires. It was so uncomfortable, notwithstanding the distance between them, that it was impossible to stay there, and little by little the guests withdrew to the side gallery, where there was tea, billiards, whist, each in front of a fireplace that it is accurate to describe as infernal. In a glass case there I saw a cane that had belonged to Charles I.

LONDON, January 8, 1875.

I have been with Borthwick to the office of the *Morning Post*. I assisted, till one o'clock, at the printing of a newspaper. It is a marvel of organization; everything is done quietly—more than a hundred compositors at the work. The MS. is delivered to them at three o'clock, and half an hour afterward is in print. Articles come in from all quarters ready for press. Every one has his appointed task. In the middle there is a director who does not touch a pen. He is a rich man who was a candidate at the last elections. Naturally he is well paid. Each compositor receives about ten francs a day. Organizations, division of labor, plenty of money, are the secrets of it.

Extracts from the Notes.

THE ILLNESS AND DEATH OF THE COMTE DE JARNAC.

The only thing that I have still to mention, is the regretted death of my superior. He had been, since the beginning of the year, suffering from an attack of asthma. Dr. Vintras advised him to take a vacation, but in vain. A run to Brighton for forty-eight hours was the only rest he took. I was struck by his exhaustion at the Hospital Banquet. At the close of his toasts, which were so full of " humor," —models of happy characterization, he had been unable to speak above a whisper. The failure of his voice had imparted an air of homely sincerity to his words about the hospital and the suffering here below. He was depressed when he took his leave, though he spoke to me of my own affairs with a genuine interest. Nothing could persuade him to take the precautions his condition demanded. On the evening of the 17th of March, notwithstanding a return of bitter cold weather, he went out before dinner, as was his habit, to make the circuit of the Serpentine. He was dining with some friends. Nobody could have foretold that they would never see him again. The next morning I was awakened very early by Vintras. He had been called in the night by the Ambassador, and had found him suffering with pleurisy; he had prescribed three leeches to minimize the local pain, and the danger of irritation from coughing. He did not attempt to hide from me that the combination of asthma and pleurisy was very serious. It was two days, however, before anybody suspected how serious, and we suffered the patient to run no end of risks in our unwillingness to believe that he was ill.

The embarrassment of my position was extreme. I had to attend the Queen's levee in the Comte de Jarnac's stead on Friday. I had to write to the Duc Decazes at once to prepare him for the seriousness of the attack. I had to reply to a host of letters that poured in from all sides, as soon as the newspapers had spread the alarm. I had to stand between the count's family, who felt as yet quite secure, and the physician, who was seriously alarmed. By the 19th an apparent turn for the better had been taken and it was announced that the count would be up the next day. . . . The sense of my responsibility was beginning to weigh on me. I took the Marchioness of Ely, who was sent by the Queen, into my confidence. Some hours later Dr. Jenner appeared; the Queen had sent him to make an examination of the patient. Dr. Vindras and I could ask nothing better.

I can see him still—the little man without a glance to spare, brusque, hurried—coming into my office watch in hand. All the doors opened at the name of the Queen. He came back soon very much excited; he almost held me personally responsible for the state in which he found the patient. " He is very bad—this can't be trifled with. I have been asked when he can get up? Ask me rather whether he will ever get up?" He gave me a telegram for the Queen and said he would be back soon. He came three times that day. Three calls from Jenner on the same day was the worst symptom possible.

I wrote to Paris the next day, the 21st: " The poor count is very low. Yesterday I notified (by telegram) the Comte de Paris and the family. I repeated the message this morning after a wretched night. The disease has attacked the lungs. Jenner came twice yesterday, leaving in my hands each time a more and more alarming telegram for the Queen. At five o'clock, he ordered a physician for the night. . . . This great misfortune is a terrible lesson to all of us. He had from the first but one ambition; he sacrificed it for twenty-six years to a sense of duty, he succeeded in it at last with a completeness that derived an added brilliancy from his long self-abnegation. He became, what he had always wished to be, an ambassador; his name, his authority, his knowledge, his experience, his social standing in France and in England, were to become at last of service to his country—he was to be permitted after all these years to do for France what he could do so well. And he had barely made a start—had just begun to come into notice; and . . . he died precisely because he had succeeded. If he had continued as an Irish landlord, simply, his asthma would have amounted to nothing. Alas! When he took up the direction of the embassy, he forgot the previous twenty-six years; he thought himself still the Comte de Rohan-Chabot, as in the days of his discussions with Palmerston. . . ."

I added, in an other letter, the 22d of March : " The disease grows worse hour by hour. . . . I was interrupted by the Prince of Wales himself who came with the Princess to make inquiries. There is nothing all these grand personages can do ! "

The same day at eleven o'clock in the evening I wrote : " The Comte de Jarnac died while I was at the door speaking with the Prince and Princess of Wales, who had come to ask how he was. He had at no time suspected he was to die. He lost consciousness ten minutes before the end, and expired without suffering. The people at his bedside did not notice that all was over till some time afterward. Yes, all was over; and, (a word to those who reach the end of their journey after a long struggle, or despair of reaching it), how cold this Protestant dying is, without a prayer, without a syllable of hope!"

The news spread immediately in the crowd in the street in front of the house and passed on to the town. Certain personages I myself notified, and they all of them either hastened to call that evening or sent messages.

I returned to the embassy by ten o'clock and found the place empty and the doors open; I made my way into where the body lay hardly cold, and nobody to stop me. One lamp was burning in a corner, but no one was there praying: he was a Protestant.

It was I who spent the night by the body of M. de Jarnac. I said all the prayers I could think of. I had leisure to look at the head (now cold and severe) that I had always seen smiling and kindly. Up to the last moment he preserved for those about him his customary playful manner. Death gave his face a beautiful and serious expression—gave prominence to his will, to which his entire life had been subordinate. He looked like an effigy upon the tomb of some old warrior. During the vigil I wrote the following official notice to the ministry:

"It is my painful duty to inform you that the Comte de Jarnac succumbed this evening at six o'clock, to the pleurisy, by which he was attacked last Thursday. The messages that I have sent you day by day will have informed you of the progress of the disease which neither the most tender care, nor the efforts of science could check. As soon as it was noised abroad that the French ambassador was ill, the Queen expressed a wish that her physician might visit the patient and give her an account of his condition. Since that time, Sir W. Jenner has followed the case hour by hour, in company with Dr. Vintras; informing the Queen directly after each visit. The Prince and Princess of Wales have not shown less solicitude. Their Royal Highnesses were at the door of the embassy making inquiries about the Comte de Jarnac at the very moment he expired. The Queen and the Royal Family have repeatedly shown their sympathy and their esteem for the Comte de Jarnac, and the public has followed their lead. There is not a public man, nor a member of London society, who has not in these last days left his name at the embassy. A note that I received from Mr. Disraëli showed clearly what impression the sudden announcement of the count's death had produced. I had sent him word of it, and he returned an immediate reply. "Your dreadful missive reached me in Parliament. The grave has closed upon a friendship of forty years. Nothing can equal the grief I feel." It does not belong to me to state what France has lost in the Comte de Jarnac; to the testimonials of the general respect in which he was held here in England I shall therefore add only an expression of the profound and sincere regret I feel myself for the death of the eminent and kindly leader under whose orders I have had the honor to serve for a time unhappily so brief."

A letter that I received the following day from Lord Derby, contained an estimate of the Comte de Jarnac which deserves to be quoted : "We have lost in the Comte de Jarnac, the most perfect representative of France in England that it was possible to conceive. His intimate acquaintance with the two nations, his invariable courtesy and finished tact, gave him an incomparable aptitude for the elevated post that he occupied. He won the esteem and affection of every one with whom he had to deal. His sudden and premature death will be felt by everybody as a national loss. . . ."

The Comtesse de Jarnac recognized in me a friend. She bore witness of it when she designated me to the Comte de Paris as the person to whom she wished to commit the custody of such of her husband's papers as at her death were to go to the Prince. Her intention in placing them in my keeping was that I should acquaint myself with them in order that I might, in case of need, make such use of them as would serve the interest of the family to which the Comte de Jarnac had devoted his life. These papers and letters extended back to the time of his entrance into public life. They related to matters that he had handled for the State and to those that he had taken charge of in the name of the Orleans family.

THE ALARM OF 1875.

I took charge of the Embassy on the 22d of March, 1875, after the death of the Comte de Jarnac. The feeling of uncertainty which began to spread through Europe, and in especial through France, after the Perponcher note of February 3d on the Duchesne affair and the pastoral letters of the Belgian bishops had not yet made itself felt in England.

One word about the Duchesne matter. I had known of its earlier stages when I was at Versailles, but had supposed it had long since come to naught. One Sunday the venerable archbishop, the Cardinal Guibert, came to my office [1] much excited, and told me of a letter he had just received from Belgium. It was signed Duchesne, and contained an offer to assassinate Prince Bismarck. The letter presented all the appearances of a trick, but as in such a matter we could not be too cautious, I promised the cardinal to treat the matter seriously, and the same evening I sent the letter to Graf von Wesdehlen, the *Chargé d'Affaires* of Germany. After some days, he came to express the gratitude of his government which he begged me to transmit to the cardinal. I do not remember what he told me was the result of the inquiries which had been made, but my present impression is that it had been discovered there was no foundation for the affair beyond a tipsy joke.

[1] M. Gavard was then chief of the Cabinet of the Duc de Broglie.

After the Perponcher note to the Belgian government, came the note to the Italian government about the insufficiency of the law respecting "guarantees," the interdiction of the exportation of German horses, and lastly a menacing article to the Berlin *Post* of April 9th. I shall not concern myself with the causes which produced the panic that spring on the Continent; I shall deal with the consequences of it in England only. On the 8th of April, without having received the least hint from the ministry, it occurred to me in the course of a conversation with Lord Derby to refer to the indications of an alarming attitude on the part of Prince Bismarck. I found the chief of the Foreign Office quite without anxiety on that score. I sent an account of this first conversation to the Duc Decazes in a private letter written at the Athenæum immediately on my departure from Downing Street. According to my custom I sent to the ministry by despatch the substance of this conversation. Here is, according to my report of April 8th, Lord Derby's conversation:

" 'No news, good news.' I see nothing on the Continent to alarm us for the preservation of peace, I repeat what I said to you a year ago; I have no anxiety about this year. I confine myself, it is true, to this year; but in the present state of Europe peace even for that short period means a great deal. Of the two notes with which you are so preoccupied, the one seems to have disappeared—at least the Italian government denies ever having received it, the other will prove of no consequence. It was simply a threat of Bismarck's to his adversaries at home; he wanted to make them believe they are vulnerable to him on every side; he, too, felt a wish to publish an *encyclical.* He has got his hands full with the Catholic Church. In order to understand events in Germany one must consider two things: the nation is aware, since its success, that it has alarmed all its neighbors and is pursued by the idea that they are preparing to combine; Germany sees a coalition in everything and wishes to conjure it away. On the other hand Bismarck's temperament must never be lost sight of; he has become more and more irritable; he is no longer master of his nerves. He is credited often enough nowadays with calculations and combinations when he is merely yielding to an outbreak of temper; such for example is the interdict put upon the exportation of horses: a measure conceived in a moment of passion, which harms nobody but the German producers. Don't fancy it an indication of extraordinary preparations or of an immediate establishment of the German army on a war basis. . . ."

Passing finally to Emperor William's trip to Italy, Lord Derby said: "Considering his age and the state of his health it is easier to explain why he has given over the trip than why he ever undertook it."

As to the maintenance of peace during that year, or rather during that parliamentary session, Mr. Gladstone had held about the same language in conversation with me on the eve of the elections. In effect in the month of April the Tory ministry regarded the state of Europe with the same optimism and quite as little foresight as the ministry that preceded it. Meanwhile the "press" began to be excited. The interview at Venice between the Emperor of Austria and King of Italy, the professions of friendship exchanged between them, the manifest vexation of Germany, and Emperor William's abandonment of his trip to Italy, were all remarked in London by the few who at that time took an especial interest in foreign politics.

On the 9th Baron Solvyns, the Belgian minister, with whom (as well as with Baron de Beust, Austrian Ambassador), I have shared this campaign, informed me that Lord Derby had strongly advised his government, as a means of strengthening its position, to consider whether something could not be done for Prince Bismarck in the Duchesne affair. He recognized for his part the inadequacy of the Belgian law which does not protect people in other countries against threats of death emanating from Belgian territory. By the 10th I noted a general alarm in the daily and weekly papers. The *Times*, *Standard*, *Telegraph* and the *Daily News* vied with each other in the vigor of their expressions of reprobation for the policy revealed in the article in the Berlin *Post*. The *Economist* believed that the blow was rather directed against Austria and Italy than against France. This idea will make its way.

On April 12th there was a fresh inquiry in Parliament. Although it came from an Irish member, the Prime Minister thought it necessary to answer it himself. Mr. Disraëli said that the note addressed to Belgium was only a friendly remonstrance and not a threat, and that he regarded the incident as closed. He finished, however, with some bravado about the independence of Belgium, if she should ever be threatened.

Hardly had Mr. Disraëli finished with his peaceful assurances on the subject of the relations between Germany and Belgium when the report was spread that a third note had been sent to the Cabinet at Brussels. Public opinion, following the newspapers, covered Belgium with its ægis; and I never doubted, for my part, that England, whatever its government, would not allow anybody to lay hands on Belgium. So far as France was concerned, the *Times* was at this particular juncture arguing that our inability to hurl back Germany's defiance was a guaranty of the peace of Europe. The *Standard* confined itself to giving advice impartially to statesmen and to nations alike, whoever they might be, that were meditating war, not to count too absolutely on England's supposed indifference.

On the 19th, the government was questioned both in the House of Commons by an Irishman, and in the House of Lords by poor Lord Russell, who hardly counts for more than an Irishman, in public opinion. He no longer knows what he is saying, he can't hear anything that is said to him in reply, and keeps on talking even while he is being spoken to. After the ministerial explanations, Lord Granville, who is really also a bit deaf, shouted the substance of them in his lordship's ear. The House waited patiently. Such scenes (they occur often) are really pitiful; the family try in vain to avoid them. Lord Russell has his things printed, when he cannot speak

—like a superannuated magistrate who cannot bring himself to quit the bench. The odd thing is that no serious speaker in either House thrusts these shadows aside. When Lord Russell is absolutely unable to come to Parliament, Lord Campbell of Stratheden speaks. Nothing gives one a stranger idea of the political mind of this House than to see them listening patiently to the words escaping from the mouth of this invalid, bit by bit, amidst the most painful contortions. One of my neighbors called them "minute guns";—comparing his empty and solemn verbiage to the blast of a gun in an official salute. No matter who it may be that asks a question, the government has never failed to profit by the occasion, not indeed to reply to it, but to give such explanations as it may think desirable. It was after all clever enough to have the inquiry come from a member whose words do not count: the reply was less difficult.

The two questions, or at least the two replies, bore on the Belgium affair only. It has not as yet occurred to the English government that there was anything else to consider.

In the House of Commons Mr. Disraëli found himself called upon to explain the conduct of the cabinet that preceded his. He spoke of a "strong representation" addressed in February, 1874, by Prince Bismarck to Belgium on the subject of the conspiracy hatched in that country by the ultramontaine party. He did not conceal the fact that the German Ambassador had asked the Queen's government to support this representation at Brussels and that he had been politely dismissed, with expressions of confident hope that Prince Bismarck would not insist on the Belgium government's overstepping the limits, within which the government of a Catholic country endowed with free institutions must confine itself. The Premier added that no communication of the same nature had since then been received by the Queen's government.

In the House of Lords, as well as one could understand Lord Russell, the Liberal veteran, offered himself as the champion rather of Prince Bismarck against poor little Belgium. Lord Derby declared that he considered the third and last communication from Belgium as perfectly friendly. He did his best to put a damper on the fire of public opinion and assured the House that the conclusions "of the incident left no ground of anxiety as to the integrity and independence of Belgium."

The next day Lord Derby assured me again that he saw nothing especially threatening in the Perponcher note; he confessed, however, that the author had so wrapped his meaning up in generalities that he (Derby) could not tell with any exactitude what it was all about.

He referred again to the advice he had given to Belgium to fill any gap there might be in her legislation in the matter of affording protection to persons residing beyond her limits. I profited by the occasion to ask him if he believed that English law, as it stood, covered the Duchesne case, as Lord John Russell seemed to think. Inasmuch as Prince Bismarck seemed to wish to raise a question of general interest apropos of the incident and was disposed according to all appearances to address himself to other governments, I felt it important to know if the English considered themselves as not involved in the question. Without replying to my inquiry Lord Derby observed to me that Germany voluntarily offered a guaranty of good faith, since she proposed to submit her own legislation to revision. I could not help pointing out to him that it would be easier to have recourse to the Tribunals at Brussels than to those of Berlin. He agreed.

Not having received as yet my instructions from Paris, I did not dare to push Lord Derby any further, and I asked the Duc Decazes whether he thought it well for me to continue to draw out the cabinet at London. Without waiting for his reply I took up the conversation once more at the Foreign Office on the 28th of April; I began by admitting with Lord Derby, that the Belgium matter was in a fair way of settlement, but I added that it was none the less important to know the purpose of these notes, these experiments of all sorts, newspaper articles, knowingly indiscreet remarks which are spreading alarm through Europe. Whatever their cause might be, Lord Derby admitted their bad effect. I added that these singular measures might well be intended simply to put one on the wrong scent. He in his turn spoke of the armaments Germany was adding with such haste. To my question "Why these armaments were being pushed" he replied, "you know that the interview at Venice caused much discontent at Berlin; Prince Bismarck's irritation was much noticed, and it confirmed the opinion already held by the men best in a position to judge of the state of affairs in Europe ; they think that the storm which sometimes threatens France, and sometimes Belgium, will burst at last over Austria. After having excluded Austria from the German Empire, Bismarck now reproached her for contracting alliances with other nations. Meanwhile I do not believe in immediate war ; I give you however only an opinion." The conversation then turned on the German army which Lord Derby did not believe proof against a prolonged war. " There was much discontent among the *landwehr*,"[1] he said, " at the close of the siege of Paris ; and if you could have held out for some time longer, there would have been an outbreak." After that he spoke of the fear of a coalition which seemed to haunt Bismarck. I replied that it seemed natural he should fear a coalition. Following his train of thought, he added, that Napoleon I. was always astonished to see coalition after coalition formed against himself, though he never ceased to provoke them by threatening or crushing his neighbors.

I reported in full this long conversation, which started with the fears that the conduct of Germany had excited in all Europe, and ended in recollections of the coalitions which had resulted in the fall of the first Empire. In forwarding it to Paris I took care to put the ministry on its guard against any premature conclusions about the designs of the English Government. The report, I insisted, was significant

* Militia.

only as indicating the state of mind of the Secretary of State of the British government, and his opinion that neither France nor Belgium was threatened, but only Austria. Lord Derby's position was elsewhere developed in an article that had appeared the preceding Saturday in the *Spectator*, under the title: *Germany and Austria*. " Germany," said the *Spectator*, " knows that she owes in some measure her prodigious success to the diversion made by Italy in 1866, and to the incapacity of the French commander in 1870. She is preoccupied by the danger to which a coalition might subject her, and believes that the only way to be beforehand with this peril is to develop her army to the point of being able to defy a coalition. Prince Bismarck's scheme is to profit by the fears inspired by France's rapid recovery; but he does not seriously dread aggression on that side, so long as France remains without allies. If he should overrun France to-day, he would simply be forming another Poland on Germany's western frontier. To triumph over Russia, or to take permanent possession of the provinces on the Baltic, would demand a long war which would offer to France the occasion and the alliances of which she has need. Austria remains, and Prince Bismarck might, by a rapid campaign, win back into the Empire ten million Germans, who would be charmed to share in his success. Germany might stretch from Hamburg to Trieste before the neighboring powers could bring their armies into play ; and Germany with that addition would have no further coalition to fear."

The similarity that all this bears to Lord Derby's

language was striking. More than that, the considerations developed in the article are far from being without value to-day ; they were sound in 1875, they are not less so in 1879.[1] Prince Bismarck seems to have pursued the policy these ascribed to him, excepting only that he has abandoned armed occupation and employed conciliation in its stead.

He has made the Emperor of Austria enter Germany and accept a position such as the Margrave of Brandenbourg held in the old Confederation. He was assured that Austria would henceforth hold Russia in check with the connivance of England ; he had, therefore, no further coalition to fear.

My first instructions came on the 30th of April. They consisted in a series of extracts from the correspondence of our Ambassador at Berlin, ending with the strange and voluntary admission snatched from Prince Bismarck's confidant, M. de Radowitz. I hastened to communicate all these bits to Lord Derby, without comment. I knew I must not try to coerce him by arguments—that the best way was to put him in possession of facts, simply, and let him draw his own conclusions.

He still held fast to his former opinion, for the time being, that Austria alone was threatened, and that the danger for Austria even was not immediate. He called my attention to the fact that the ammunitions of war that the Cabinet of Berlin had recently been in such a hurry to get ready had come precisely from Austria. When he insisted on the salutary influence Russia might exercise at this moment at

[1] It was in 1879 that M. Gavard wrote these notes.

Berlin, I replied : "As much as England." In the diplomatic corps, the impression that Austria was in danger spread rapidly. There were persons who averred, however, that it was Turkey that would have to pay the price of an understanding between the three powers. Every one was guessing, and guessing wrong.

On the 6th, a private note from the Duc Decazes contained the following passage: "Hohenlohe came to tell me, before leaving for Munich, that Herr Von Bulow finds Gontaut very optimistic, and that the German Government is far from being entirely convinced of the inoffensive character of our armaments." This communication convinced me that the moment had come to try every means to induce the English Government to speak out. Strong in my convictions, I hastened to Lord Derby, and spoke to him with an emotion which was genuine. I believed there was immediate danger ; I fancied I might be of real service to my country. Lord Derby was moved (or did I only imagine it?) and came, before I left, to share my alarm. I give his words, the look and intonation with which he accompanied them I cannot give.

He said first that our fears, so far as the immediate future was concerned, were not shared by Lord Odo Russell.[1] Lord Odo, indeed, rather gave his Government reason to suspect that what Bismarck was at the moment aiming at was not so much a war, but a war scare. Lord Derby persisted in believing that if the Chancellor wanted the war, his first blow would be directed at Austria. He admitted, how-

[1] Lord Odo Russell was Ambassador at Berlin then.

ever, that the secret purposes of Bismarck, whose will was beyond control, were by no means plain, and that the present state of Europe reminded one of the days when her fate hung on the will of the First Napoleon. This justified me in suggesting: "And suppose the first blow should be levelled at France?" "Such an act of aggression," said Lord Derby, "would exite universal indignation in Europe, and nowhere more strongly than in England. Germany herself could not brave such an outburst of public opinion." When I urged him to be explicit—to say what form the manifestation of England's sympathy would take : "You may count on me," he said, "you may rely upon it that the Government will not shirk its duty. I give you all the assurances that a minister in a Constitutional Government can give." This declaration he made to me repeatedly and in various forms. The last words are literal.

I observed to Lord Derby that there are events that can be prevented by being foreseen, and that it was time England should declare herself. "Certainly," he said, and added : " I have already spoken to Count Munster. I told him that we did not take seriously the scare they were trying to foster in Germany on the subject of the armaments in France, that everybody knows France's present attitude is not a threatening one, that all this uproar looks too much like a pretext, and that I did not understand what interest his government could have in keeping Europe unsettled." Then I spoke of the meeting of the two Emperors at Berlin. Lord Derby assured me that he founded great hopes on Emperor Alexander's influence. " In especial," I added, " if it is supported by that of other powers who are not directly interested in peace." Lord Derby made it evident to me that he understood the importance of this addition and promised to inform me of whatever step might be taken. The conversation ended in a discussion of the evil Prince Bismarck might be meditating against France and Europe. I made a memorandum of all Lord Derby had said, and thanked him for his friendliness toward France.

In the account of this conversation I sent in a private letter to the Duc Decazes on the 7th, I said: " It would, of course, be a mistake to regard Lord Derby's words as a guarantee of effective aid in case of need ; but they are at least assurances such as were not given to us in 1870. It is an overture to be made the most of in case things take a bad turn."

My impression of Lord Derby's attitude was confirmed by a conversation I had with Count Beust, in which he spoke only of our just anxiety, and not of the dangers with which Austria might be threatened.

On the 8th appeared a long leader in the *Times* à *propos* of the correspondence published by Blowitz, at the instance of the Duc Decazes. It aimed at dissipating the alarm that publication had occasioned. A little more and it would have thrown the responsibility on us. Its language resembled that of Count Munster, who spouted smoke and flame, denouncing our armaments, and affirming that during negotiations for peace, Prince Bismarck would have consented to reduce the indemnity in exchange for an engagement on our part in relation to our effective military and naval forces. Cardinal Manning communicated to me a mandate that he intended to issue against Germany, and an appeal that the Catholic clergy of England were to address to the Catholics of the world against the persecution of which the church is the object in Germany. I confess I did not feel hopeful about the effect this manifestation would produce in England.

We had evidently touched the point where the crisis must, for good or evil, be faced, and the evening of the 9th, which was Saturday, I went to Lord Derby's reception with the firm intention of eliciting fresh explanations. He saved me the trouble of making the attempt. The moment he saw me he came forward; the people about us discreetly turned aside. Every one understood the gravity of our conversation, above all when, after some minutes, he called Lord Lyons, who was present at the reception, in order to repeat before him what he was telling me. He begged me to state to my government that his anxieties for the moment were at an end. He had just received from Lord Odo Russell, in reply to his last instructions, a telegram which left no room for doubt that the danger had been averted. He added that he had not been satisfied with this assurance, but had sent a telegram that same evening, advising the most energetic declarations in support of the Russian Emperor's peaceful counsel. He did not endeavor to disguise the fact that Russia's action had been more efficacious than that of his own government in this crisis. He wished, however, to demonstrate to me how it could not but be so ; Russia being prepared to support her remonstrances by arms. I could not help replying that he did not seem to me to attach sufficient importance to the English navy, which could not indeed prevent a war from arising but could prevent its long continuance. Lord Derby was silent. Presently, however, he added that aggression against France, under existing circumstances would have excited an outburst of moral indignation throughout the whole world that would have checked the Chancellor of the Empire himself. I made the observation that up to the present speaking obstacles merely moral could scarcely be said to have sufficed to block Prince Bismarck. "I expressed myself badly," he replied ; " what I meant was that there spreads abroad now and then an universal sentiment of uneasiness ; every one feels that he is in danger, and the result is such a coalition as that to which Napoleon I., in spite of his genius, was forced to succumb." *That* evening, at the Foreign office, I was " cock of the walk ; " everybody had divined the topic and drift of our conversation there in public.

Two days afterwards, Monday the 11th, Lord Derby gave me a copy of a telegram he had received from Berlin. The substance of it was as follows : Prince Bismarck thanks you for your kind services, but says they are unnecessary, and that he has not dreamed of disturbing the peace. " This is the reply," said Lord Derby, " to the instructions I sent on Saturday to Lord Odo, that he should back up

Russia. I know that Emperor Alexander's influence has been brought to bear on the same side as our own, and that he had decided to speak energetically if it should be necessary. All fear of conflict, however, is for the present at an end, the incident is closed. I do not believe, to say the truth, that Prince Bismarck dreamed really of attempting such a war; he wanted to feel public opinion simply—*and he has done it!*" Lord Derby pronounced the last words with marked emphasis.

Some hours later the same explanations were given in Parliament, amidst "cheers." The House testified by its evident satisfaction (and so also did the Press) the gravity of its fears. The general disapproval excited by the manœuvres of Prince Bismarck was not less marked than the general alarm. I closed my report for May 11th with the reflection, which was just and not immoderate, that: "During this last week we have not run more risks than we had the week before, but England had not taken account until now of the danger which threatened France and Europe. The revelation of this crisis, and the intimate communications it has occasioned between the two governments will leave some trace, I hope, in the minds of the Cabinet."

The next day, the 12th, confirmation of the good news reached me from every side. In the first place, Lord Derby expressly sent for me to come to see him. After telling me that the most favorable information on the score of peace was coming in from all quarters, he took on a diplomatic air which was not in the least becoming, to reveal to me in great confidence, that he had obtained no co-operation on the part of Austria, and that it had proved to be beyond his power, frightened as Austria was on her own account, to make her speak to Berlin.

It was Count Schouvaloff's turn next. He had arrived two days before on his way to Berlin. He commenced by handing me a telegram from Emperor Alexander, sent the same day, at the moment of his departure from Berlin. He said to his Ambassador, in express terms, that he took his leave completely assured of the maintenance of peace. Here, according to my despatch for the 12th of May, is what Count Schouvaloff said in the course of conversation. He thought all danger of war for the present at an end, but he did not try to conceal from me that it might well make its appearance again at almost any moment. He spoke then of the cause of this recurrent menace, and in what direction we should look for safety. "The danger," he said, "lies in Bismarck's fixed idea, that France is disposed to attack Germany, and unhappily (which is more unfortunate), the idea is shared by Von Moltke. He believes you will be ready by 1876, and that the moment will be so much more favorable for you because you will still have a class of older soldiers who have already seen service. The Chancellor believes you will wait till 1877; but both he and Von Moltke agree to anticipate you. They pretend that you are the aggressors according to this theory, which is not new in their mouths that the real aggressors are not those who make the attack, but those who make the attack necessary;

and they propose, as the result of a fresh campaign, an overwhelming indemnity and a prolonged occupation. . . . The "guarantee for peace" is that Russia does not want war. She is opposed to an aggression on either side. You know what the Emperor said to General Le Flo. I was commanded to repeat it in Berlin. I saw the old Emperor who seemed much astonished at our anxieties. He really did not believe the war imminent, but he is the only one in Berlin who was so ill-informed. It was not difficult to bring him to the point we wished when once he perceived how matters stood. As for Bismarck he knows that he can neither attack Russia because of you, nor attack you if Russia opposes him. Therefore I consider peace as assured, in spite of the alarms that may come up, for the reason that Russia does not want war, and that such an attitude on her part is not a Platonic one." Then followed an examination of the relative force of the respective powers, and of the straits in which Germany would find herself, if she endeavored to act either against Russia or without her help, or not at least without her kindly neutrality, as in the last war. He then spoke to me of revenge. He finds it natural that the desire to recover our lost provinces should lie at the bottom of every French heart, but he does not believe we shall be able to hasten it. He believes that we ought to wait till the occasion offers itself in some European complication. It was thus that the Treaty of Paris was annulled (in 1871, after fifteen years waiting), by Russia without striking a blow. Count Schouvaloff then brought the conversation back to Belgium to tell me that the opinion generally current in Berlin, and shared by men in a position to know, was that Bismarck had conceived the notion of bringing about a state of things which would allow him to offer Belgium to France in the hope of satisfying our rancor at that price. But he added that he had explained matters to Bismarck, who had disavowed the intentions that were attributed to him.

I replied to Count Schouvaloff that one could not attribute to a politician like Prince Bismarck motive's other than serious, and that his conduct in regard to Belgium seemed to me inexplicable. The Russian Ambassador said, that since we no longer understood Prince Bismarck, we had better look for the explanation of his conduct or of his purposes in the overexcited condition of his nerves, or in the nightmares that haunted him on restless nights. . . . On sending an account of this to the minister I reminded him that my interlocutor's speech was commonly as daring as it was abundant—that he affected to touch without reserve on the most delicate subjects, and that I could not be certain of anything about him except of his desire to see me fail in my promised discretion.

On the 14th, Lord Derby informed me that he was on his way to Knowsley[1] for ten days, and observed that his departure testified to his feeling of security, and asked me to keep him informed of anything that might occur during his absence. "You know," said he, "that at Berlin no one wishes to confess ever having even thought of war. Prince

[1] Lord Derby's country place in Lancashire.

Bismarck blames it all on Von Moltke, in which he is perhaps not wrong; but, however true it may be, as he affirms, that he never thought of war himself, he has in any event talked a great deal. . . .

This is the way I ended my despatch for that day: "Perhaps it would be advisable, the present crisis (which will doubtless be followed by others) being at an end, to ascertain where we stand and precisely at what point we should wish to begin our confidential communications with the English government in case the danger at present conjured away should reappear. No doubt we have escaped war this once because Russia refused to act in complicity with Germany; but it is no less certain that England has spoken, at Berlin and elsewhere, in favor of peace. . . . (the Queen's letter to Emperor William). I am confident that it is not alone to me that Lord Derby has given reason to suspect the coming of one of those European coalitions that issue from time to time out of the common danger, and that triumph over Empires supported by genius even. In any event, I believe that it is greatly to our interest to take account of what England has done for the maintenance of peace; we should perhaps even do well to encourage her by expressing our recognition of the course she has pursued. The cabinet has showed itself very sensible of the notices in the press, on its firm attitude in this affair. My colleagues in the diplomatic corps have echoed them too in their conversations. It would be well if the French press would not forget to mention England's share in the results obtained."

The Duc Decazes, in a long letter dated the 14th and which did not reach me till late, replied to the wish I had expressed. It contained words of thanks for Lord Derby and also for Mr. Delane of the *Times*, whom I had also recommended to his gratitude. He charged me to tell Lord Derby with what sentiments of gratitude we had welcomed the news of his intervention, etc., etc.

I replied the same day, May 15th: "I am enchanted with the messages you have authorized me to deliver to Lord Derby in your name. They are all that could be desired. I shall send him, in the country, an extract of your letter which says so happily and justly all that is necessary. Are not the deceptive promises you speak of essentially contained in the gossip about Belgium Count Schouvaloff took the trouble to collect at Berlin? I replied, you know, that I could not attribute other than serious purposes to Prince Bismarck. I am very much on my guard with this brilliant talker—he does not inspire confidence in any one here. That is in especial the opinion of the Duke of Cambridge. Here is what the Duke said to me day before yesterday: 'What a week we have just been through! It is said that things are settled, and that Russia has preserved the peace of Europe. But I do not believe that anything is settled: it will all begin again at the first opportunity. I no more count on Russia than I do on the beautiful speeches of her ambassador.' 'Let me at least count on England,' I said. He exclaimed: 'What can I say to you of England. The Tories are in power, the danger is flagrant, the people realize it, and would refuse us money for an army.'"

Lord Derby answered me by private letter dated at Knowsley the 17th. ". . . . assure the Duc Decazes that it is for me, and for the government of which I am a member, a double pleasure to have done what was in our power for the maintenance of peace in Europe and to have done it for and in concert with the French nation. . . . We shall have to take precautions and to be prudent on all sides to avoid a renewal of the dangers from which we have escaped. But personally I do not admit the pretended necessity of a European war. I think (this is my personal opinion) that very few wars have been necessary and very few just. . . ."

This letter shows that Lord Derby believed he deserved the thanks that I had sent him. We shall see the whole Cabinet (after the event) banking on the gratitude due them for what he has done.

This incident, which began near the middle of April and which reached a crisis during the first week of May, was at last closed. It is interesting, however, to consider the consequences of it. Every one was looking at it and using it from his own point of view. Count Schouvaloff was pleased that it had all happened; it had shown England and Russia what their standing together could do. He added that England and Russia's uniting together in support of France had accomplished the result which was the object of his mission to England, the bringing of the two governments closer together. He disavowed or disowned (it is neither the first nor the last time) the famous testament of Peter the Great. He protested that his government has no other object nor interest in the Orient than to prevent the establishment at Constantinople of a great power such as might embarrass or threaten Russia. "Who," continued he, "could better fill this programme than the Porte?"

After the event I was anxious to resume with Lord Derby the exchange of confidences, and to discover how far he might be disposed to go in return for my demonstrations of gratitude.

He began in very much the same tone as in his letters, and as he was going on with his usual scepticism about the inefficiency of intermediation in general, I checked him and asked him to make a distinction between an impartial intermediation between two powers who are discussing a doubtful point and an intermediation inspired by a profound feeling that one of the parties is in the right and a profound disapproval of the threats uttered by its antagonist. I observed that such an intermediation engaged the intervening powers too deeply not to be of consequence in some way or other. Lord Derby did not deny it. The review of the situation led him to speak energetically, *à propos* of Belgium, against any country's attempting to shackle liberty of speech and the freedom of the press in any other country. He seemed satisfied with the contrast I drew, in closing, between the attitude of the Government and public opinion under the Liberal Ministry and under the Conservative Cabinet since the close of the war : On the one hand public opinion hesitating, and the Government extreme in its reserve; on the other, the movement which has swept away public opinion in these last days, and the encouragement and the support we have found in the Tory Cabinet. Lord Derby seemed to relish the compliment. Subsequent events prevented him from forgetting it, and one may see (in the course of these notes) how, as time went on, he came, in 1875, to extend rather than to diminish the scope of his intervention in continental affairs. One may see to what use he put my testimony, to justify himself against the reproach of indecision, of pusillanimity, of inaction, with which his adversaries overwhelmed him when he went out of the Cabinet,

On the evening of May 29th, a question of Lord Russell's, quite as unintelligible as any of its predecessors, gave Lord Derby an occasion to produce before the public, information which had been received and kept secret by the Cabinet.

Here are my comments, the next day, on the interview, of which I had given an account that evening by telegram: " If the declarations of Lord Derby revealed to us nothing that we did not know before, they at least constitute an avowal in public of much that previously we were not in a position to affirm. For the future nobody can deny the existence of the danger, which the *Times* did not exaggerate in the correspondence from Paris, that created so much excitement; nobody can deny the existence of the menaces which the German Ambassador echoed in London. On the other hand, England's feeling about the projected act of aggression, her conviction respecting the purely defensive character of our armaments, her intervention with the power which had provoked the alarm in Europe, the initiative that the London Cabinet took in relation to Russia, her making common cause with that Government, are at length made certain. Also the dangers of the future are equally foretold. The intention of the English Government to remain no longer an indifferent spectator in continental affairs is evident from Lord Derby's last words, which were received with unanimous approval. . . . I consider the publicity which he has given to his convictions and to the conduct of the Cabinet at London of serious importance. Trivial causes, these past weeks, have been producing great effects. When Lord Derby first admitted that he was becoming anxious, but affirmed that the object of Germany's hostile preparations was at least not France, he was far from anticipating the steps Lord Odo has had to take in co-operation with Russia.

Bismarck's thanks (which did not sufficiently hide a tone of irony) provoked a fine and sarcastic retort from Mr. Disraëli, when he was questioned on the subject of Count Munster's speech at the *National Club*. Circumstances have lent this speech, which in itself was nothing but a piece of stupidity, the proportions of a serious incident. The reverberation of Lord Derby's words will help rouse public opinion and magnify afterwards the importance of this first step of England's in favor of justice and peace.

After the danger had passed, everybody grew bolder—in which of course I saw no harm.

Neither did I think it useful to investigate the reason for the unanimous approval meted out to Lord Derby's language. If the defence of the European equilibrium possessed its serious partisans on the benches where, what is left of, English Toryism sits, no doubt the cheers of the partisans of 'peace at any price' swelled their applause. The radicals cheered too—cheered the cessation of a peril—the termination of the affair. It might have terminated as in 1871 by a second amputation of France, and they would still have cheered.

The danger passed, Lord Derby became more and more expansive. He said to me on June 4th: " I really believe that our intervention contributed to the maintenance of peace, and I also believe, whatever may be said now, that the danger was great." I questioned him about what guarantee we possessed for the future against the recurrence of similar dangers. " The Old Emperor," he said, " does not want war, but we have seen that he is not kept informed of what goes on about him. Prince Bismarck does want war, and is anxious it should come off during Emperor William's life. The Crown Prince is a just man, not at all bellicose, but he is pursued by the idea that it is necessary to put the finishing stroke to German unity by reducing to subjection to the Empire the states which still retain a semblance of autonomy, and he does not believe that that can be done except by a foreign war. For the present, our main lookout must be to keep the old Emperor from being circumvented. England possesses means of letting him know the truth, and, as you know, she has used them. As for the Crown Prince, the matter is more difficult, since, notwithstanding his antipathy to war, he agrees with Bismarck. England has stood in this last crisis with Russia and also with Italy. It is probable that we should continue to stand with Russia as long as Alexander lives. He aspires to the rôle of peacemaker in Europe; he does not dream of the conquest of Constantinople. We must believe that his moderation will suffice to overbear both the ambition of the Russian people and the spirit of perfidious intrigue abroad;—but who will come after him! Lord Derby confirmed me in my belief that Austria had done nothing. Was it from pure timidity, or from a secret hope of coming to some better understanding with Germany?

I had been especially careful not to hint at the responsibilities that England's honorable conduct might involve her in, but the newspapers were not so reserved. The *Standard, Post, Pall Mall Gazette, Fortnightly, Spectator* and some radical organs, put the question squarely, and the *Spectator* solved it by saying: " It is England's duty for the future to stand on guard to maintain the balance of power on the Continent, and on guard in uniform, not in citizens' clothes."

My conversations with Lord Derby continued on this friendly footing till the arrival of the new Ambassador, the Marquis d'Harcourt (June 25th), put an end to my administration. The intimacy which had established itself between the First Secretary of

State and me, during this crisis, survived the Marquis's arrival; it survived even his term of office. I know that I made great progress in Lord Derby's confidence by not trying to see Mr. Disraëli during the crisis. He was pleased that I had trusted the affair to him and had spared him the difficulty of having to agree with the Premier on what they should say. I was advised to act thus and the issue proved that the advice was good.

The Duc Decazes wrote me the following letter:

"June 24. My uncle leaves to-morrow by way of Boulogne. I make a point of announcing it to you. I take this occasion to tell you how much we have appreciated the wisdom, the prudence, the efficiency of your administration.

"You more than any one else had deplored England's long silence in continental affairs; it was right that you should assist at her glorious awakening; and indeed you had in a sense a hand in it."

Extracts from the Correspondence.

LONDON, April 7, 1875.

What struck me most in my expedition[1] was the waving of the handkerchiefs from the windows as long as the Prince of Wales's train remained in sight, and the cheers from every one physically capable of a cheer. We arrived at Chatham in the rain, with nothing but umbrellas to shelter Bylandt's and my

---

[1] M. Gavard had been invited to Chatham to be present at the launching of a vessel.

finery. We had to walk four kilometres through the crowd, in the mud, our swords under our arms and gold-braided pantaloons turned up at bottom. We were "guyed" at by a double row of thirty thousand people, but the most of it fell to our colleague, the Shah's share. After this little pedestrian Odyssey we arrived at last at "Stand A;" the threshold crossed we became princes once more. At first I did not understand what the great wall was that we were lining up against; on reflection I perceived it was the keel of the "Alexandra."

At the appointed hour the cannon boomed; the princes and princesses arrived. The Archbishop of Canterbury said a prayer; but the tide was not full, and even their Royal Highnesses must wait. At last the "Godmother"[1] pressed a spring and a bottle of champagne covered with flowers was broken over the prow. Heavy blows resounded from right to left, almost like so many explosions; it was the sound of the supports giving way under the hammer. The mass began imperceptibly to move; smoke rose behind her; the explosions swelled a frightful fusilade: there was no further need to try and draw the spikes—they broke like so many matches under the moving weight. Finally she went with a rush. The view opened out and presently the "Alexandra" was floating tranquilly three hundred mètres from the stocks. There were cheers and booming cannon, and a solemn parade (in the mud) between a double row of sailors and volunteers toward the Admiralty. We arrived at

[1] The Princess of Wales.

last, escorting the ladies, at a handsome red and white tent where lunch was served; there was not too much wind blowing and we had music, toasts, and a speech from the Prince. After lunch we smoked; the Prince paid me some agreeable compliments. We were offered a place for the return trip in the Royal train: there was no time to be lost, so we hastened madly through the crowd and mud. Bylandt, Ransès and I arrived a good first. Schenk same too late; like a true " Yankee," he wanted to get on the moving train; but the guard pulled him away from the door. He found Musurus, the Greek, and the other wastes and strays of the Diplomatic corps, to console himself with.

LONDON, April 22, 1875.

Yesterday at a dinner at the " Foreign Office " I sat at Lord Derby's right, near the Duke of Cleveland, who is not exactly impecunious, and next to the Marchioness of Exeter, who told me that she possesses the most beautiful country house in England, and to the Countess of Galloway, who has immense estates in Scotland and a castle overlooking the sea from three sides. Opposite me sat the Duke of Norfolk, who has more than two hundred thousand pounds a year; a little farther on was Lord Ellesmere, successor of the Duke of Bridgewater, who owns four forgotten Raphaels in an abandoned town house. Mlle. Meyer de Rothschild was also there; she has more millions to her dowry than I have pence in my pocket, and last of all, plain Mr. Disraëli, the Prime Minister. I shall not speak of the diamonds that sparkled in the lights and were reflected in the silver service. A rumbling military band filled the gaps in the conversation. I forgot to say that the Duke of Cambridge entered with "God Save the Queen." By the way, I asked my neighbor about Lord Bedford's fortune: it is more than 300,000 pounds a year—that is 7,500,000 francs; and Lord Derby has only a little less, between 200,000 and 300,000 pounds a year.

LONDON, April 26, 1875.

I dined with Mr. Baillie Cochrane. . . . We talked of this scandalous mission of the two revivalists, Moody and Sankey, two genuine "Yankees". The one sings and sells organs and music; the other converts sinners, male and female! After the meeting, they hold consultations without music. The ordinary Conference-Hall is no longer large enough. It is in the Opera-House that they meet now in the daytime; it is there that they meet the master. Sometimes it is Moody, sometimes Sankey, who gets up, illuminated, and announces that he sees the Lord. After each meeting Sankey telegraphs to his manager in New York: So many organs sold, so many souls saved!

LONDON, April 27, 1875.

Yesterday evening I went to the Opera to hear Moody and Sankey. There was only a substitute present so I found a seat easily. It seems that it is Sankey's music that produces the miracle. A handsome blond opened the meeting in his stead, and edified the meeting with his pious gesticulations. Sometimes he asked for singing, and sometimes for prayer.

At the signal for song, a "spinster" (what we should call *une vieille demoiselle*) sat down at the organ, and played a devout tune and everybody sang. The man on my right had evidently come to make his high notes heard; the one on my left, to come out strong at the end of a verse with a sing-song bass; but there were those also who had really come to the Opera-House to find God. After the music, every one began to pray out loud; weariness and sleep overtook the assembly, and as no miracle seemed forthcoming, the young blond hurriedly dismissed the meeting. There is only one God and one Moody.

Day before yesterday I was talking with Kinnaird, M. P., and heir presumptive of a peerage, in one of the lobbies of the House of Lords. We both had our hats on. The Marquis of Lansdowne came by with his on too; he is very young. Kinnaird passed the time of day with him and talked a bit, taking his hat off; but the Marquis did not give the slightest evidence of intending to run the risk of catching cold by taking off his.

LONDON, May 13, 1875.

Count Munster's toast is creating a stir. He was so imprudent as to accept an invitation to the National Club. It is an association of eccentrics who meet to the confusion of the Catholic clergy. A bit touched by what he heard around him on the politics of Bismarck, he pronounced a panegyric on that statesman, and mistook for a testimony of national sympathy the applause that this lot of simpletons gave to his glorification of the *Kultur Kampf* and to his declamations against the black men. Encouraged by their cheers, he forgot himself and proposed as an example for England the policy of the Chancellor, enforcing his advice by alarming insinuations relative to the situation of Ireland.

LONDON, May 21, 1875.

The Irish deputation having provoked an explanation in the House of the duties of an ambassador the debate came up yesterday in Parliament. Mr. Disraëli replied to the questions of the Irish members. Entirely recognizing that it is not usual for ambassadors to make political speeches at public gatherings, he hastened to add that he was too strong a partisan of liberty of speech to complain of the innovation which was being made. Then passing to the object of Count Munster's remarks, he gratuitously attributed to him an intention of taking a trip to Ireland, and he expressed the hope that he would be convinced, after the trip was over, that there was not the least analogy between the situation of the Catholic subjects of the German Emperor, and that of the subjects of the Queen. I do not know whether Count Munster fathomed the purpose of Disraëli's speech, but he went about everywhere protesting that he never dreamed of taking the trip.

I had a very interesting conversation with Lord

Derby, in relation to the future. Speaking of recent events, he said that he had perceived how deeply I felt everything I said, and how sincerely I believed it.

Yes, the crisis is over. Meeting me some days ago in the Foreign Office, Munster took me in his arms, thus certifying the peaceful intentions of his government.

Extracts from the Notes.

A journal of the life I led during the months of May and June would have this interest—it would show what can be done with twenty-four hours a day. The pleasures of the morning, of the day, of the evening, of the night occupied me no less than business itself. After all, the dinners and parties of the "season" are the business of a diplomatist who wishes to have an ear and an eye open on everything. What complicated my pursuit of pleasure and business was the preparation for the sale in Leicester Square for the French charities. At the death of Comte de Jarnac, everything fell on me. I had to procure in France things to sell; in England, people to sell them and to buy them. I never made a greater hit. The booths at the Embassy were loaded down, the most elegant ladies of English society, Protestants and Catholics alike, acted as saleswomen and that with enthusiasm. The ladies of the diplomatic corps and of the Embassy threw themselves into it with devotion, and so too did my society friends; and the mob poured in. Royalty was an acquisition as everywhere. The Duchess of Edinburgh came in person, and I can testify that she and the Duke showed their generosity. She was most gracious to France and to her representative. In brief, the sale was a great success, socially and financially. I profited by the first and the charities of the second. The sale brought in 60,000 francs, of which nearly 52,000 francs are net. These figures have not been equalled since.

Extracts from the Correspondence.

LONDON, October 25, 1875.

I have made a trip with Beust, and here is some information for Klaczko: When Count von Beust was still in the service of Saxony, the Emperor of Austria gave him, immediately after the battle of Sadowa, a message to Napoleon. He was to ask Napoleon not to declare war against Prussia, but to send the camp at Chalons to the frontier, and to oblige Prussia to recognize him as a mediator. He found the emperor in a state of complete physical and nervous prostration. All he got from him were the words, repeated again and again, "I have no army, I can do nothing."

I have been to the theatre with Austin Lee. The scenery played protagonist. You saw a prisoner go through a wall, then the wall turned and the prisoner was outside, where an electric moon and the villain of the piece were waiting for him. Happily he drowned the villain; and though he was himself killed two or three times, he came to life again and,

Fenian as he was, embraced, in the final apotheosis, and was embraced by, an officer of the Queen. They made a mess of a scene in the pantomime which might have produced great effect. It was an Irish wake. The corpse lay there exposed in the miserable hut which in life had been his home ; an old hag improvised a lamentation in strophes in honor of his memory. A chorus of women, relations and neighbors, responded in antistrophes, lifting their arms to heaven. Unhappily, every time the hag turned her head the corpse sat up and emptied the pot of beer at her elbow. It seems that in Irish wakes the beer-mugs are replenished often. It ruins the solemnity of the ceremony.

LONDON, November 10, 1875.

I have been to the City to a banquet at London Tavern. The commissioners of the Guild-hall Library invited me this year as usual. I was very kindly welcomed from the time I stood up, and was cheered when I spoke of the 'Journal of the Proceedings of the Common Council': "It begins in the year 1485 and reaches to your meeting last night. It is beautiful to be able to follow across four centuries, the uninterrupted deliberations of your municipal parliament, which, under every change of government, has preserved the charter of its liberties, which it has never attempted to abuse in an effort to encroach upon the rights of the nation. . . ."

There were certainly a hundred and fifty people present—members of the corporation, doctors, men of letters and artists. The chairman, a champagne merchant, proposed a very gracious toast in honor of me as a representative of the diplomatic corps, and he added a eulogy of Comte de Jarnac. Then there was music by four men who sang together without an accompaniment. It was semi-devotional but fairly well done. Then my turn came. I had not anticipated the eulogy of M. de Jarnac, and I had to begin with some words in honor of his memory. Then I pulled my little *extempore* speech out of my pocket and went ahead. One of the men next me drank nothing but water; he is an active member of the temperance movement—what they call a "teetotaller." Explain that word who can! He did the clown in the evening's entertainment—supplied a mixture of the ridiculous, and finished his toast with a glass of water. Many glasses were turned down in sign of agreement with him, but the assembly stood true to the "good bombards."

WESTONBIRT-HOUSE,[1] November 14, 1875.

It was foggy and rainy when I started and grew worse *en route*. There was nothing but an endless expanse of water to be seen. I felt as if the entire country must be inundated, from London to Tetbury. But the important thing is not to miss the station. The rain came down in torrents; it was impossible to distinguish anything or to put one's nose outside. Even the guards stayed in. I got out, however, at my station, and found the door. The only person I met was a little girl crying, whom I took in charge,

[1] Mr. Holford's country house.

though her gibberish was beyond me. She wanted to go back to Tetbury, and the coachman took her up by him. For ten miles nothing but rain. Then I saw the little town of Tetbury with its pointed roofs and windows in the style of the Renaissance. After an hour and a half I arrived at the park, and then at the house. It seemed like a palace to me. They live in one corner of it only.

The young ladies came down in long flounced dresses. After dinner Evy played some Gounod for me and the sonata which they call here "Moonlight." Then the mother sang from her Italian repertoire,—she manages her contralto with much art. It was exquisite. Mr. Holford talked with me first about his pack of hounds, forty spaniels; then of "poor rates," and "school-boards," in English, if you please. I am now here in my room. The wind whistles around the house. I am going to sleep in a bed big enough for fifteen, and in a room of like dimensions.

SUNDAY.

The storm did not let up all night, and avalanches of water fell on the roof; but it stood firm. I have not been able to go out, except in a carriage to Malmesbury, a little town six miles from here, where I found mass in a little wooden chapel, hard by the splendid ruins of an ancient abbey in which the Anglicans have fashioned for themselves a chapel. These little English villages without manufactories are not without their charms. The ruins of the abbey, with the ivy, broken arches, and antique sculptures, possess a beauty of their own.

Then I had leisure to see the country. It is good fox-hunting ground—meadows with hedges that can be leaped, barriers everywhere that can be lifted. One may ride anywhere across country in a hunt: except in a hunt it would not be permitted. Practically the English are fox-worshippers: six days in every week they adore him, and on the seventh kill him, or kill themselves in the attempt. Nothing is sacred; the church loses its right of refuge, the home even is not respected; they kill their prey wherever they run it down—before the altar or on the hearth, even if they have to break in through the roof.

The Duke of Beaufort, who lives at Badminton near here, hunts every day. To-morrow if the weather is fair I am going six miles to see the start of the men in red, the women in riding-habits, the dogs and the horses. When I say, if the weather permits, I refer to myself, for the others think nothing of weather.

This morning I have lost no time. Sometimes Mrs. Holford, sometimes Evy, took me about the house, which surpasses in magnificence any that you know. There is a hall, a sort of conservatory three stories high, something like the great apartments of Louis XIV. The most original room in the house is the one painted by Mrs. Holford, in a bizarre, fanciful style, something between Delacroix landscape and Rouen pottery. When the mother sat down the daughter played cicerone in her stead, going on before with her long braids down her back, her shawl thrown over her shoulders after the fashion of a Roman peasant. She is very agreeable and seems to have become stronger, though you have the feeling that if you were to look at her very hard you might see through her. Minnie is not very well and shows herself but seldom. The mother decidedly has distinction, one understands where the daughters get theirs.

MONDAY.

The sun shines—" Alleluia ! " and then your letter of Saturday has arrived. The ground is frozen, covered with white frost. I have been sent for to go about the place. The house is an old palace surrounded by gardens, with ponds and fountains, etc. The architecture is like Versailles and decorative in effect. Then there is the park—endless, undulating stretch of verdure with great clumps of trees which extends for I don't know how far.

The hunt! I can really say that I hunted with the Duke of Beaufort's pack. It is the same as if I had. At half-past ten I started in a carriage with my two small friends and their grandmother. We reached the " hunt " six miles away, in a neighboring park. As we drew near we could see, coming here and there through the fields, a man in blue uniform with gold buttons, round hat, and white breeches. The roads were dotted with pony chaises and victorias; and lastly, there were all the children and working people of the country round, all going to the " hunt." We found already gathered a goodly number of gentlemen, and of farmers who have none the less good horses. The friends only of the Duke wear his uniform ; others wear the red hunting suits of the neighboring hunt. Grooms with reserve horses for the second portion of the day, stood behind the cavaliers who were waiting for the hunt to begin. The ladies of the party wore white breastplates on their habits. The pack arrived at last. The first " whip " came on ahead in green, then all the dogs with their tails in the air. The second " whip," the Master of the Hounds, is also Marquis of Worcester, the Duke's son ; he takes personal charge of the hounds. The horsemen moved about bowing and chatting with the occupants of the carriages. The Duke of Beaufort, who has handed over the direction of the hunt to his son, regretted the absence of a number of the customary hunters, who had been kept away by the grounds being softened by the rain. One of the huntswomen, Maid of Honor to the Princess of Wales, came to our carriage to pass the time of day. When the signal was given, the column moved toward the woods, where they expected to start a fox. It was a helter-skelter squadron of one hundred and fifty, dressed in all all colors ; gentlemen, farmers, ladies and " girls "— almost babies. A regular mob accompanied them. Gamins, soldiers in red coats, peasants all keeping up as best they could. Our carriage took a road at one side. We saw the column stop on the borders of a wood, waiting for a sign from the dogs who had disappeared among the trees. Many of the stragglers cut across lots and caught up with the main body of the hunt ; others looked on from a distance in hopes the fox would come their way. Fancy our luck! The dogs swept toward us, a herd of cattle helter-skelter along with them. They crossed the road two hundred feet ahead of us. The cavalcade came after—bore down back of us on a fence which they trampled to pieces beneath their horses' feet. As we were directly in their way, they turned right and left to avoid us—some down into the ditches, others headed by two little girls of twelve to fifteen years of age leaping the hedge. They found the dogs in fields on the other side of the road. They came up with them and opened out—the dogs had lost their scent! They hesitated, hunted, and took the second hedge. One red-coat had a fall, but was on horseback again before I had noticed him. One or two ladies took advantage of an opening, and the whole crowd disappeared,

And it will all be done over again to-morrow and the day after. There are always the same horsemen five times a week. The Marquis of Worcester will not miss once for four months running; then—he will return to his regiment. Decidedly, it is more than a pastime—it is a passion, it is a national institution. High and low, everybody shares it, beginning with the good people whose fences are knocked down, whose turnips are trodden underfoot by a hundred and fifty horses, not to mention the mob on foot, that keeps up I don't know how! It is dusk as I write. The hunt is scarcely over yet. And every one is coming back, at the cost of six, seven or eight miles more, in addition to those he has galloped during the day over flooded country, over walls and hedges and fences. I ought to say that when I saw the start and the cavalry charge I had a strong desire to be in it. I understand the attraction ; but every day for four months is steep !

After luncheon my friends took me in a pony chaise, across the beauties of the park to the keeper's lodge. I saw conservatories without end, then a lake, a bit of a wild, heaps of rocks that it seems have been newly brought there. And the lake too is a thing of yesterday. The pheasants were so thick we fairly trod on them. At last we reached the Head-keeper's lodge, and saw a pack of thirty spaniels with legs short enough to make the rabbits dance for joy !

It is all so beautiful and so well cared for that in the heart of the country, one loses the sense of nature. The hand of man is visible everywhere though he himself is not in sight. I returned on foot, walking by Mrs. Holford in the chaise.

I must close, because of time and space, not from lack of matter.

Extracts from the Notes.

I had charge of the Embassy for some time, in November and December. I undertook the responsibility in the most complete ignorance of what attitude the French Government wished maintained at London, and the situation of affairs was delicate. Relations between the conservative cabinet and Russia were visibly strained. Everything indicated that England had given up the doctrine of non-interference in matters of foreign politics, and that she was prepared to give a sign of life, or rather of resurrection from the dead, in the East. It went hard not to be authorized to put in a word at London; but I tried at least to make it understood at Paris that the situation was grave. This was the object of a dispatch, or rather of a memorandum, which I sent the home Government on the 19th of November, concerning the state of mind and attitude of each party in England toward foreign politics. Their interest in the European equilibrium, the Colonies, the Eastern question, *i. e.* the Indian Empire, the two routes leading there, the one for Russia by Central Asia, the other for England by the Suez Canal; what England will tolerate and what she will not tolerate in Europe and elsewhere. . . . My observations still seem to me to be correct, and have thus far been confirmed by events. In any event they were at the moment extremely *à propos*, reaching Paris as they did five days before the buying in of the Suez Shares belonging to the Khedive.

I did not stop, however, with this general warning, I sent at the same time under date of the 20th a more precise account, which was intended to open their eyes to the attitude the cabinet was prepared to take in the East, and in especial in Egypt. The morning of the 20th I received word from Duc Decazes asking me what effect the company's action in pushing the Khedive's stock would have on the English Government. The declarations I obtained from Lord Derby may be read in my despatch of the 20th. It is recorded in the French Yellow Book for 1875. They were categorical, and marked clearly England's intention if the Khedive should be obliged to dispose of his shares to meet the threatened demands upon his treasury, not to let them go into other hands than their own, and in especial not into French hands. But in spite of my urgent desire for authority to open up the subject again with Lord Derby, the Duc Decazes neither replied to my telegram of the 19th nor to my letter of the 20th, of which I here give some extracts.

" November 20, 1875.

" MONSIEUR LE DUC :

" The conversation in my interview to-day with Lord Derby, having drifted from the financial difficulties of Turkey to those of Egypt, Lord Derby told me that the Khedive was trying to mortgage his Suez shares at the Bank of the Ottoman Empire. I then asked him if there was not also in contemplation a sale of them to the company. He said : ' I must not conceal from you that I see serious inconveniences in the way of anything of that kind. You know my opinion of the French company. It has borne the risks of the enterprise; the honor of the achievement belongs to it, and I do not contest one of its titles to recognition, but our interest in the canal is greater than that of anybody else ; we use it more than any other country. Keeping that passage open has become for us a point of capital importance. I should look forward, however, with great satisfaction, to the time when it might be possible to buy out the shareholders at a generous figure, and to replace the company by some sort of joint administration, or syndicate in which all nations should be represented. In any case, however, we must do our best to prevent a matter that our interest depends on from being monopolized. The guarantee resulting from the Porte's control is no longer of insignificance; if we should lose also the guarantee from the Khedive's participation in the control, we should be absolutely at the mercy of the M. de Lesseps. The French company and shareholders have already 110 millions of the 200 which represents the capital stock; that is enough."

After some words in reply to the subject of the Suez Canal company, I went back to the mortgage loan of which Lord Derby had spoken. He replied that he did not want the Khedive to mortgage his titles, but that, after all, a mortgage is not a transfer of the titles, and that they could always be bought back. He insisted in closing on the bad effect that would be produced in the present circumstances by a sale of the titles to a French company, and expressed also his desire not to reawaken sleeping jealousies which a matter of this kind would inevitably provoke."[1]

Meanwhile the English government lost no time. It was Saturday, the 19th, that Mr. Disraëli, dining at the Rothschilds, allowed the Baron to suggest to him the idea of England's buying the shares up. The idea pleased him; he immediately summoned Lord Derby and Lord Salisbury. The former hesitated, the latter grew excited. Baron Rothschild took

[1] It is the step related in this letter which was the occasion of Mr. Disraëli's complimenting M. Gavard publicly in the House of Commons (see later letter of February 9, 1876).

the purchase on his own responsibility, pending the approval of Parliament; it was concluded during the 25th and communicated to the press that night. The news astonished all London the morning of the 26th. It had been perfectly unexpected. It was a theatrical stroke of the sort Dizzy delights in, devised as a business stratagem by Rothschild. The ambassador [1] returned the morning of the 26th.

Extracts from the Correspondence.

LONDON, November 29, 1875.

I dined with Count Beust. Everybody had the blues. . . . The celebrated Burton was there; you may have met him in your excursions into Central Africa. China remains for him still to see; but for that, he would be a prey to *ennui* it is his resource against the spleen. At present he is on his way to Zanzibar. He knows Lake Nyanza as I know the Bois de Boulogne. He has lived intimately with the Mormons. Yesterday he was in Ireland, and two months before he discovered some antiquities in Greece.

He has learned one after the other all the languages there are. He began with the three Arabic dialects of Afghanistan; and afterwards, with the aid of these, made his way to Mecca. He has received, in his travels, from arrows and lances, as many wounds as he knows languages. His face is tattooed with scars. He acquires the use of a new tongue in ten

[1] Marquis d'Harcourt.

days. He leases out his memory to a language for so long—takes as many months' worth of any given idiom as he wants, and with it all speaks French better than I do English.

I was amused this morning on reading the news of a mishap to an English iron-clad. A little more and the "Iron Duke" which sunk the "Vanguard" three weeks ago would have been on its way to join her at the bottom of the sea. She was on the verge of foundering, the distress signal was at the mast-head; the pumps could do no more. Then it was discovered that they had simply forgotten to batten down a hatch. The best thing is that the vessel was going down in plain sight of the shore and of the dockyards without any one's dreaming of sending help; nobody saw the signal, and they had forgotten to take powder aboard, and could not fire an alarm-gun! It is to be hoped that the English fleet will be better equipped when it leaves to conquer Constantinople.

LONDON, November 27, 1875.

England has bought the Khedive's shares in the Suez stock. It is a masterly stroke for Disraëli at home. Every one here approves it, without distinction of party; and he is safe for the next session. All his weaknesses are forgotten. Well, from the point of view of foreign politics,—it is certain that it is the first step that has been taken over and above negotiation in recent years. England has provided for herself; I hardly think the other powers will not do the same. All right, they will say, because they have never made any claims on Egypt.

But it has not been proven that the barrier between Servia and Montenegro is not to be raised,—a fact which England has no doubt taken into consideration. As for ourselves, my advice is, not to sulk; our ill-temper would do no good. For my part, I anticipated England's design, if not the way in which she has carried it into effect.

LONDON, December 14, 1875.

I spent an uninteresting evening yesterday with Solvyns at a Geographical Society. It takes the English to listen for hours together to the journal of a trip to New Guinea. Neither the author nor the reader put into it anything to ward off sleep. One member read in a monotonous voice, while another pointed out the places on a large map with a long stick. The female public, especially, felt it necessary to applaud from time to time, but no one knew why. Then a gentleman who was acquainted with the country, gave an account of his trip, drawling a great deal; feeling the need to make his travels interesting, he referred frequently to human flesh. It ended with the wish that the British flag might soon float over this land of cannibals. It gives one a clue to the taste for geography these insatiable land-grabbers have.

I spoke with Mr. Oppenheim at the club; he is the originator of the Suez affair. He suggested the idea to M. Disraëli and gave the Rothschilds a hint what to do; their commission is 2,500,000 francs. He confirmed my belief that Lord Derby knew nothing of it when he talked with me on Saturday.

THE YEAR 1876.

Extracts from the Correspondence.

HATFIELD-HOUSE,[1] January 3, 1876.

When I used to leave you to go to the country, my one idea was to have done with it as quickly as possible and get back to our apartment. It is entirely different now. Here I am in the country, nothing draws me back to town, since your letters reach me just as well here, and no one waits for my return.

I occupy the same room as last year, the same mausoleum of a bed, same Cyclopean fire. . . .

The first familiar faces I found were those of the two daughters. The elder, who is almost pretty, has the same frank manner as always. She is perfectly natural. I succeeded in sitting next to her at table. There were thirty-six of us. I sat directly under the four French flags, which were not put there out of politeness to the French ministry. They were a gift from Wellington.

After dinner the band played waltzes. Every one danced. I took a turn with one of the Reverends.

It was time for me to stop. I saw already thirty-

[1] Residence of Lord Salisbury.

six candles, and . . . "the years' irreparable wear and tear!"

To-morrow there is to be a dance with eight hundred people invited. It ought to be worth seeing the "yeomanry" in petticoats. There will be a hunt no doubt in the morning. Do not be alarmed, I shall not get into the way of any of the members of the cabinet. I shall pay more attention to the hunters than to the game. Eustace Cecil, the under Secretary of War is here. We are to come back it seems even to the English army knapsacks.

The weather is beautiful for this season of the year, and the walk will be pleasant. It is not the bishop's tree that you visit here but the queen's.[1] She was there when they told her that she was rid of her sister, which cannot have given her much pain. It appears from the last things written about her that she was eminent for none but moral attributes and that it was Lord Cecil, the founder of this house, that was the brains of the administration.

HATFIELD, Wednesday Morning,
January 5, 1876.

First let me tell you the great events that the Marquis announced to me last night. Lytton[2] is appointed viceroy of India. I shall be able to recommend Eydin[3] at my leisure. This appointment will not be refused. For five years, at least, our friend will be the greatest and most powerful

[1] Elizabeth.
[2] E. R. Bulwer-Lytton, English Ambassador to Paris, where he died in 1891.
[3] Consul-General at Calcutta.

sovereign in the world—one hundred and eighty million souls at his mercy. Also he can recruit his fortune there, thanks to an enormous salary. But the poor young wife will often think, in her Asiatic palaces, of her dear Knebworth and of her mother whom she will leave here ill!

Yesterday I fired all my cartridges and we brought down six hundred *pieces*. It is needless to say that I shot like an *oyster !*—it's enough to drive one to despair. All the same, toward the end of the day I found my account in watching the others.

This park with its old trees is superb; I should not have roamed about it in this way but for the pretext afforded by the rabbits and pheasants. I chatted mostly with Mr. Rally, M. P., who is of Greek descent; with the oldest son of Lady Derby, Lord Lyonnel Cecil (whom I mistook for Mr. Beresford), son and heir to £40,000 a year—as you might guess by looking at him; he has an aplomb! His two sisters are here; poor things, they are so much more agreeable than he!

The hunt over, I sat in front of my fire till dinner. During the day the house has been transformed for the ball. Everything goes here by rule and commandment, as at a theatre. As there were forty-six of us we were divided into three tables. Toward ten o'clock the whole of Hertfordshire began to arrive. Whoever leaves his card at the house is invited. It is at this annual fête that the young people who do not go to court nor to London are presented. . . . The only improvement that I noticed is that the ladies hold their dresses under their arms when they dance. I danced some quadrilles, nay, a lancers even—one must be useful. Martino[1] and his wife joined us. The two orchestras played till three o'clock in the morning. There were certainly eight hundred persons and nearly as many carriages on the place. The castle was lit with electric light.

WEDNESDAY EVENING.

This has been a beautiful sunshiny day. The hunt gave me a pretext to take the air at my ease; I say pretext because I was as clumsy as yesterday. I shouldn't have minded if I had not had an attendant behind me, who could scarcely conceal his contempt. He did not know that I was a member of the Society for Protection of Animals, and that every time I missed fire it was so much gained. There were only seven of us and we only killed two hundred and fifty *pieces*. The Marquis is at Hertford for the "quarter sessions." There are not many here to talk with.

Martino has been called back to London. Beust is running to Knowsley after Lord Derby.

When we re-entered the gallery the orchestra began to play a waltz, and I had to dance. If I should stay a few days longer I should be the successor of Vestris; but not in the lancers. I succeeded in putting everybody out, but it helped on the fun.

THURSDAY.

Another day of hunting and of dancing. As for the hunt it is horrible; more than six hundred

[1] Chargé d'Affaires d'Italie.

pieces brought down by seven shooters, not counting those which have been killed since. I contributed the least possible to the massacre, though still too much for my conscience. These days in the open air are certainly doing me much good, although nature is not very natural in this country. The gas-lights hardly end where the thickets begin. The hunt was without incident or possible accident. Pigeons were shot—a great many. The only unexpected item was the sudden appearance of a fox; whereupon there followed frightful cries, and every one abused everybody else, but without levelling a gun. The beast is reserved for his lordship's pack.

Before dinner, we had music which was poor, and then visited the famous "Cecil papers"—the entire correspondence of Cecil with Elizabeth and James I.; the order for the execution of Leicester, for that of Mary, entirely in the Queen's hand. One can't speak one's mind about Elizabeth with perfect freedom here, because Elizabeth was really Cecil. He flattered her passions to the point of bloodshed, to keep her in the humor of allowing him to reign.

LONDON, January 10, 1876.

While I was dining at the club Schouvaloff came in and took possession of a seat. Conversation ran so high while he ate and drank that it soon became general. For an ambassador, he is amusing. He told us of the entertaining time he had in Paris, in 1856, when the Emperor commanded Bacciochi to entertain him. In the midst of these edifying tales, he dropped a few words about the Austrian memorial. Was he making game of it, or speaking in its support?

Lytton's appointment is generally well-liked. It falls in line with the old tradition of divining the "rising man." How old were Pitt, Palmerston, Canning, Gladstone, when they took hold of public affairs? He was not the nominee of Disraëli only. Derby said some time ago to Reeve, that Lytton would be called to a high post.

Lord Amberley is dead. I wonder if he will be cremated as his wife was? He is the oldest son of Lord John Russell. He and his wife have made a specialty of blasphemy and of rearing their children as agnostics.

Yesterday I dined with the Vaughan family. They had invited the daughter of X. for me to meet. Her eyes, tongue, imagination, head, toilet, all were spirited; a true Parisian mouth, but with German brains grafted on English humor and Italian audacity. She believes in nothing but her own reason; reads everything, knows everything and takes council of no one. She began by saying that so far as she could consent to marrying any one is concerned, she would prefer Salvini; after him, she thinks Wagner possible, and a certain prophet of Wagner's, a German pianist, who has married a Greek and has baptised his children each with the name of some opera of the god of music. She believes also in George Sand. Does she admire the morals of *Lélia* and *Indiana?* Yes, she believes in the free woman in the free state, and talked about it. She is a German, and a German in sympathy with Bismarck and the German Emperor. In short, she is a complete Salmagundi. You would only find this sort of thing in England. I thanked my friends for letting me see so diverting a spectacle.

This morning, I received an amusing letter from Lytton, who is very anxious to know how to manage his "white elephant"; he seems to be very happy.

LONDON, February 8, 1876.

Just back from the ceremony.[1] Well, it does not stir one's risibility, and that is saying not a little when one recollects the heralds, the throne, the crown, the genuflections, etc., etc. I left home at one o'clock, and made my way through the human current to Westminster. No bells rang, because of the illness of Lady Augusta (Stanley). The House was full. At first I saw nothing but women; the day was so dark I could scarcely make out anything else, even after I had been there for some time. I sat on the Bishops' bench, up high. The Justices were in the centre in their wigs, and looked like a drove of enormous sheep; next came the ermine robes, and then the peeresses. Toward two o'clock the hall was filled with a continuous murmur; everybody had recognized everybody else. Exactly opposite me sat Lady Ilchester, with a flash and sparkle of diamonds about her neck, and eyes as brilliant as her gems. By her side sat Lady Lytton. Lytton himself was conspicuous among the ermine robes, his brown head rising black above the white.

[1] Opening of Parliament.

I met them on my way out; they leave next month.

To return to the ceremony: it began with the arrival of the two Princesses Mary—Mary, Duchess of Edinburgh, coming in second. They seated themselves in front of the throne on the woolsack. Mary of Teck was spiritually much at her ease, convinced that she was exciting admiration; the Duchess seemed bored, because of her second rank. Then entered the heralds, then the sword, and the crown, all backwards—and not one fell! The Queen was not more majestic than usual, but in the midst of all this silence and respect she was very imposing. She mounted her throne, where her robe was in waiting. Her two daughters, one on either side, assisted her. The Princess of Wales took her place on the woolsack opposite. The Queen gave orders to notify the Commons. The door at the bottom opened, and from the throne you could see the Speaker in the chair. The Commons kept the Queen waiting some time, for the reason simply that they always *had* done so. Presently we heard them coming. The Speaker came forward deliberately; the mob followed with a great noise which they kept up the whole time, as they crowded at the bar.

The Speaker stood opposite the throne in his official costume and bore himself with great dignity.

The Lord Chancellor knelt down and received from the Queen's own hand the speech that he had himself brought there under his arm. He read it; but there was no: "Oyez, la reine le veult!"

What has become of the ancient formula? There was nothing in especial in the speech itself; it was just what one might have expected, except, perhaps, for a reference to the title that is to be conferred upon the Queen as Sovereign of India. It will be *Empress* no doubt. The ceremony ended, as it had begun, in perfect silence. A slight bow to the right, a slight bow to the left—that was all. Those who had come in backward, went out backward; and I found myself in the midst of a flood of peers and peeresses, and was much flattered to see how many great people I know: Aberdare, Vernon, Lytton, Salisbury (who called me Bishop, because of where I sat); Carnarvon, Bedford, Brett, and then the young ladies. I found the Marchioness of Bristol very pleasant, and a sister of the Duke of Norfolk not less so. I presented my homage to the two beauties, Ilchester and Galloway, all in the hubbub of our exit. The place was fairly overflowing with peeresses.

LONDON, February 9, 1876.

Here is what you will find in the *Times* this morning if you read Mr. Disraëli's speech at the meeting last night: " On the 20th of November, the official Representative of France, not the ambassador, who was absent, but a gentleman whom we know and respect highly, M. Gavard, was absolutely instructed to call on Lord Derby, I will not say to pump him (laughter), but to learn whether England would submit to the French company's purchasing. . . ."

In any event they weren't obliged to crown a

poor devil of a *Chargé d'Affaires* if they didn't want to.

LONDON, February 10, 1876.

I found myself, at dinner to-night, sitting near Mr. Corry,[1] Mr. Disraëli's secretary. He promised to transmit my gratitude to the minister, who will, he said, appreciate it highly. He added: " It seems that you have some friends in the House, for, after the compliment, Mr. Disraëli was interrupted by cries of: 'Hear! Hear!' " I have decidedly missed the biggest day of my life. A plague on colds!

I forgot to tell you of the jostling of the M.P.s when they reached the bar. The ministry were swept away by the crowd. Mr. Disraëli found himself at the door, happy to have preserved his hat. During this time Dr. Kenealy was in evidence outside. Mangin's carriage had been permitted to come nearly to Westminster because somebody had thought they recognized the doctor in it; he was following it really in a cab, which the people drew home on his return. The electors of the future!

There was a " spelling bee " (a game in orthography) yesterday at Lady Cambermere's, with three judges and prizes. These great big English simpletons amuse themselves with this sort of thing tremendously. Can you fancy Mr. Lowe, with his albino eyes, standing up to spell, *braisé*. It seems that the word has been naturalized.

LONDON, March 10, 1876.

The sight of a little Jew promoting the Queen

[1] Baron Rowton in 1880.

of England and giving her a second crown is not to be seen every day.[1] So of course I went yesterday to Parliament. I thought Dizzy very weak: he did not give a single good reason, not one. His refutation of objections lacked amplitude, but the trick was well played. To refuse the imperial title to the Queen, they would have to ignore her prerogative, compromise the position of the ministers in regard to her, and what is more serious, in finding fault with the title they would seem to refuse to the population of India the rights of citizenship. Mr. Gladstone replied with abundance and completeness, without, however, in my opinion escaping from the absurdity which permeates the whole discussion. This notion of making the Queen an Empress is as difficult to defend as to combat. On Dizzy's part, it is the whim of an artist in royalty, of a King-maker; on the Queen's part, it is the whim of a sceptred parvenu; she thinks she will be a more considerable figure with the title of Empress, and that her children will make better marriages. My impression is that they made a great mistake to lift the veil which ought to cover the origin of claims to sovereignty. What has been done can be undone. One doesn't play quits with matters of that sort. Kings and Emperors are born: it is dangerous to be specially created one. Decidedly, Disraëli has made a mistake : everybody feels already that the thing is a pill; and they are not going to thank the ministry for making the country swallow

[1] He refers to the project of giving the Queen the title of Empress of India.

it. As the discussion was rather long, malcontent members went to dinner to escape having to vote. It was once more Stafford Northcote who made the best impression with his air of good sense and straightforwardness. After he sat down, murmurs began to make themselves heard, and timid cries of "Divide, divide; " and after Kenealy had spoken nobody would listen to anything. At half-past two we were shut in for the voting. The Speaker made the last call for the "noes," and there were none, there was no need to go out into the "lobbies."

When they took up other matters I went home and dressed, and then came back again to "Mrs. Speaker's." The House was still in session. M.-P.s deliberate, take tea, and chat, all at the same time; the bell warns them when they must go to vote. There were a number of girls there whom I found I knew. From the windows one saw the boats on the Thames glide by, noiseless, lightless, mysterious: it was very picturesque. I went out at midnight to dinner.

LONDON, March 10, 1876.

I saw the good Mme. Lionel[1] yesterday. She has no desire to make the journey at this windy season, and I fancy she will give it up. She told me of their majesties' visits to Northumberland.[2] I think Easton Newton is the name of the castle that has been rented for them. The Queen of Naples is to occupy one wing. There has been a great deal of money laid out on good hunters and more are in

[1] Baroness Rothschild.
[2] Empress of Austria and the Queen of Naples,

demand at any price. Every day you find them at the meet of some hunt in the neighborhood, the Duke of Grafton's, or Lord So-and-so's, etc. The Empress has already fallen twice, but as she has not yet broken any bones, she is not yet satisfied.

To-day the Empress came back to pay a visit to the Queen at Windsor. There was some misunderstanding at the beginning. The Queen could not receive her at the date the Empress had fixed, and so the Empress left without waiting for Her Majesty's day. It is evidently the presence of so many Majesties or Imperial Highnesses that has turned the Queen's head. A Queen by birth, she aspires to the title of an upstart! The result is deplorable; the Ministry will never recover from a success like that. I am much put out, because when all is said the conservatives are our party really. A mere comparison of Granville's and Gladstone's language with that of Lord Derby, Salisbury and Dizzy's, make me decidedly a Tory in this country.

When you are not meeting Queens, with or without subjects here, you are jostling against Princes. I reached Farm Street[1] this morning, a little before the storm. There came a large man with a ferocious look, who went straight to the front bench, followed by two aides-de-camp with pointed moustaches, waxed with Hungarian wax. He made the sign of the cross again and again at the beginning and at the close, but other than that he was not more attentive to the mass than a lion in his cage would

[1] Church of the Jesuits,

have been. He stood up, made play with his arms, looked about whenever he felt inclined, then left as he had entered, with his aides-de-camp, who hastened after him. He looked as if he were threatening the sky because it rained on a monarch who cannot even be said to be " fallen." It was Don Carlos. His face is handsome enough, but the expression is hard and evil.

LONDON, March 14, 1876.

Sunday's storm brought to light the bitter-sweet relations between the Empress[1] and the Queen, who aspires to be an Empress. I think I told you of the Empress having, on her arrival, proposed an hour for her visit to the Queen, and of the Queen's refusing to see her then, and appointing another time. Diana, the huntress, did not wait. The breach was to be healed on Sunday, but the interview was very short. Diana left without stopping for lunch, in spite of the storm and the hour of service. To punish her the heavens unchained the winds as against the invincible " Armada." The train was stopped on the way. Not to let their mistress die of hunger, the Empress's people borrowed the station master's luncheon. She has had no better success with Derby. She tried to make an appointment with him for Sunday. With the dignity of Minister to the Queen he replied : " It is not possible, I go to the country."

Yesterday at the Club, I found Schouvaloff. There is always something worth remembering in his rambling talk. It appears from his account that

[1] Empress of Austria.

Bismarck has, from the beginning, contended for intervention in the revolted provinces. Schouvaloff himself favors Austro-Russian intervention. The fantastic part of the talk turned on the English naval force and the means of overpowering it.

LONDON, March 16, 1876.

Yesterday, at dinner, I sat by a very agreeable but very obese lady, who asked me, when the meal was over, to help her get up. "Here," she said, "you see a queen of beauty." It was the Duchess of Somerset, queen of beauty at Lord Eglinton's famous tournament. She is the sister of Lady Dufferin. You could see that she had been beautiful. Her conversation was not without interest. She told me she had sixteen small children. Then she corrected herself, and said nineteen; she had forgotten three. The Duke of Somerset wore his Star of the Garter. I should have taken him for a substantial tradesman if I had not known that he publishes books in refutation of the principles of religion.

LONDON, March 19, 1876.

I have been to an official city banquet. When the Lord Mayor made an allusion to the title of Empress, there were cries of "Queen! Queen!" Such a manifestation is very extraordinary in this country.

LONDON, May 9, 1876.

Yesterday I read a curious history of a fanatic "Orangeman" in the Parliament of 1832. Alone, with the help of one acolyte, he forced the House to divide seventeen times on an insignificant bill, that is to say, to vote, by all the "ayes" going into one room to be counted, and all the "noes" going into another, with an average expenditure each time of some twenty minutes. Between every two "divisions" the wretch apologized, but said that he could not do otherwise, having sworn to hinder the bill by all means in his power. Then Palmerston and some others tried to argue with him on his "case of conscience" and to prove to him that he might, without disloyalty to his oath, let the House go to bed at a reasonable hour. He would not hear to it. Finally, after the seventeenth division, the bill was carried, and the House adjourned at four o'clock—in the morning. The terrible man apologized once more and promised "never to do so any more." You fancy the House was put out with him? Not in the least. The incident was the origin of his popularity. There you have an Englishman for all the world—among Englishmen! Read also a very haughty letter of Macaulay to the electors of Leeds, soliciting their votes. He will have no commerce with the mouthpiece theory of representation; he approves of the principle of division of labor; says you ought to choose a legislator as you do a physician, and your choice once made, to rely on his judgment because, in the matter in hand, he knows better than you.

Schouvaloff told me a capital saying by a Prussian general to justify flogging his soldiers. "What will you have? Die Canaille haben studirt" (The blackguards have been to school!).

LONDON, May 13, 1876.

"Prussia House."—The secretaries were not powdered, but wore breeches. They waited on the Empress Augusta. We were penned up in a drawing-room and I *cooked in my juice* (as we elegantly express it) all evening; I scarcely saw more than the backs of my colleagues, or their wives, crowding to exchange a look or word with her Highness. My modest reserve did not cost me much as you may imagine; I could contemplate Augusta's fabulous diamonds in silence. They make one feel that they must belong to the House of Hanover. For the rest she was painted and powdered, and tricked out with a black wig and beautiful speeches: "These chairs seem to reproach you, ladies, for not being seated." That is how one says: "Sit down," in the Prussian court. The ladies took good care not to profit by the invitation. There was a whole string of phrases quite as simple and profound.

She asked Beust his opinion of the exposition, after telling him what she thought of it herself; he said it was like a promenade concert minus the music. He is the only one who knows how to come off with honor; he makes up for his obsequiousness by a certain air of making game of their Majesties. I found my very young friend Maud (Cecil) again; she grows beautiful. That is the one incident I treasure of the evening.

I live, you see, in a round of pleasures. It is a shameful existence for a man of my age: so much the more so that one loses the thread of one's serious work. I do nothing and I learn nothing. . . .

LONDON, LOCKINGE-HOUSE,
October 28, 1876.[1]

Here are the *dramatis personæ:* Loyd Lindsay and his sweet young wife, always with her little air of melancholy; Mrs. Holford and the beautiful Alice; her mother and Lady Mary Crawford, who are on their way to Italy; Lady Alice Ayre and her husband; Morley[2] and his young wife, also on their way to Italy; and Lord Oberstone who remains in England. That is the list of the family simply, and I breathe happy in their midst. Nothing happened on the way, and I saw nothing except a treeless landscape hidden in fog, and a charmingly rustic village.

I reached the house at nightfall. The road disappeared beneath great trees of which I could see no more than the trunks; bright lights reflected on the water reached me through the darkness. Finally we made a turn and I found myself in front of what I took at first for a large factory with every window lighted and reflected in a basin. I was mistaken; it was the house of which I could distinguish nothing. First we entered the hall; it is two stories high, all in wood, and decorated with beautiful tapestries. While I was talking with Colonel Lindsay, I saw a face at the window on the second floor—or rather I heard the rustling of robes on the gallery over our heads. The beautiful Alice affirms that the place is a bad one for the honey-

[1] Residence of Colonel Loyd Lindsay, now Lord Wantage.
[2] Earl Morley, who married Miss Holford.

moons, because everything can be seen and heard from above. Even while I was talking, I descried a large Murillo, the counterpart of the *Assumption*. The Virgin and the Child had been cut out by the monks to save them from the French, but not from the English, who bought the piece and sold it to Lord Oberstone. The drapery of the Angel or rather of Love, which formed the bottom of the picture, was left. They did not escape to Marshal Soult. After long years of waiting the second piece joined the first, and they were put together without showing. I must wait till daylight to judge the picture and give you an account of all I have not seen this evening.

FRIDAY MORNING, October 29, 1876.

This morning I began to reconnoitre. I said yesterday that the house resembled a large factory illuminated by a thousand fires; the truth is that the design—the architecture is nothing to speak of, but the interior is perfect. The gardens are perfect in their kind, with little cascades every few feet; the park is Woburn or Hatfield over again, with a surface more diversified, indeed, but exemplifying everywhere the sort of artificial nature they go in for here, the poverty of invention, the perpetual presence of the hand of man. For the rest, the total effect is rich, opulent, in a supreme degree; there are swans on the water, the herds of cattle in the meadows, vegetable gardens that I drove through, a second park beyond the first, with a country house in it given up to Colonel Lindsay, father of the beautiful Violet;[1] two villages, one at each extremity of the park, entirely made by Loyd Lindsay, regular Trianon-villages; some schools that he maintains without aid from the state, and his flag floating over his possessions at the top of a flag-staff as big as a mast. Here is one who is "called" to inhabit the earth; in especial when he has a father-in-law who owns a hundred times as much.

Yes, but they have no children, and everyone is curious to know to whom they will leave their possessions. If you could have seen the joy in Mrs. Holford's face when she told me to-day that she would soon be a grandmother.

I shall leave at one o'clock and will be in London at four and at Gunnersbury for dinner. It may seem jolly to knock about in this way, but I would rather stay in one place; I never knew such a madman as I am to be always leaving the place where I am happiest.

GUNNERSBURY ACTON,[2] October 30, 1876.

Saturday Night. Here I am at Gunnersbury. The material part of it, the establishment, is superior to any other I know. It makes one positively happy, it is so comfortable. It is ideal, the triumph of well-being. Fancy a room in which you should find everything; a library in three languages, and all sorts of "cabinets." But the thing that pleases me more than the comfort is the cordiality with

[1] Now Marchioness of Granby.
[2] Residence of Baron Lionel de Rothschild.

which the husband and wife welcomed me. They apologized for inviting me, without other guests than their children. It is precisely this intimacy that warmed and touched me. What will they do to-morrow to entertain me? Yesterday, under the roof of Lord Overstone, to-day, under that of Rothschild ! The latter tells me that Overstone is the richest man in the world : Overstone has, he said, about eight millions a year. I wanted to ask : " And you ? "

SUNDAY.

This morning we visited the beautiful cedars, the ponds and the ducks. I was told a story of four swans that were driven away from one pond after another by the older occupants. They kept together and moved on till they should find a place where they would be allowed to stay. Finally, they came here ; but they stir up the bottom—ill-smelling exhalations from it seem to be complained of, and this morning I found a gardener seriously engaged in perfuming the pond with violet water. At eleven o'clock a brougham took me to mass at Chiswick; then I had a stroll with the Baron in his little carriage. They wanted to take me to see the Duchess of Cleveland, but I refused.

GUNNERSBURY, October 31, 1876.

We had a reunion here yesterday, of all the powers of England ; capital was represented by our host; the government by Beaconsfield ; the press by Delane; the opposition, by Villers ; and the populace by Menabrea, etc. It is true that the powers have talked very little except to each other. At sight of the *Premier*, Delane who has, of late, not spared him especially, retired into another drawing-room ; but the *Premier* followed, and I fancy we shall see the result of the conference in to-morrow's *Times*.

I know, from the Baron, that Dizzy is well satisfied, that the armistice is accepted, and that he has no doubt that peace will be preserved. What is certain is, that Rothschild seems to me to be inclined to send orders to all the Rothschilderies in Europe.

Am back in town. L. de Rothschild brought me back in his phaeton. All the omnibus-drivers saluted us. I hear that he gives them an annual dinner. Good way not to be impeded on the road.

LONDON, November 2, 1876.

Lord Salisbury came into the club and went silently and alone to his corner. I read to him the Duc de Broglie's reply to his compliments. He asked to be allowed to keep it, and this morning I got it back with the following note.

" November 3, 1876,
" India Office.

"MY DEAR MONSIEUR GAVARD :

" I did not find you at the Athenæum to thank you for permitting me to read this interesting letter from M. the Duc de Broglie. It has given me much to think of. What is called free thought in France is truly a mysterious and terrible phenomenon.

" You must not judge from the newspapers here, and in especial not from the *Times*, of what British opinion really is on affairs in France. There is a lively sympathy felt here for the efforts and desperate struggles of the conservatives.

"Believe, my dear Monsieur Gavard, in my devoted friendship.

"SALISBURY."

(The letter is in French.)

LONDON, November 8, 1876.

Salisbury at Constantinople![1] I was not far from the mark yesterday; I ought to add even that I was more confident really than I appeared. The appointment will not be very agreeable to Russia. It is in the interests of the Tory programme that he goes. It is mistrust of Russia, almost the desire to come to blows with her, if it can be done within range of the fleet, and occupation of the Bosphorus at the first signal. As for Egypt, England may take her time if she holds Constantinople. Salisbury is certainly the man to hold Ignatieff in check. But whom are we to send? Absolutely the Duc de Broglie is the only one possible.

There are two persons in Salisbury: the simple, charming gentleman that every one finds when they talk to him in tête-à-tête, and the violent, bitter orator, one listens to in every assembly in which he speaks. Which of the two will sit at the Conference in Constantinople?

LONDON, December 17, 1876.

Have you not heard me jokingly suggest that in-

[1] Lord Salisbury was sent to Constantinople as First Plenipotentiary at the conference charged to revise the treaty of San Stefano.

stead of the disestablishment of the English Church, Gladstone and others would do better to disestablish the double consonants that are not pronounced in English, the entire syllables that are swallowed in the speaker's haste to reach the accented ones. The last London school board has seriously called on all the other school boards to join it in petitioning Parliament, inasmuch as it regulates weights and measures, to reform English orthography. It is one more symptom of the centralizing movement which shows itself here, and which tends to bring England down to our political level.

Solvyns capped my suggestion on the disestablishment of the double consonants with a German story. Some one asked in Germany the name of an English traveller and the reply was: " Er heisst Schmidt aber das schreibt sich Douglas." (He says his name is Smith but he writes it Douglas.)

THE YEAR 1877.

Extracts from the Correspondence.

LONDON, January 22, 1877.

Yesterday I dined with the Dean [1] and his sister— the one who has been converted to Catholicism. It came about by her seeing the Sisters of Charity at their work in the Crimea. It seems that these sainted sisters did all the hard work while Miss Nightingale reserved herself for the notabilities who were wounded and would advertise her.

Near me [2] as I write, I see the cardinal in an armchair, reading a magazine; Darwin, who does not especially resemble an ape; two or three old men who swore; a little farther on Emly, who laughs to himself while reading a satirical life of Dizzy; near the other fireplace, the director of the National Gallery; Leighton, their only painter, writing at one of the tables; and a card-party is going on in the other room between Hayward, Solvyns, Trollope and Forster. I leave the bishops whom I do not know unnamed. As for myself, I am having a cup of tea at my writing-table. It sets me up well when I forget to breakfast. . . . There is Murchison, the

[1] Stanley, Dean of Westminster,   [2] At the Athenæum,

physician, crossing the hall; there poor Delane, who creeps along, looking very unlike himself, toward an arm-chair; and Wade, just back from China. But I shall never have done if I do not seal this up.

LONDON, February 2, 1877.

Last evening Schouvaloff read me his dispatch giving an account of his talk with Lord Derby. Lord Derby had set forth England's present attitude. I went home and wrote out what I had heard and sent it to Lord Derby, saying that I had just bought it for one hundred pounds. He sent it back immediately with two corrections in his own hand, thus testifying to the perfect exactness of the rest. . . .

The dinner at Reeve's was interesting. Wade, who has just returned from a seven years' residence in China, fairly took me a trip through China—answered all my questions. It is the system of education that puts a damper on the masses there. They exhaust all their faculties in learning the books of Confucius; after which they can do no more; and when they ought to reason, they remember. For the rest we shall see them overrun the earth with cheap labor and coal. A Peter the Great is needed, simply, to put down their customs and prejudices, and to launch their two hundred or four hundred millions of human beings on the way to progress. Motley held forth on the other side without much tact on the justice of the return of Alsace-Lorraine to Germany; Villiers opposed him. I seemed not to be listening, but I thanked him afterwards. He is Clarendon's brother.

There was also a certain Grant Duff there, a political personage, who gives away his works bound in full leather.

LONDON, February 21, 1877.

Last night I reached Parliament at five o'clock and left at midnight. The speeches are always pretty much the same, and I do not see that one is any further along at the end than at the beginning. Discussions they are not—the speakers never cross swords. Somebody fires off a speech, early in the evening, aimed at a member of the party opposite, who in turn replies—but not to the man who has attacked him. When one member has finished speaking he may leave his seat, and that is precisely what he does, while his opponent is dressing him down. I heard Salisbury, who is the best speaker of them all; his language is effective and perfectly natural, and imbued with passion. Beaconsfield, on the contrary, is at the farthest remove from naturalness; he has nothing but art, possesses an extreme address, plays with difficulties—without the least scruple in regard to fact or veracity. He entertained me highly at first by the daring flights, in which he spoke successively of France and of Germany, and recalled the war of 1870 and the conquest of Prussia in 1807, à propos of the doctrine of the integrity and independence of nations. One did not know whether to laugh or to cry. Then he struck into his Guildhall speech, changing his tone and his accent and playing the lamb. To me, who saw him as lion in the City this turn was particularly amusing.

Toward ten o'clock I went in search of Schouvaloff whom I found cooling his heels at the foot of the throne; I brought him back into the gallery and translated for him as well as I could the striking passages. For my pains, he confided to me a conversation of the utmost importance that he has just had with Beaconsfield.

LONDON, February 22, 1877.

Banquet at the chamber of commerce! The meeting possessed a more important character than I had dared to hope. Salisbury spoke with much charm and in the account he gave of his mission he gave us to understand what actually took place,— the matter that Schouvaloff spoke to me about yesterday. Then there was an exchange of compliments and polite speeches between Salisbury and Forster. You ought to read the two speeches, which are models in their kind. Be it known in France that these are the two principal orators in England, and belong to the opposite extremes of political opinion: the Commoner almost a radical and the Marquis an ultra Tory. It was charming— in such good taste; always in the tone of pleasantry and always very earnest at bottom. Forster's speech, as it happened, took a turn that for me was serious. He brought me in a sense into the discussion—he began to praise France, spoke with admiration of her energy, her patience, her self-possession, and emphasized each word by looking at me. Terror took possession of me; I had to reply, but, if I should say one word on politics, I should be lost; if I made a false step, I could not recover it. There was no time for reflection, and good-natured neighbors were backing me up for all sorts of subjects. At last the moment came for me to get up. Salisbury said he anticipated much pleasure in listening to me. I pulled through somehow—patched it up.

Salisbury is very cordial. Did I tell you that I sent him this morning an important correction of his Tuesday's speech? I had not understood it as the newspapers seem to have done, and I was right. We talked of his interviews at Berlin with Bismarck; for an hour and a half he said the Chancellor talked with a raciness, a crudity, a wit, a grossness, unparalleled, but every word bore the stamp of a superior man. Meanwhile he said nothing about what he had most at heart, he neither spoke of France nor of the Pope. At which of them is he aiming? He made indirect offers after the Biarritz fashion to all comers, even to England, to whom he tendered Egypt on her restoring to Russia the mouths of the Danube. Will every one be able to resist the bait? Germany caused the conference to fall through by dint of persuading the Turks that the Russian army could not hold the field. "But in the last resort," I asked, "if he succeeds in his attempt, shall we have nothing but right on our side?" "You are beyond reproach," he replied. "And you know to which side my sympathies lean; but it will not be the government here that will decide the matter, it will be public opinion. You have the same means of knowing it that I have; look to it for your information." That is precisely what I myself keep repeating.

LONDON, April 8, 1877.

Solvyns has just spent three charming days in the country with Leveson Gower, brother of Lady Georgina. Gladstone arrived, while he was there, with his box, his umbrella and his axe; yes, his axe, to fell trees with. Happily he spared the cedars in the park; they handed him over to a neighboring forest. As for the rest, the host's talk was marvellous, inexhaustible, incomparably various and interesting At midnight last night the walking-match which has been going on for six days and nights came to an end. It is an exhibition of brutality simply, and people here would risks their neck to see it. It is true that they hoped to see at least one of them expire before the end.

LONDON, May 20, 1877.

Yesterday at the club there was a ballot taken— it was very funny. I never before took part in such a ceremony. The candidate was discussed. Nobody said a word against him, quite the contrary. There were only nine of us present; we voted, and the candidate was black-balled. Everybody looked at everybody else; and I did not confess that I had noticed who had put in the fatal ball.

I spent two hours yesterday at Burlington. It reconciled me a little to our Exposition. If there is too much of the nude with us, there is not a bit here—not a serious picture, not a genuine attempt;

design, style are absolutely lacking. Such painting really is not worth while. Nothing can equal the puerility of the subjects, except the naïve absurdity of the public, who languish before them with admiration. It was a holiday and the crowd was enormous; not a shop-girl out for the day from behind her counter but was there, jotting down items in her note-book.

One picture represents a gigantic gun, standing bolt upright, a shako, a haversack, a sword; the title is: " The guard dies and does not surrender! " It is by the brother of the Duke of Sutherland.

LONDON, May 27, 1877.

Had a charming time yesterday from ten in the morning till nine at night out in the open air under a mild sun; listening to the cadenced fall of the horses' hoofs upon the road for three and four hours at a stretch. My old friend, Henry Lacaze, could not have driven more sedately and slowly; but a truce to regrets when one is looking out on the English landscape from the roof of a coach. Once beyond the London streets, the country is one great unbroken park, except the large villages, till you reach Waterford. I cried out in admiration, and secretly anticipated that we should find the Country of Brett[1] situated between a public house and a brothel; but be assured, it is a bit of meadow hidden between the parks of Lord Clarendon and Lord Essex—two considerable domains that have come down undisturbed from King Harold's time,

[1] Sir R. H. Brett, Judge of Appeals.

and that nobody will interfere with them till the end of the world, or till the coming of universal suffrage in this country. There was nothing in sight but verdure and trees, and beyond, a canal with boats on it passing silently, and a river. The current was swift, the water clear, the bottom covered with reeds, and the banks shaded by trees dating from before the flood. One could spend one's life watching it flow, and nobody to see one but the birds, the rabbits, and the trout. We took a stroll in Essex Park, and came out, by an avenue of centenary beeches, half as broad again as a boulevard, upon an old Tudor Manor. In one place we stumbled upon some archery practice, in another upon a cricket match among the people of Waterford; practically the park is theirs, except that they are not called upon to take care of it. We returned through Clarendon Park, and saw another antique manor fitted up, however, with all modern conveniences. Here and there we found a charming cottage for some younger son. As for the inhabitants of the country, if the neighboring lord is not gruesome and denies them admission to his park they have the high-road to stroll in, which is not, thank God, exactly a high-road for the traveller with a taste for the picturesque. It is a narrow way bordered on either side with beautiful trees which belong to the landlord and of which he disposes at his will. The public have permission, to walk on it and keep it up,—that is all.

But let us go back to our one-story villa, opening on a carpet of grass which stretches away beyond a vegetable garden with apple trees in bloom as far as the eye can reach. I thought I had never seen anything so beautiful. What ravishing flowers! what combination of pink and white! We went boating, too, on the canal. And finally home again behind our four chestnuts. Our coachman seemed to lose caste a little when he was not on his box. He has twelve chestnuts alike and seventy-five mares on his estate. The estate used to bring his father an income of 1,200,000 francs: but his father managed it injudiciously and it now brings in no more than 300,000. It is true that the son has other resources besides, but he too has committed his little follies; among others he married a nobody with whom he does not live, and as he is Catholic he cannot get a divorce—worse luck! This original, for all his hundred horses, inhabits a hole in Manchester Street. I would not live there twenty-four hours. He owns, however, castle after castle.

LONDON, June 2, 1877.

Had a conversation with Salisbury. He is uneasy and believes that we shall be attacked before winter. Nothing could be more legitimate than the dissolution,[1] but, to manage a democracy, it is not good to have been reared among constitutional traditions. ... England is letting things take their own course in the East the better to stand on guard in the West. Will the Russians know where to stop? Won't the hand that forced them into war, force

---

[1] In France.

them into some other imprudence? Will they be contented with what is given them?

LONDON, June 4, 1877.

The dinner [1] yesterday was indeed charming. They have a beautiful house fronting on Sloane Square; the dining-room is in the back, opening on a paved terrace, with a background of large trees. I was between Leighton and Lord Granville, then there was Alma Tadema, Barington, Chamberlain to the Queen, a poet, and, of course a reporter for the *Times*, and finally Martino, all of them at the house of the champion of radicalism. The dinner was very good—asparagus as large as the trees, a whole forest of it, and strawberries to correspond. While we talked and ate, the stars came out, and we could see them, but could hardly realize that it was night, the weather was so mild. Unfortunately, I could not follow all the conversation back and forth. The most entertaining bit for me was my discussion with Leighton about the *Nocturnes* in the Grosvenor Gallery. I made him talk in all languages, but reserved my own as a weapon of attack, which flattered, singularly enough, his self-love at the cost of the cause he was defending. Do not forget that our amiable host went to Leipzig to cremate the young wife who received me so graciously when I was here the first time. It embarrassed me for some time, but I do not make a point of being more faithful to the memory of dead and incinerated wives than their own husbands are.

[1] At Sir Charles Dilke's.

LONDON, October 28, 1877.

Last night I was going to sleep with great difficulty about one o'clock, when there was a bang, bang! bang, bang, bang! It was like the knocking at the gate in Macbeth. " Good," I thought, " it is only a telegram; they will drop it into the box, I will wait until to-morrow morning." But the banging continued. I went to my window and saw a policeman knocking at a neighboring house. For half an hour this noise continued with the same vigor. Everybody in the neighborhood must, I was sure, have been aroused. Finally I lost my patience and went downstairs. " What is the row?" " A shutter is open in the next house on the street floor." " But the house is empty." " That makes no difference, the shutters ought to be shut." And they went on knocking vainly at the door. I am sure that it is only in England that an entire street could be wakened because of an open shutter.

HATFIELD, November 6, 1877.

Here I am, after three years' absence, back at Hatfield, only I have the Hornbeam instead of the Hazel room. It is a little nearer the sky; all the other floors are taken by the representatives of the great powers. I made the journey with the Marquis of Salisbury, reached the station at the last minute with Schouvaloff and his wife, who arrived after the last minute. The train was already moving, and I had to lend " Russia " a hand or they would have been left. What an amount of light and space for so few people! That was my first impression. My second was to reflect on what a small creature I am, considering the associations and the splendors I enjoy. We arrived at night. All the windows were illuminated—that is enough to give you an idea of the grandeur. Tea was served. Odo Russell and his wife formed the third couple of Ambassadors. " Eat and dawdle, dawdle and eat," is the order of the day; so much so that my letter has been interrupted by it twenty times. It rains and there is a strong wind, but that makes no difference. They have played lawn tennis just the same all morning. It is all as innocent as that. You go to the tennis court, where a man awaits you with costume *ad hoc*; you return for luncheon, and then you have a choice between horseback-riding, walking, a visit to the rabbits or to the schools. I'm off to the schools.

Tuesday evening, November 7, 1877.

My letter was interrupted by a drive. The visit to the schools was put off till to-morrow, and a party in three carriages drove about the park. There were trees everywhere older than the house; they were a hundred years old when Elizabeth awaited the crown beneath their shade. We dined in the large dining-room with the gallery, and the French flags in it. There are a good many more besides these, alas! that we have lost.

I sat by Lady Maude, who has come out now, and is very agreeable. After dinner there was a little of everything, promenading in these endless galleries, music in one corner, games in another. I was with the Countess Schouvaloff, who is a singular person, and attractive. She will return to St. Petersburg in fifteen days, and England will never see her again. I do not understand her very well as yet. After the evening party was over, the smoking began. It is the custom for every one to change his clothes before going to the smoking-room. It was a happy time for Schouvaloff. He told some of his stories. They are always amusing. . . . He told about a trip in Germany with His Majesty Wilhelm I. This is the manner of it: His Majesty addresses everyone that is presented to him with: "Your regiment?" The person addressed, with a violent kick, replies: "*80th Fusilier, dritter Battalion, erste Compagnie.*"[1] Then he passes to the next and the same dialogue begins all over again. Whenever they arrived at a station the municipal corps was always on the platform. The burgomaster lines them up, orders number three to retire, number five to advance. They all mark time, and then: *Still!* At last the Emperor arrives: *Hut!* (Salute.)

Thereupon I slept like a rock until morning prayers, which I heard from the gallery. I have perhaps scandalized the X.'s, but I believe that one always gains something in the company of people at prayer. The Marquis came in first, then his sons, then the guests, the domestics, the chaplain, the organist,—no one was missing. There is a time for everything in lives laid out on a grand scale.

LONDON, November 18, 1877.

There is general admiration for the Duc de Bro-

[1] 80th Fusiliers, 3d Battalion, 1st Company.

glie's speech. Here is a witticism on Gladstone:
"Certainly, he is an honest man, in the worst sense
of the word."

I have at last met Lady Howard. I shall receive
a card to-morrow for the ceremony.[1] A card is quite
indispensable as London and its suburbs will be
there. Let me tell you how this match was made.
The young lady was an intimate friend of the Duke's
sisters, with whom she spent some months. She had
first the grace to allow them to convert her to the
Church, and then the luck to make the acquaintance
of their brother. Her face became familiar to him—
he ultimately came to think her pretty—which she
is not: she has a beautiful figure, simply. A year
ago he was on the point of putting a period to his
indecision. It was at a ball at Lady Early's. I was
there and did not in the least suspect what was going
on under the ducal coronet. The evening advanced;
at last, it is said, he opened his mouth to declare
himself when an ill-omened fellow came to claim a
waltz from Lady Flora. She left and the Duke
recovered his senses. The season ended, and another
occasion did not present itself.

Fortunately they met again in the country. Lady
Flora went to Arundel, and stayed two months
waiting and hoping. Her father grew angry and
ordered her to come home. She announced her
departure for the next day, with red eyes. The
next day came, the packing was done; she went—

[1] The marriage of the Duke of Norfolk, First Duke and Earl,
Hereditary Earl Marshall and Chief Butler of England, with Lady
Flora Hastings.

into the garden—to say good-bye to the children. The Duke followed; at last he declared himself— he did not have to do it twice. A telegram was sent in all haste to 'papa.' " I remain, serious matter, see letter!" Papa replied " Stay!" And that was a clever stroke—to become at a stride the first Duchess of England.

And now, day after to-morrow, before half-past ten, to the oratory. The doors will be closed for half an hour before, and even thus I am told there will be no place for the bridegrooms when they come.

WOBURN-ABBEY,[1] December 16, 1877.

We walked across the park; under the great trees it was very beautiful in the moonlight. The frightened deer passed like shadows. Dinner was served in the large dining-room, with the lights pouring down on the service of vermilion and silver. I spent the evening with Lady De-La-Warr, one of the most beautiful blondes in England,[2] and with Lady Tavistock who is clever, dresses well, and possesses, I believe, great wealth.

On retiring to your own room you find everything comfortable—an open fire. There are open fireplaces all over this great cloister, and every one ablaze from morning till night. I am always amazed at the array of buckets, basins, and bath tubs,— enough for the Heroes of Homer, if they ever bathed. I am supplied also with a wooden tripod to hold

[1] Residence of the Duke of Bedford.
[2] Elizabeth, daughter of Lord Lamington, married to the seventh Count De-La-Warr.

my light, and sit snugly in front of my fire and read!

At lunch I had to have hare soup, made just for me alone. You see my poor stomach has been out of order for over a week. After luncheon, took a walk, paid a visit to the stables, to the horse-gear, to the tennis-courts, to the gardens, to the gallery, to the gold statue,[1] to the kitchen-garden, to the conservatories, etc., all in this immense park. We should think it in France a good deal for one family.

Everything is done by rule and scale. I find that there is an ex-poacher in the park. He is installed as gamekeeper, and has given up his vocation of poacher to somebody else; and will soon be the best of guards against the interlopers, who do so much spoil the hunting. There was a high wind going, and rapid clouds; the great trees in the avenue skirting the crest of the park stood out against a troubled sky. As we mounted toward the avenue, the background of the picture rose, elevation after elevation, each more sombre than the one preceding, and all of it, as far as the eye could reach, belongs to His Grace the Duke of Bedford. And he was wishing to walk with a poor devil like me, and went to the kitchen himself to order a soup for me.

WOBURN-ABBEY, December 17, 1877.

There is a lack of music here, as they say. The piano is open and the candles lit, but no one touches the keys. There is a lack of spirit in everybody, of

---

[1] Of the Duchess of Bedford, by Boehm.

reaction against the heaviness after dinner, against the repose of Sunday, and the apathy of the day following. Everybody is full of good intentions, but there is a dearth of invention. The dressing for dinner yesterday has been the great event: they opened a new treasury; the Duchess carried another firmament in her hair; Lady Hermintrude wore a dress with an apron; the beautiful blonde, a long-trained blue satin gown, and the beautiful Tavistock a gown sown with pearls and a long train set off with knots of ribbon : a court-dress, which was especially becoming to her.

There will be no playing to-night as it is Sunday. The only exceptions in England are for chess and fishing. They fish with a hook, for fish with a ring in their snouts, in a sheet-iron tub. While in France we should dance, play charades, or crambo, or music. In any event the ladies would not be forgotten.

This morning I accompanied Tavistock on a hunt. As I was coming across country without waiting for the end of the chase, I saw a sheep with its legs in the air. I thought the poor thing was dead. Not at all, he had tumbled on his back, simply, and was waiting for a good Samaritan to come and set him on his legs. I did not fail him. He made me think of some men I know.

. . . .

We will delay our meeting no longer, my dears.[1]

[1] M. Gavard was called from London by M. Waddington at the close of 1877.

If I am obliged to hew wood and raise cabbages to earn our bread, it will no doubt be the happiest time of my life. It will occupy hands and brain both.

THE END.

INDEX.

Anson, Col., 111
Anson, Mrs., 63
Amberley, Lord, 287
Athenæum Club, 49, 306
Austria, Empress of, 293, 294, 295

Balfour, Rt. Hon. A. J., 215
Beaconsfield, Viscount, vid. Disraëli.
Beaconsfield, Viscountess, 94, 111
Bedford, Duke of, 222, 263, 321
Belgium, King of, 150
Bernstorf, Count, 41, 98, 118
Bisaccia, Duc de, 159, 162, 165, 166, 168, 195, 200
Bismarck, 27, 234, 242, 244, 245, 247, 249, 258, 296
Blenheim, 20
Broglie, Duc de, 2, 3, 11, 12, 22, 32, 38, 95, 97, 100, 101, 156, 160, 207, 303
Brunnow, Baron, 35, 160, 199
Buckingham Palace, 110
Bulwer-Lytton, E. R., 283, 287, 288
Burlington, 311
Burton, Sir Richard, 279

Cambridge-Oxford boat-race, 102
Cardwell, Viscount, 135
Carlos, Don, 295
Chartres, Duc de, 21, 22

"City," the, 89
Clarendon, Lord, 169
Communists — their secret understanding with the Prussians, 26
Covent Garden, 49
Crystal Palace, 109

Dakin, Sir Thomas, Lord Mayor, 59, 60, 62
Derby Day, 115
Derby, Lord, 117, 182, 188, 233, 234, 238, 239, 241, 242, 243, 244, 246, 248, 254, 255, 258, 263, 307
Dilke, Sir Charles, 174, 194, 315
Disraëli, 92, 111, 116, 117, 183, 235, 236, 237, 265, 278, 280, 281, 290, 291, 303, 308
Duff, Grant, 308

Eu, Comte and Comtesse d', 16

Favre, Jules, 1
Fullerton, Lady Georgiana, 51

Gavard, Charles, Duc de Broglie's notice of, iii; notice of, in the *Moniteur*, vii; meets Duc de Gramont, 7; entrance of Prussians into Paris, 8; goes to Morgan House, 9; evening at Lady

Burdett-Coutts's, 14; red flag in Paris, 15; visit to Oxford, 17; beginning of the Commune, 21; returns to France, 22; remarks on the government at Versailles, 24; removes his family from Paris, 25; returns to England as Chargé d'Affaires, 26; cuts down expenses in the Embassy, 29; business at the Foreign Office, 31; rout at Lord Mayor's, 32; daily routine at the Embassy, 33; dines at Lord Granville's, 34; Rothschild's place, 35; visits the Central Telegraph Office, 36; goes to banquet in Duc de Broglie's uniform, 38; idem, 40; in Lord Granville's office, 39; telegrams on the fight in Paris, 42; getting London firemen off, 43; disappointment at their departure's being countermanded, 44; English sympathy with the defeated communists, 44; visit to Parliament, 47; conduct of public business in England, 48; the Athenæum, 49; Covent Garden, *ib.*; at Walmer Castle, 51; trial of artillery, 54; visit to Old Men's Home, 55; visit to church at Eaton Place, 57; visit to Westminster Workhouse, 58; at the Mansion House, 59, 60; makes his speech, *ib.*; visit to fire-brigade station, 62; also to fire-tug, 63; criticises "The Rivals," 64; dines at the Rothschilds', *ib.*; project in aid of French charities, 65; criticism of English drama, 66; idem, 67; takes part in sham battle, 68; Boxing Day, 71; criticism of the English drama, *ib.*; behind the scenes, 72; visit to slums, 73; Sunday in London, 86; present at the opening of Parliament, 88; evening party at Gladstone's, *ib.*; visits Rothschild at his country house, 89; an evening at Lady Cork's, 94; thanksgiving for Prince of Wales's recovery, 95, 96; banquet at the French hospital, 97; a levee, 98; dines at the Rothschilds', 99; dinner at the Embassy, 101; Cambridge-Oxford boat-race, 102; remarks on the conduct of public business in England, 108; visit to Crystal Palace, 109; visit to Buckingham Palace, 110; interview with the Empress of Germany, 113; in the country, *id.*; dines at Lord Granville's, 117; negotiation for the treaty of commerce, 119; banquet at Guildhall, 137; dines with the Duchess of Cleveland, 141; visits Speaker's house, 144; dinner at Lord Granville's, 145; Court of Common Pleas, 147; dines at Rothschild's, *ib.*; Jewish school in Whitechapel, 152; English drama, 154; French bazaar, 155; spring exhibition, 156; English stage, 163; English Christmas, 164; dissolution of Parliament, 171; follows a political canvass, 172; fire in London, 179; visits Lord Derby, 182; dines with Lord Salisbury, 184; review of troops from Ashantee, 187; Livingstone's funeral, 189; dinner at the

French hospital, 190; the Duc de Bisaccia's ball, 196; culottes, 198 ; the Czar of Russia, 199; Guizot, 205; dinner with Schouvaloff, 208; Ritualists, 211; at Hatfield House, 212; at Woburn Abbey, 217; Henry VIII., 224; visits the offices of the *Morning Post*, 225 ; illness and death of Comte de Jarnac, *ib.;* the war-scare of 1875, 232; launching of a vessel, 260; dinner at the Foreign Office, 262; Moody and Sankey, 263; sale in Leicester Square for the French charities, 266; English drama, 267; banquet at London Tavern, 268; going to the "meet," 272; negotiation for the sale of the Suez shares, 276 ; purchase of Suez shares by England, 280; evening at the Geographical Society, 281; at Hatfield House, 282; at the opening of Parliament, 288; is complimented by Disraëli, 290; a spelling-bee, 291; debate on offering the Queen the title of Empress of India, 292 ; fanatic "Orangeman," 296; waits on the Empress Augusta, 298; at Lockinge House, 299; at Gunnersbury Acton, 301; English spelling, 305; at the Athenæum, 306; tricks Lord Derby, 307; Wade on China, *ib.;* debates in Parliament, 308; banquet at the Chamber of Commerce, 309; conversation with Salisbury, 310; English art, 311; coaching party, 312; conversation with Salisbury, 314; dinner at Sir Charles Dilke's,

315; an open shutter, 316; at Hatfield House, *ib.;* an aristocratic courtship, 319; at Woburn Abbey, 320
Gladstone, W. E., 3, 38, 65, 94, 106, 117, 141, 151, 176, 181, 183, 186, 292, 311, 319
Grant, Lieut.-Gen. Sir Hope, 68
Granville, Lord, 34, 51, 52, 57, 67
Gounod, 37, 42
Guizot, William, 204
Gunnersbury Acton, 301, 302

Harcourt, Comte Bernard d', 119
Hatfield House, 212, 214, 215, 282, 316
Hayward, Abraham, 85, 115, 136, 161
Hoare, Sir Henry, 174
House of Commons, efforts to silence a member, 106; divisions, 109
Howard, H. Fitz-Alan, fifteenth Duke of Norfolk, 36, 37

Jarnac, Comte de, 200, 225
Joinville, Prince de, 15, 31

Kensington Museum, 7

Lockinge House, 299
London slums, 73

Mansion House, 32
Morgan House, 9, 15

Napoleon III., 28, 267
Nemours, Duc de, 13, 16
Northcote, Sir Stafford, 213, 215

Orleans House, 13
Oxford, 17

Oxford-Cambridge boat-race, 102

Paris, Comte de, 5, 12, 46

Rothschild, Baron Lionel, 35, 64, 89, 99, 278, 281

Russell, Lord John, 236, 238

Salisbury, Marquis of, 94, 184, 303, 304, 308, 309, 310, 314, 316, 318

Say, Léon, 56, 59, 62

Schouvaloff, Count, 203, 207, 208, 248, 286, 295, 297, 307, 309, 316

Slums of London, 73

Staël, Mme. de, 42

Stafford House, 118

Stanley, Dean, 306

Sumner, Charles, 136

Thiers, 30, 56, 91, 119, 131, 134, 156, 207

Tichborne case, 150, 161, 167

Vernon, Lady, 51

Victoria, Queen, 37, 97, 98, 100, 110, 154, 227, 289, 290, 292, 294, 295, 296

Wales, Prince of, 11, 66, 93, 95, 96, 162, 228

Walmer Castle, 50, 84

Westminster Abbey, 6

Westonbirt House, 269

Woburn Abbey, 217, 218, 223, 320, 321

January, 1897.

Henry Holt & Co.'s

Newest Books.

The Island of Cuba.
By Lieut. A. S. ROWAN, U. S. A., and Prof. M. M. RAMSAY. With Maps and Index. 12mo, $1.25.

"Excellent and timely, a clear and judicial account of Cuba and its history."—*The Dial*. "Conveys just the information needed at this time."—*Philadelphia Times*.

English Literature.
By BERNHARD TEN BRINK. Vol. II. Part 2. From the Middle of the Fourteenth Century to the Accession of Elizabeth. 12mo, $2.00.

"Has taken highest rank in its department."—*Outlook*.

Earlier Volumes:—*Vol. I*. To Wyclif. $2.00.—*Vol. II*. Part 1. Through the Renaissance. $2.00.
Ten Brink's Lectures on Shakespeare. $1.25.

Telepathy and the Subliminal Self.
By Dr. R. OSGOOD MASON. A work treating of hypnotism, automatism, trance, and phantasms. (*To be published at once.*) 12mo.

"It is with the hope of aiding somewhat in the efforts now being made to rescue from an uncertain and unreasoning supernaturalism some of the most valuable facts in nature, and some of the most interesting and beautiful psychical phenomena in human experience, that this book is offered to the public."—*From the Preface*.

A Diplomat in London. (1871-77.)
By CHARLES GAVARD. A book giving interesting light on the diplomacy of the Commune, and on the English aristocracy of the time. (*To be published at once.*) 12mo.

In India.
By ANDRÉ CHEVRILLON. 12mo, $1.50.

"A masterpiece... Such a vivid reflection of the country, its people, its architecture, and its religion, that we become unconscious of the printed page, for we see and feel that mystery of the world—India."—*Bookman*.

Henry Holt & Co.'s Newest Books.

Richard Brinsley Sheridan.

By W. FRASER RAE. With an Introduction by Sheridan's great-grandson, the Marquess of Dufferin. With portraits. 2 vols., 8vo, $7.00.

"A story of romantic and human interest."—*Atlantic Monthly*. "A marvelously ingenious and deft piece of biographical narration... Mr. Rae has told a full and interesting story, and has told it well."—*N. Y. Tribune*. "The best biography of Sheridan in existence."—*Review of Reviews*.

Social Forces in German Literature.

By Prof. KUNO FRANCKE. 8vo, $2.00 *net*. (*This book is being translated into German.*)

"We owe a debt of gratitude to the author... his exposition is admirable."—*Nation*.

On Parody.

By ARTHUR SHADWELL MARTIN. An essay on the art, and humorous selections. 12mo, $1.25.

"Of infinite delight and resource to lovers of English verse."—*Outlook*. "Full of good examples."—*Nation*.

Modern Political Orations. (1838=1888.)

Twenty-four speeches by Brougham, Macaulay, Fox, Cobden, Bulwer-Lytton, Bright, Morley, Beaconsfield, Gladstone, Chamberlain, Parnell, McCarthy, Churchill, etc., etc. Edited by LEOPOLD WAGNER. $1.00 *net*.

Russian Politics.

By HERBERT M. THOMPSON. With maps. $2.00.

"Most intelligible and interesting."—*Atlantic Monthly*.

Animal Symbolism in Ecclesiastical Architecture.

By E. P. EVANS. With 78 Illustrations. $2 *net*.

"Many a ponderous and voluminous work on mediæval history and art, requiring months for its study, is really far less valuable than this little book."—The Hon. ANDREW D. WHITE, in Appleton's *Popular Science Monthly*.

International Bimetallism.

By FRANCIS A. WALKER. 3d edition. $1.25.

"An elaborate study of bimetallism from the first bimetallist in the United States, and there is not a syllable in it that is favorable to the free, unlimited, and independent coinage of silver by the United States."—*Christian Register*.

Henry Holt & Co.'s Recent Fiction.

The Honorable Peter Stirling.
By PAUL L. FORD. A brilliant novel of New York Political Life. *Sixteenth edition.* $1.50.
"Timely, manly, thoroughbred, and eminently suggestive."
—*Atlantic Monthly.*

Emma Lou: Her Book.
By MARY M. MEARS. 12mo, $1.00.
"The neatest, closest, and most accurate description of village life in exactly the way an uncommonly bright girl would see it. It is its exceeding naturalness which is so taking. . . . We are inclined to give the book the highest of encomiums as a sound, wholesome, and most amusing story."—*N. Y. Times.*

The Buckram Series.
Narrow 16mo, with frontispiece, 75c. each.
"That admirable Buckram Series—to which a dull book is never admitted."—*N. Y. Times.*

Out of Bounds.
Being the Adventures of an Unadventurous Young Man. By A. GARRY.
"An exceedingly good story. . . graceful and interesting."—*N. Y. Commercial Advertiser.* "A story which none will read but to enjoy."—*Boston Times.*

Earlier Issues.

Anthony Hope's Romances.
6 vols. The Prisoner of Zenda (31st Ed.). The Indiscretion of the Duchess (10th Ed.). A Man of Mark (9th Ed.). The Dolly Dialogues (9th Ed.). A Change of Air (9th Ed.). Sport Royal (3d Ed.).

A Man and His Womankind.
A novel. By NORA VYNNÉ.

Sir Quixote of the Moors.
A Scotch Romance. By JOHN BUCHAN.

Lady Bonnie's Experiment.
A quaint pastoral. By TIGHE HOPKINS.

Kafir Stories.
Tales of adventure. By WM. CHAS. SCULLY.

The Master-Knot (2d Edition).
And "Another Story." By CONOVER DUFF.

The Time Machine.
The Story of an Invention. By H. G. WELLS.

Tenement Tales of New York.
By J. W. SULLIVAN.

Slum Stories of London.
(*Neighbors of Ours.*) By H. W. NEVINSON.

The Ways of Yale (6th Edition).
Sketches, mainly humorous. By H. A. BEERS.

A Suburban Pastoral (5th Edition).
American stories. By HENRY A. BEERS.

Jack O'Doon (2d Edition).
An American novel. By MARIA BEALE.

Quaker Idyls (5th Edition).
By Mrs. S. M. H. GARDNER.

John Ingerfield (6th Edition).
A love tragedy. By JEROME K. JEROME.

Sixteenth Edition of a New York Novel.

The Hon. Peter Stirling
And what people thought of him.

By PAUL LEICESTER FORD.   12mo.   Cloth, $1.50.

The Nation: " Floods of light on the *raison d'être*, origin, and methods of the dark figure that directs the destinies of our cities. . . . So strongly imagined and logically drawn that it satisfies the demand for the appearance of truth in art. . . . Telling scenes and incidents and descriptions of political organization, all of which are literal transcripts of life and fact—not dry irrelevancies thrown in by way of imparting information, but lively detail, needful for a clear understanding of Stirling's progress from the humble chairmanship of a primary to the dictator's throne. . . . In the use of dramatic possibilities, Mr. Ford is discreet and natural, and without giving Stirling a heroic pose, manages to win for him very hearty sympathy and belief. Stirling's private and domestic story is well knit with that of his public adventures. . . . A very good novel."

The Atlantic Monthly: "Commands our very sincere respect . . . there is no glaring improbability about his story . . . the highly dramatic crisis of the story. . . . The tone and manner of the book are noble. . . . A timely, manly, thoroughbred, and eminently suggestive book."

The Review of Reviews: " His relations with women were of unconventional sincerity and depth. . . . Worth reading on several accounts."

The Dial: " One of the strongest and most vital characters that have appeared in our fiction. . . . A very charming love-story. To discern the soul of good in so evil a thing as Municipal politics calls for sympathies that are not often united with a sane ethical outlook; but Peter Stirling is possessed of the one without losing his sense of the other, and it is this combination of qualities that make him so impressive and admirable a figure. . . . Both a readable and an ethically helpful book."

The New York Tribune: "A portrait which is both alive and easily recognizable."

New York Times: " Mr. Ford's able political novel."

The Literary World: " A fine, tender love-story. . . . A very unusual but, let us believe, a possible character. . . . Peter Stilring is a man's hero. . . . Very readable and enjoyable."

The Independent: "Full of life. The interest never flags. . . . It is long since we have read a better novel or one more thoroughly and naturally American."

The Boston Advertiser: " Sure to excite attention and win popularity."

HENRY HOLT & CO., 29 W. 23d St., New York.

Anthony Hope's Romances
In Buckram Series.
18mo, with Frontispieces, 75 cents each.

The Prisoner of Zenda.   32d *Edition.*
"A glorious story, which cannot be too warmly recommended to all who love a tale that stirs the blood. Perhaps not the least among its many good qualities is the fact that its chivalry is of the nineteenth, not of the sixteenth, century; that it is a tale of brave men and true, and of a fair woman of to-day. The Englishman who saves the king . . . is as interesting a knight as was Bayard. . . . The story holds the reader's attention from first to last."—*Critic.*

The Indiscretion of the Duchess.
10th *Edition.*
"Told with an old-time air of romance that gives the fascination of an earlier day; an air of good faith, almost of religious chivalry, givees rality to their extravagance. . . . Marks Mr. Hope as a wit, if he were not a romancer."—*Nation.*

A Man of Mark.   9th *Edition.*
"More plentifully charged with humor, and the plot is every whit as original as that of Zenda . . . returns to the entrancing manner of 'The Prisoner of Zenda.' . . . The whole game of playing at revolution is pictured with such nearness and intimacy of view that the wildest things happen as though they were every-day occurrences. . . . Two triumphs of picturesque description—the overthrow and escape of the President, and the night attack on the bank. The charmingly wicked Christina is equal to anything that Mr. Hope has done, with the possible exception of the always piquant Dolly."—*Life.*

The Dolly Dialogues.   9th *Edition.*
"Characterized by a delicious drollery; . . . beneath the surface play of words lies a tragi-comedy of life. . . . There is infinite suggestion in every line."—*Boston Transcript.*

A Change of Air.   9th *Edition.*
With portrait and notice of the author.
"A highly clever performance, with little touches that recall both Balzac and Meredith. . . . Is endowed with exceeding originality."—*New York Times.*

Sport Royal.   3d *Edition.*
"His many admirers will be happy to find in these stories full evidence that Anthony Hope can write short stories fully as dramatic in incident as his popular novels."—*Philadelphia Call.*

HENRY HOLT & CO., 29 W. 23d St., New York.

www.ingramcontent.com/pod-product-compliance
Lightning Source LLC
Chambersburg PA
CBHW030325240426
43673CB00040B/1273